REINVENTING HUMAN RIGHTS

Stanford Studies in Human Rights

Reinventing Human Rights

Mark Goodale

Stanford University Press
Stanford, California

STANFORD UNIVERSITY PRESS
Stanford, California

Printed in the United States of America on acid-free, archival-quality paper

Library of Congress Cataloging-in-Publication Data
Names: Goodale, Mark, author.
Title: Reinventing human rights / Mark Goodale.
Other titles: Stanford studies in human rights.
Description: Stanford, California : Stanford University Press, 2022. | Series:
    Stanford studies in human rights | Includes bibliographical references
    and index.
Identifiers: LCCN 2021029537 (print) | LCCN 2021029538 (ebook) | ISBN
    9781503613300 (cloth) | ISBN 9781503631007 (paperback) | ISBN
    9781503631014 (ebook)
Subjects: LCSH: Human rights.
Classification: LCC JC571 .G639 2022 (print) | LCC JC571 (ebook) | DDC
    323—dc23
LC record available at https://lccn.loc.gov/2021029537
LC ebook record available at https://lccn.loc.gov/2021029538

Typeset by Kevin Barrett Kane in Minion Pro

Cover design: Notch Design

Cover engraving: Glascow, ca. 1880. Roth. Adobe Stock.

In memory of Sally Engle Merry (1944–2020)—
mentor, colleague, friend.
~ *Festina lente* ~

For now we see through a glass, darkly; but then face to face: now I know in part; but then shall I know even as also I am known.

1 Corinthians 13:12

It is easier to imagine the end of the world than the end of capitalism.

Fredric Jameson

Contents

Preface

In her improbable and yet pioneering ethnographic study of human rights activism among Myanmar's LGBT community, *The Politics of Love in Myanmar: LGBT Mobilization and Human Rights as a Way of Life* (2019), the Singaporean sociolegal scholar Lynette Chua introduces us to two activists whose intertwined lives and experiences constitute the central thread of her work. Tun Tun is a former English literature student at Rangoon University, the son of a prominent family with deep connections to the country's authoritarian regime. During the prodemocracy movement, which began in 1988, Tun Tun joined the mobilizations against the ruling junta along with thousands of other protestors.

When the Orwellian State Law and Order Restoration Council—known as the dreaded SLORC—decided to "pacify" the prodemocracy movement, which was led by the future Nobel Peace Prize winner Aung San Suu Kyi, the regime turned to mass roundups and the widespread use of torture against activists. Tun Tun fled Yangon for the dense jungles along the Myanmar-Thailand border, where he took up arms as a rebel fighter within a wider guerrilla struggle against the military government.

Tun Tun spent years engaging in dangerous and ultimately fruitless attacks on government installations, strikes in which many comrades were killed or captured. By the mid-1990s, the military regime in Myanmar had destroyed most of the rebel camps and suppressed the prodemocracy movement. Tun Tun formed a close relationship with another man in the camps, and the intimate attachment had to be kept secret, even if other rebel soldiers in his unit sensed the nature of the relationship.

For almost twenty more years, Tun Tun lived in exile in Thailand, where he eventually became a leading human rights activist and one of the first openly gay Burmese. Although he had begun his human rights work as a prodemocracy activist, he eventually made the decision to create the first Burmese LGBT movement. Stirred by human rights as a new language of empowerment, Tun Tun worked with others to build a fragile transnational LGBT network against a background of homophobia and political violence.

Fifteen years younger than Tun Tun, Tin Hla grew up at the very center of Burmese military life. Raised in a strict military family, his grandfather was an army major whose unit played a central role in maintaining law and order in the one-party state. As a boy and then as a teenager, Tin Hla grew up in constant fear of his grandfather and other children in the military compound, who subjected him to years of physical and emotional abuse. Although he tried to hide his true sexual identity from others, he was still bullied and ridiculed by others on the military base, who called him *achauk*, a derogatory Burmese word for gay men.

Ten years after the brutal military crackdown of 1988, deep in the midst of internal political and cultural repression, Tin Hla's grandfather retired from the military, something that released Tin Hla, in a very real sense, from twenty years of bondage spent in isolation from his true self. He passed much of his twenties wandering the country, doing odd jobs, and exploring his sexuality through a number of furtive same-sex relationships. By his early thirties, Tin Hla had returned to Yangon, where he eked out a living working in a mattress shop.

Yet with each passing year, Tin Hla had become more confident in his queer identity, despite the pervasive social discrimination. Volunteer work with an international NGO implementing HIV/AIDS programs in Yangon brought him, for the first time, into contact with gay Burmese activists, some of whom maintained connections with the exiled Burmese LGBT community in Thailand, led by Tun Tun. Finally, in 2013, the lives of Tun Tun and Tin Hla were brought together when the exiled LGBT activists came home. Tin Hla soon joined the transnational organization and went on to become one of the founding members of Myanmar's LGBT activist network.

The stories of Tun Tun and Tin Hla, and those of many others far from the centers of dominant human rights theory and policy making, were an ever-present source of inspiration and guidance as the proposal to reinvent human rights coalesced over the years. This is because the interconnected narratives of Tun Tun and Tin Hla offer a glimpse into the forms a reinvented human rights might take in the future based on an account of how human rights *is already being transformed* beyond the boundaries of political and legal institutions, without regard for international treaties and monitoring bodies, and without any commitment to a flattened conception of the abstract "human." Under the most implausible and onerous of circumstances, queer Burmese have built a new social community in which "human rights" functions as a metaphor for translocal action and moral renewal amid the realities of social suffering, a metaphor through which they manage to find joy and meaning in their lives.

But if the unlikely transformation of human rights in authoritarian Myanmar into a "way of life" reveals the possible future of a reinvented human rights in the present, it also offers a critical lens through which to better view more troubling developments in the centers of global power, particularly those closely associated with the invention of existing human rights. If *Reinventing Human Rights* was written with one eye on the ways in which human rights can *and must* be radically reconceived in the face of manifold long-term crises, both those we must confront now, and those looming just over the horizon, it was also written with another eye on a crisis with more immediacy: the intellectual and moral crisis of the—largely Euro-American—political left.

With the failure of international human rights—its tribunals, its international bodies, its ethics of naming-and-shaming—to fulfil its apparent destiny as the grand replacement framework for a traditional left-wing politics anchored in redistributional socialism and a vision of conflict shaped by historical materialism, what remained was an increasingly fragmented series of oppositional movements, many fighting among one another to reclaim the mantle of revolutionary change. The problem, however, was that the remnants of the old political left, betrayed by the well-intentioned but ultimately false promises of international human rights, turned inward and toward categories of exclusionary difference—ideological, social, racial—as the grounds on which the struggle for emancipation would be waged.

Despite the fact that categories of *inclusionary* difference can form an important initial basis for collective mobilization, as the case of Myanmar's LGBT activists reminds us, the tragedy of the erstwhile left shows what happens when categories of *exclusionary* difference become both the means and the ends of political life. Leaving aside the inability or unwillingness of many well-meaning progressives to respond meaningfully and coherently to the foundational problem of global capitalism, the more pragmatic concern is that a politics based on categories of exclusionary difference is fundamentally incapable of producing the translocal alliances that will be absolutely necessary for meeting the most serious global challenges: economic and social inequality, conflict over natural resources, ethno- and religious nationalism, and the rapidly escalating consequences of climate change.

A reinvented human rights, by contrast, can never be circumscribed by categories of exclusionary difference. Even though the idea of the universalizing "human" turned out to be a completely misbegotten grounds on which to try and build the postwar moral—if not political—world order, it at least had the virtue of projecting beyond the kinds of ideologies of difference that had fed the catastrophe of world war, militarism, and genocide. For that is the great lesson from history: categories of exclusionary difference can never, in the end, form the basis for true emancipation, which requires solidarity, empathy, and understanding *across* the many lines that divide us. It is this spirit of translocal belonging and action that animates the proposal for a reinvented human rights, a proposal that is made with a keen sense that it is getting very late in the day, that the intellectual and moral crisis besetting what replaced the traditional political left shows no signs of abating, and that the window of opportunity for forging a radically different future is fast closing.

Château-d'Oex
May 2021

REINVENTING HUMAN RIGHTS

CHAPTER 1

Human Rights against the Maelstroms

IN EARLY 2019, Ai Weiwei, the hounded Chinese artist and global social activist, sounded a cri de coeur on behalf of human rights. Taking stock of the contemporary condition, he lamented that societies and states around the world were succumbing to a pervasive moral failure—the unwillingness, or inability, to live up to our collective responsibility to "uphold human dignity," as he puts it.[1] He cited, as current evidence, the global refugee crisis, a degrading global ecology, armed conflict, "unrestrained expansion under a nationalist, capitalist [global] order," economic and social inequality, and the use of technological innovation by authoritarian states to "tighten their grip on people's thoughts and actions."

The only way to overcome these painful realities, according to Ai Weiwei, is to embrace—and then act on—the truth that "human rights are shared values," that "human rights are our common possession," and that the "dignity of humanity as a whole is compromised" every time an abuse, of whatever form, is committed against individuals, against communities, against vulnerable states, and against marginalized ethnic groups.

For Ai Weiwei, who has become one of the most highly visible and influential voices of anti-authoritarianism, there are only three possible explanations for our collective failure to defend and realize our human rights: first, we—both individually and collectively—are too selfish, "too benighted"; second, we understand the truth of human rights but lack the courage to organize our lives and systems around this truth; or third, we are insincere, "we don't really love life enough." As he puts it, in a widely read opinion piece, "we con ourselves into imagining we can get away without discharging our obligation to institute fairness and justice, we fool ourselves into thinking that chaos is acceptable, we entertain the idea that the world may well collapse in ruin, all hopes and dreams shattered."

Without wanting to make selfishness, cowardice, and insincerity the painful moral realities around which the interventions in this book are based, I do think that Ai Weiwei's reflections—shaped, importantly, by his own well-documented life as a target for Chinese state censorship—reinforce the seriousness, even gravity, of our rapidly changing times. Long gone are the halcyon years of the first decade of the post–Cold War, in which contemporary human rights in their different legal, political, and moral forms burst onto the global landscape after decades trapped within the straitjacket of Cold War Realpolitik. Yet when what former United Nations Secretary-General Kofi Annan confidently proclaimed as the "Age of Human Rights" came to an end, it did so with something like the opposite energy.[2] Instead of a dramatic implosion, the Age of Human Rights slowly, but seemingly inevitably, faded.

The optimistic certainty—which, in retrospect, seems dangerously naive—that a "spirit of brotherhood [sic]" had, after nearly five decades, finally captured the moral imaginations of people and nations around the world, dissolved into various forms of agonized "insincerity" in the face of overwhelming countercurrents and symbolic gestures: the rise of the national security state after September 11, 2001; the unforgettable images of soldiers from the Shining City on the Hill gleefully engaging in perverse acts of state-sanctioned torture; the accelerating impacts of human-induced climate change; a world increasingly divided between the socioeconomic haves and have-nots; the recognition that old demons like structural racism are still very much alive; and, more recently, the manifest failure of the "truth" of human rights to provide any international basis for responding to the ravages of a global pandemic.

And if this book is in full agreement with Ai Weiwei's diagnosis of the perilousness of our times, it too shares his unwillingness to simply capitulate, to simply come to terms with the fact that human rights are obsolete and "chaos is acceptable," that the best we can do is to prepare for a world that will increasingly be in ruins. Yet if the challenges and provocations of the benighted, cowardly, and insincere age that replaced the "Age of Human Rights" are formidable, so too must be any counter-response, any proposition for an alternative future that is not destined to remain captive to the "brutality and complexity" of the present.[3]

What follows, therefore, is just such a proposition. It is a proposition animated by two broad empirical and critical imperatives. First, the various interventions in the book—which are meant to crystallize into a distinct alternative account of human rights as the most important global framework for justice-seeking at all levels—are inspired by an anthropological orientation. By this I mean much less an orientation that is anchored in the discipline of anthropology as such, although different kinds of research from the anthropology of human rights over the last thirty years provide an important evidentiary source for a number of key arguments in the book. Rather, by "anthropological orientation" I mean much more a sensitivity to the plural, idiosyncratic, and, above all, hidden lives of human rights as these have been documented through research and participatory engagement across a broad spectrum of contemporary political, social, and legal contexts.

Moreover, an anthropological orientation is one that insists on, and privileges, the inclusion of the most diverse range of voices and experiences possible on the question of the future(s) of human rights. Although this book is superficially the work of a single author, I view the approach developed here as a collective one; it is a framework that ultimately synthesizes a number of unacknowledged possibilities for human rights through a kind of appreciative channeling.

And second, the book is also meant to be a thoroughgoing critique of two kinds of persistent, interconnected, and debilitating quietism. The first is an often-well-meaning quietism found within the relatively bounded world of human rights scholarship, in which proposals for reform or modification are tightly connected to the existing international human rights system, itself understood in narrow legal and political terms. With the increasingly rare exception of instances in which the existing international human rights system is defended by scholars with full-throated and even stubborn enthusiasm,[4] it is much more common that scholars adopt a pragmatic approach to human rights reform, in which improvements are suggested but the elaborate framework of international human rights remains intact.[5]

The second type of quietism—alluded to by Ai Weiwei—is obviously much more consequential and globally diffuse. This is the quietism that marks different segments of the equally diverse political left, which has seen its "hopes and dreams shattered." Quietism, in this sense, is the final stage in a process of collective leftist grieving, the acceptance that we are more likely to witness the end of the world itself (as Fredric Jameson pithily put it) than the end of a political economic world order whose complex brutalities are the root cause of a long list of ramifying crises. By contrast, this book represents a rejection of acceptance, a rejection of the naturalizing pretensions of global capitalism, and a rejection of the ideological inevitability through which what I will describe as a "G20 world" has come to extinguish any remaining vestiges of post-1945 internationalism.

Indeed, given that the contemporary political economic world order—with global capitalism at its very core—feeds voraciously on these broader forms of quietism, the proposition for an alternative approach to human rights developed in this book is inspired by a radically different spirit, one that the late critical sociologist Erik Olin Wright described through the paradoxical category of "real utopias."[6] To "envision" a real utopia, according to Wright, is to strike an intellectual and ethical balance between practice and idealism, pragmatism and the imagination, and the present and the future. Above all, "envisioning real utopias" means pushing against the apparently fixed boundaries of what is possible, since imagining what can and should lie beyond has always been the necessary—if not sufficient—condition for realizing meaningful change.

This brings me to the central arguments of the book. I describe the proposition for an alternative approach to human rights as a "reinvention" in order to reinforce two basic points. The first is the important acknowledgment that, as Lynn Hunt put it, human rights were "invented."[7] Without necessarily adopting Hunt's specific intellectual and cultural history of the gradual invention of human rights from the late eighteenth century to the promulgation of the Universal Declaration of Human Rights (UDHR) in 1948, what I embrace instead is the underlying constructivism of Hunt's analysis. The result is a perspective that is immediately marked by a tension that has proven problematic.

Much like taking a sociological approach to the emergence of religions, one that offers an explanation for the human invention of doctrines that specifically deny the possibility of their invention by humans, so too with a constructivist approach to human rights, which insists that human rights were invented within particular historical conjunctures, for particular social and political reasons, by particular people, organized within particular collectivities. And yet, as Hunt shows, what was invented over the *longue durée* was a political, legal, and moral doctrine that had at its center a normative conception of "man" that denied its—and "his"—essential contingency.[8]

In proposing a reinvention of human rights, I convert this essential contingency—which is excluded by the vast doctrinal and institutional system that the UDHR gave birth to and forever molded—into a fundamental virtue, a key that unlocks the possibilities for reimagining human rights in starkly different terms. Of course, in so doing, the approach takes leave, once and for all, of any remaining attachments to the naturalistic ontology of "universal human rights," which imagines its power to be derived from the quasi-biological claim that human rights are "*natural rights*: namely, rights (entitlements) held simply by virtue of being a person (human being). Such rights are natural in the sense that their source is human nature."[9]

Instead, the kind of reinvention of human rights I believe is urgently called for is an acknowledgment that we have no choice but to make a virtue of social contingency; that it is far too late in the game to be doubling down on quaint late eighteenth-century inventions (no matter how august);[10] and that we must not fear what the resocialization (and denaturalization) of human rights will lead to because of our fear of what contingency is typically associated with: political manipulation, pervasive bad faith, and, more recently, the ideological attack on the facticity of truth itself.

But if human rights can be reinvented, the question becomes: should they? Notice that the question itself already presupposes several important concessions, the most important being that the polyvalent project of "human rights" is both coherent and valuable enough to be reimagined, beyond the more historical starting point of Hunt's analytical framework. Yet the more direct answer to the question, the answer that grounds everything that is to follow in this book, is *yes*, human rights can and, indeed, *must*, be reinvented.

Reinventing Human Rights between Disenchantment and Defiance

Before explaining why I see this as the only possible answer to this question, the only way forward, it is worth stepping back to recognize that this is an answer that will prove unacceptable to many scholars and activists, especially those who—from a variety of perspectives, for a variety of reasons—have crossed the Rubicon and have effectively given up on human rights.

Leaving aside both the vital long-standing skepticism toward human rights from postcolonial writers and intellectuals, and the variety of critiques of human rights associated with the political right-wing and authoritarian governments of all stripes, what concerns me here is the posture toward human rights of critics whose position reflects a form of conversion. The starting and end points of this conversion vary, but what this anti-human-rights approach has in common is an evolutionary process of disenchantment through which otherwise progressive intellectuals come to realize that the promise of human rights, the promise to remake the world under the sign of universal human dignity, was a false promise, one that was doomed to remain unfulfilled. From this entirely understandable perspective, the task should not be to reform, let alone reinvent, human rights. Rather, the task for both progressive politics and for the scholars who track and support it is either to develop a replacement for human rights as the dominant framework for global justice or to abandon the search for such a framework altogether.[11]

Yet as will be seen throughout this book, although I adopt any number of the same historical, conceptual, ethical, and ethnographic critiques of the existing international human rights system as many from the disenchanted left, where I part ways is in the response. The proposal to reinvent human rights is neither an argument for an entirely new framework for global justice nor an argument for abandoning the search for an organizing framework altogether; indeed, quite the contrary. But to part ways with disenchanted critics of human rights is by no means a way of aligning the propositions developed in this book with the still-dominant approach to human rights of those scholars and activists who view any problems, let alone structural crises, to lie outside the international human rights system itself. On this view, any failure to realize the promise of human rights at a global level is ultimately the cumulative effect of bad faith at all scales. From this perspective, the history of human rights in the postwar period can be read as a long and doleful list of evasions, manipulations, unaccountable atrocities, and political special pleading, interspersed with just enough counterexamples to give us "evidence for hope."[12]

This is an approach to the future of human rights to which the framework of this book is unambiguously opposed. Indeed, contrary to the argument that criticism of international human rights is much worse for the cause of global justice than the alternative of redoubling our collective commitment to the "long, drawn-out effort," the position in this book is that, in fact, the opposite is true. The unwillingness to take seriously the extensive and multifaceted criticism of human rights represents, from my perspective, the greater long-term obstacle. This is because, to the extent to which human rights remains the dominant political, legal, and moral framework within which justice (in all of its forms) must be pursued, we are confronted with what I believe to be a devastating Hobson's choice. Without any alternatives with equal global legitimacy or scope, it is either existing international human rights or nothing. Even if criticism of human rights is rarely accompanied by the articulation of an alternative vision for reaching the same—or similar—objectives, at least it has the virtue of acknowledging the manifold problems with the international human rights system, no matter how disorienting this might be.[13]

Justice-Seeking, Reinvention, Translocality

In light of these different starting points, the proposal for a reinvented human rights is guided by three general principles. First, I believe that "human rights" can and must be retained as the framework for global justice-seeking, both now and in the future, even if what is meant by human rights will look very different in relation to the current orthodoxy of treaties, declarations, legal tribunals, and UDHR-derived political ethics. In other words, I want to maintain the shell of human rights rather than central parts of the existing core. To do this, the proposition to reinvent human rights begins with a deep critique of human rights institutionalism and political theory and ends by giving priority to what anthropologists describe as the "practice of human rights," which is not the same thing as "practice-dependent theories" of human rights.[14]

Second, by using the admittedly provocative concept of "reinvention" to describe this vision for the future of human rights, I intend to make an unambiguous argument: only a completely reformulated approach to human rights will prove adequate to the monumental task, which is to (re-)establish the grounds on which the most consequential global problems can be confronted and, ideally, overcome. This must remain the goal, even if few people have any experience of "global problems." In fact, the most local of problems are often tightly intertwined with regional and global processes, from economic inequality to forced migration to climate change. Nevertheless, the point is that human rights can and must be retained as the most fundamental framework through which these problems are faced, but only if the meaning and potentialities of human rights are thoroughly reconceived.

And third, the proposal to reinvent human rights is structured by an ethical principle that I describe as "translocality." What I mean is that the globalizing logic of existing human rights must be maintained, but in starkly different terms. Instead of an a priori claim to universality, the vision for the future of human rights that I develop is one that requires people to form lines of alliance that justify collective action beyond established boundaries of community, nation, race, or religious identity, among others, yet without the need to extend these lines out to what the Preamble to the UDHR describes as "all members of the human family." In this, I don't believe there is another option, that is, in relation to the fundamental goal of confronting and overcoming the most consequential global problems. Yet instead of rearticulating some version of the natural rights heritage that finds expression in existing human rights, the argument is that the very claim of universality itself should be abandoned.

To replace universality with translocality is not, however, to give greater importance to categories of difference. On the contrary, similar to existing human rights, the alternative I propose recognizes that a more enduring framework for collective belonging and social action can never be one defined by difference: national, class, racial, religious, and so on. Yet even if specific moments of mobilization will emphasize difference strategically, this will only be consistent with a reinvented human rights as an initial call to arms, as a way to accelerate the formation of new lines of alliance beyond these same boundaries of difference.

A People's History of Human Rights

Before establishing the political, economic, and social contexts of the book in more detail, something should be said about its orientation to history. This is important not only because the argument for reinventing human rights is partly inspired by a particular history, a history of their invention. Even more, it is necessary because the broader history of human rights reveals rich, diverse, and largely hidden parallel histories that will be used as a resource for reimagining what human rights can and should be in the future. What this suggests is that part of what it means to "reinvent" human rights is to engage in a process of recovery, to understand differently and give legitimacy to the many trajectories of human rights that continue to unfold far beyond the walls within which the postwar international human rights system was conceived, institutionalized, and set into motion.

In doing so, I am also making a historiographical argument that necessarily has a sharp edge. In this, my approach to the history of human rights is influenced by the work of critical historians like Howard Zinn, who shined a light on a set of historical perspectives on the United States that had been hidden from view because these perspectives challenged long-standing narratives about the United States and its national values.[15] In this case, what I emphasize is that at different points in the history of the invention of human rights, various microhistories were sprouting in the shadows of the high profile activities of the UN Commission on Human Rights (CHR), which oversaw the drafting of the UDHR, and then, after 1948, in the shadows of the international human rights system to which these early postwar years gave birth.

Some of these microhistories remained either unacknowledged or suppressed because they problematized the official narrative: that a diverse international community coalesced around the basic truths of universal human rights between 1945 and 1948; that this consensus was expressed in the UDHR, which Eleanor Roosevelt (the chair of the UN CHR) called the "Magna Carta for all mankind";

that the implementation of the international human rights system was paralyzed during the decades of the Cold War, a long period of irrelevance symbolized most notoriously by the glacial pace at which the UDHR was eventually broken into two parts and rendered into international law through the two covenants; and that, with the end of the Cold War, the universal human rights movement was finally given a chance to flourish, a period of expansion marked by historic world conferences, the increasing power of "activists beyond borders,"[16] the establishment of standing human rights tribunals (including the International Criminal Court), and the proliferation and influence of specialized human rights categories such as Indigenous rights and women's rights.

Although recovered counternarratives from the diffuse and deeply heterogenous people's history of human rights will, in various ways, be interwoven into the book's alternative vision for the future of human rights, let me give just three examples of how these microhistories reveal more diverse, more contested, and yet more suggestive possibilities for human rights over this same period. During the roughly two years in which the UN CHR was organizing a largely state-level process through which a declaration of universal human rights was debated, drafted, and then presented to the UN General Assembly for adoption in December 1948, a parallel process was taking place whose inner workings and eventual revelations would remain unknown for more than fifty years.

Under the guidance of Julian Huxley, its charismatic and complicated first director-general, the United Nations Educational, Scientific, and Cultural Organization (UNESCO) took it upon itself to conduct a global survey of a wide range of thinkers, religious leaders, trade union activists, political leaders, and artists. The objective was to generate cross-cultural data in response to a questionnaire that asked respondents how the project to draft a statement of human rights fit with their own political, ethical, cultural, and religious sensibilities. After responses were received, UNESCO convened a small meeting of experts in Paris in June and July 1947 to examine the responses and then draft an analysis to be sent to the UN CHR, whose work on the declaration was moving rapidly forward. In 1949, a year after the UDHR had been adopted, UNESCO published a selection of the responses to its 1947 survey, but apart from this, the work of UNESCO during this period, and especially the full implications for human rights of what the survey revealed, were lost to history for decades.

The UNESCO human rights survey was later rediscovered under fraught historical circumstances. Despite the fact that many human rights scholars and activists experienced the 1990s as a kind of Hesiodic Golden Age, this was also the decade in which a number of distinct critiques took shape, most notably the critique—which took both political and academic forms—that the expanding human rights movement was actually a continuation of Western imperialism cloaked in the language of universal values.[17] Worried that this critique was gaining traction just at the moment in which the postwar human rights movement was finally breaking free of its Cold War shackles, pro-human-rights scholars and activists redoubled their efforts in the search for a definitive, and irrefutable, response to the charges of Western bias.

Although some tried to argue that the highly political machinations behind the drafting of the UDHR nevertheless revealed real consensus on the universal nature of human rights, it was the UNESCO human rights survey that was offered as a kind of trump card.[18] Perhaps without wanting to know more about the fascinating actual history of the UNESCO survey, scholars selectively interpreted certain parts of the UNESCO 1949 publication as documentary proof that human rights universality was discovered completely independently of anything that the UN CHR was doing at the same time.[19]

The problem is that more comprehensive research on the UNESCO human rights survey revealed a profoundly different situation, both in terms of what the responses to the survey said about the question of universal human rights, and, more important for my purposes here, what they revealed about the wide range of perspectives on the relationship between human rights and especially socioeconomic justice. Far from demonstrating that a global consensus existed about the value of the particular approach to human rights that would soon find expression in the UDHR, the UNESCO survey documented wide-ranging skepticism toward this approach, preference (especially among Western leftists) for Marxist or socialist alternatives, and often creative suggestions for how the UN human rights project could evolve beyond its perceived late eighteenth-century European origins.[20]

A second subversive microhistory is to be found in challenges to the part of the conventional historical narrative that reads the decades of the Cold War to be a kind of human rights wilderness, with cracks of light coming from the cloistered towers of the UN, in which intrepid international lawyers worked through the long night to keep the flame alive while laboring away over drafts of treaties, optional protocols, and hard-won ratifications.

But as counternarrative human rights historians have shown, this Geneva and New York–centric perspective on the decades of the Cold War obscures the ways in which human rights discourse—if not necessarily law—was mobilized in highly productive, and highly contextual, ways throughout the Global South. These microhistories of dynamic appropriation were most clearly associated with political decolonization, but, as one scholar puts it, were also part of a loosely organized movement throughout the Global South that sought nothing less than the "reconstruction of global values."[21]

A final category from the wider people's history of human rights, one that constitutes a fundamental source for many of the approaches and perspectives developed throughout the book, is what might be called the "ethnographic history of human rights." This is to be found in the wide-ranging comparative database of ethnographic case studies that tracked the practice of human rights after the end of the Cold War through its stunningly complex ramifications, from the use of human rights language as a rhetorical weapon of ethnonationalism in the very first post–Cold War constitutions to the campaign to translate the UDHR into Aboriginal Australian languages.[22]

The ethnographic history of human rights is a rich resource for reimagining the future of human rights for several reasons. First, ethnographers documented the practice of human rights largely by following its lived realities wherever and however they took shape, without being constrained by preexisting normative or political assumptions. This epistemological and methodological openness gave ethnographers the capacity to capture the extraordinary range and depth of human rights practices far beyond the boundaries of courts, political campaigns, and advocacy networks.

Second, this comparative ethnographic record reveals in granular empirical detail the many ways in which the practice of human rights is marked by transformation, innovation, and what might be described as "organic reformulation." Some of these organic reformulations stretch the meaning of human rights beyond what would be recognizable within the international human rights system, which is why they receive so much attention throughout this book.[23]

And third, the ethnographic history of human rights is arguably the comparative database that best coalesces the voices and visions of ordinary people around the world who have harnessed what I have described elsewhere as the "connotative power" of human rights, that is, the capacity to gesture toward, or invoke, what are believed to be essential values of human rights without making any specific reference at all to human rights as such.[24] As will be seen, the prevalence of connotation within the ethnographic history of human rights forms the starting point for a number of the book's key propositions.

For Now We See through a Glass, Darkly

In his thoroughgoing dissection of the multiple incapacities of the international human rights system in the midst of what he calls the "neoliberal maelstrom," Samuel Moyn argues that the greatest threat in the world today is the explosion of global economic inequality, a threat for which conventional human rights provides only weak and ultimately insufficient answers.[25] Although Moyn does not suggest that the postwar international human rights system was responsible for the eventual dominance of neoliberal capitalism as the world's governing political economy, he observes that their close historical interconnections raise troubling questions. As he puts it, "human rights became our highest ideals only as material hierarchy remained endemic or worsened. . . . Human rights emerged as the highest morality of an unequal world, in a neoliberal circumstance its partisans could struggle to humanize, only to find themselves accused of complicity with it."[26]

However, despite the critical importance of Moyn's intervention, which supercharged debates about the fundamental moral crisis of global economic inequality under conditions of capitalist hegemony, I don't believe that the structural ravages of global capitalism are the only maelstrom that a reinvented human rights must be prepared to confront. Moreover, it is not clear that "brutality and complexity in the global economy" function as the root cause of the other maelstroms,[27] despite the fact that the "expulsions" of capitalism are implicated in a range of other chronic global problems, from human-induced climate change to resource conflicts to the increasing use of data technologies to both surveil and manipulate consumers and voters alike.[28]

Nevertheless, regardless of how one positions global economic inequality in relation to the other contemporary maelstroms, the basic fact remains: we are living through dark times without either seeing a light at the end of the tunnel, or, apropos of existing human rights, even having the realistic capacity to see it. It is this fact, more than anything else, that lends a sense of urgency to the proposal to radically refashion human rights in such a way that it recaptures what Moyn calls its "defensible importance" as one of the "main keys to unlock the portal to the world's future."[29] Yet beyond the obvious importance of global capitalism, there are three additional parts of the wider social, political, and economic background that are of particular concern.

The first is the return of nationalism as a predominant ideology of collective identity, albeit an ideology that jostles with those that center on religious and ethnic or racial identity. It is striking how quickly nationalism returned as a force for political and social mobilization and also how widespread nationalist ideologies have become, uniting—in this sense, if not in others—a vast range of political currents from the United States to India, and from China to the United Kingdom. If the causal relationship between the rise of human rights and the explosion of global economic inequality is still in some doubt, the relationship between the collapse of existing human rights and the suffusion of nationalist ideologies around the world is not.

The end of the "Age of Human Rights" was first and foremost the end of a fragile historical period in which concepts like global citizenship and transnational identity were given a serious hearing, although never in ways that ever challenged the underlying Westphalian system of autonomous nation-states, a chronic defect in the postwar international human rights system. Rather, the snuffing out of the embryonic flames of cosmopolitanism left an ambiguous field on which the many existing and transmogrified forms of nationalism could flourish. The critical problem for any reformulated account of human rights is that despite the many variations, nationalism, at its core, relies on a hard and fast ideology of difference, which runs completely counter to any efforts to imagine—let alone act on—forms of collective belonging animated by the principle of translocality. And if the problems and violence of what might be called the "inner face" of nationalism are well known, what is even more worrying, from my perspective, is what might be described as the "outer face" of nationalism.

As historians of the rise of nationalism in mid-nineteenth-century Euro-American international relations have emphasized, nationalism was the driving impulse behind colonial expansion. Beyond the need to secure access to natural resources for burgeoning capitalist economies, colonialism was also a competition for symbolic political capital among certain state powers.[30] In these terms, nationalism defined and justified categories of immutable difference between "nations" while compelling "nation-states" to impose their national values on others, since every nation viewed its values as the true ones—and there could only be one truth. The character Shatov in Dostoevsky's novel *The Possessed* (published in 1873) describes this "outer face" of nationalism in its purest, most chilling, form: "If a great people does not believe that the truth is to be found in itself alone . . . if it does not believe that it alone is fit and destined to raise up and save all the rest by its truth, it would at once sink into being ethnographic material, and not a great people. . . . A nation which loses this belief ceases to be a nation."[31]

A second ominous part of the wider global landscape on which a reinvented human rights would necessarily have to take root is the increasing importance of bioenvironmental crises, which impose their own logics of transformation and also seem to defy our best (and worst) efforts to confront them. Leaving aside for the moment the ongoing and future catastrophic effects of human-induced climate change, the most obvious example of how bioenvironmental crises pose an existential challenge to any future vision for human rights is the global COVID-19 pandemic. The pandemic carries lessons for how the role of current international institutions must be understood and for how a spirit of existing human rights influences the way people act toward one another, especially during a sudden and unprecedented crisis of global scope.

Although different points of fracture can be emphasized, I think it is unarguable that the UN system manifestly fell short of its Article 1 raisons d'être in the face of one of the most consequential global emergencies since the founding of the United Nations in 1945. If the United Nations was created to "take effective collective measures for the prevention and removal of threats," to "achieve international co-operation in solving international problems of an economic, social, cultural, or humanitarian character," and to function as a "center for harmonizing the actions of nations in the attainment of . . . common ends," then we must acknowledge that the United Nations tragically failed to achieve these purposes in the midst of a new global crisis.[32]

In a way, the global COVID-19 pandemic simply laid bare all of the weaknesses and contradictions in the postwar international system, which embeds formal inequality among nation-states—most clearly through the UN Security Council—and claims to be working toward the creation of a global political and social order based in human rights, while remaining structurally hostage to the violent vicissitudes of national sovereignty. Although these fatal flaws have often been minimized or obscured by the rhetoric of internationalism, the global COVID-19 pandemic pulled back the curtain to reveal the actual hollowness behind the international system; what remained was a frightening scenario in which states competed on a vastly unequal playing field in a nasty, brutish struggle to survive.

But apart from the institutional failure of the international system to realize its grand cosmopolitan visions, what did the experience of the global COVID-19 pandemic have to teach us about the ethical underpinnings of this system, that is, existing human rights? Even if we agree that our "highest morality" has proven incapable of effectively confronting the long-term implications of global economic inequality, what about the more immediate circumstances of a global pandemic, in which decisions about life and death are made in every home, in every neighborhood around the world, for the same reasons, at the same time?

Here, I think the evidence was surprisingly much more mixed. Indeed, I would suggest that many of the responses to the pandemic in the localized and intimate spaces of everyday life showed a deep desire and willingness to form lines of alliance based on common purpose, solidarity, and the refusal to accept the crushing realities of social suffering—all glimmers of possibility that support the ethical core of the alternative approach to human rights developed throughout this book.

Finally, the proposal to reinvent human rights takes shape against a wider political background in which the contours of progressive political ideology and practice are as confused as they have been for arguably 150 years, when the bloody suppression of the Paris Commune of 1871 ushered in a half century marked by political agitation and violence, the rise of a consumer-oriented and exclusionary bourgeoisie during the Gilded Age, and the fearsome expansion of empire as a pervasive mechanism of international power.[33] Clarity on the political left only pierced through this period of ambiguity with the 1917 Russian Revolution, which, among other things, showed the world what a successful nonliberal revolution can look like.

This legacy and its afterlives bear on the current moment in ways that carry uncertain implications for any project to refashion human rights as a reconstituted framework for global justice. As the political philosopher Nancy Fraser predicted during the early years of the post–Cold War, the rapid collapse of revolutionary socialism gave rise to a politics of recognition in which justice was no longer framed along political economic lines, but along lines of identity.[34] The politics of recognition quickly came to replace the socialist politics of redistribution as the dominant ideology of the left, especially in countries like the United States and the United Kingdom, where traditional leftist parties were co-opted by their "new" successors, which found ways to combine support for human rights with the promotion of neoliberal economics. Moreover, political mobilization during this period, which coincided with the broader "Age of Human Rights," took place largely through institutional channels: legislative reforms, the courts, and through support for political candidates (at least in democratic countries).

Yet with the gradual waning of the Age of Human Rights, a number of consequential transformations took place on the political left. On the one hand, as early as the Occupy movement and associated mobilizations in the aftermath of the Great Recession of 2007–9 (in which the anarchist anthropologist David

Graeber played a leading role),[35] the political left began abandoning institutional engagement, whether on behalf of human rights activism or otherwise. What replaced institutional engagement was a kind of anarchist revolutionary politics, yet one shorn of the ideology of the traditional revolutionary left, that is, the ideology of Marxist or socialist struggle grounded in some version of historical materialism.

And, on the other hand, although these initial mobilizations were inspired by anticapitalist logics that were anchored in broader demands for economic justice, this brief glimmer of a new politics of redistribution quickly ebbed. What remained, however, was the methodology, the oppositional imperative, the deep distrust—especially by young activists—of institutions, associations, even traditional political parties. Without a clear commitment to a revolutionary confrontation with capitalism, whose hegemony was only reinforced after the Great Recession with the stunning strengthening of the G20 as a postinternational node of global power, the political left continued to fragment into many smaller movements, not all of which were mutually reinforcing.

If questions of economic justice were relegated to the peripheries on this diffused, even chaotic, political left, a certain coherence was established through the way in which identity discrimination—both historic and structural and more recent—became the central focus for social action. In this, the language of recognition justice—racial, gender, sexual orientation, disability rights, among others—became what Axel Honneth described as the "moral grammar" of resistance and progressive action, which implied new means of coordination, new criteria for participation, and especially new methods of intervention, including those that harnessed the fraught power of digital technologies.[36]

The centrality of a politics of recognition on the contemporary political left creates a twofold dilemma for the proposal to reinvent human rights as a reconstituted framework for global justice. First, although members of vulnerable groups experience the violence of discrimination as a dehumanizing harm that can take both more subtle and immediately brutal forms, it is difficult to generalize the nuances of identity discrimination beyond specific histories, specific political contexts, and specific cultural formations. One of the virtues of historical materialism, at least—a virtue that cannot be simply reappropriated through a kind of nostalgia for simpler ideological times—was to provide a means for understanding how highly diverse conflicts in different parts of the world were ultimately the effect of class struggle, of the efforts of certain parts of society to control the means of production through exploitation, alienation, and structural exclusion.

And second, and perhaps even more problematic, the politics of recognition is structured by a logic of mobilization that comes into immediate tension with any proposal to forge wider—if not necessarily global—lines of alliance, which demand solidarity and affiliation beyond categories of difference. Although the proposal to reinvent human rights is not based in an abstract concept of universal personhood, it does, nevertheless, require a commitment to translocal common purpose and a reaffirmation of the critical importance of "thinking and feeling beyond the nation."[37]

The task, therefore, is to keep the current spirit of resistance at the very center of a reinvented human rights, a spirit that evokes what Dr. Martin Luther King Jr. called the "fierce urgency of now,"[38] while at the same time imagining how this spirit can and must animate social and economic action beyond the categories of difference in which specific histories of injustice and specific movements for justice are inescapably embedded.

CHAPTER 2

Human Rights, Capitalism, and the Ends of Economic Life

> The first man who, having enclosed a piece of land, thought of saying "This is mine" and found people simple enough to believe him, was the true founder of civil society. How many crimes, wars, murders; how much misery and horror the human race would have been spared if someone had pulled up the stakes and filled in the ditch and cried out to his fellow men: "Beware of listening to this imposter. You are lost if you forget that the fruits of the earth belong to everyone and that the earth itself belongs to no one!"
>
> Jean-Jacques Rousseau, *Discourse on the Origin of Inequality* (1755)

IN THE FIRST MONTHS OF 1947, the newly formed UNESCO undertook what became a remarkable study of the philosophical, cultural, and historical bases of human rights. Although the UN's Commission on Human Rights (CHR), under the leadership of Eleanor Roosevelt, had been constituted specifically to oversee the drafting of a new "international bill of rights" (the description of the planned declaration changed over time), the actual process through which this would happen remained uncertain. Specifically, questions swirled around how the widest possible level of participation could be guaranteed for this most consequential of early postwar efforts, beyond the roles played by state-level representatives within the nascent international system.

Into this ambiguity stepped UNESCO, under the leadership of its cosmopolitan first director-general, Julian Huxley. Huxley, at the time a renowned scientific humanist and controversial eugenicist, was the product of a family at the very center of English social and intellectual power. His paternal grandfather was T. H. Huxley (Darwin's "bulldog"); one of his brothers was the novelist Aldous Huxley; one of his great-uncles was the cultural critic Matthew Arnold; and his half brother

Andrew would go on to win the Nobel Prize in Medicine. Huxley, who had played a leading role in advocating for the creation of an international educational, scientific, and cultural organization as the cornerstone of the postwar world order, viewed UNESCO's central purpose as promoting the "emergence of a single world culture, with its own philosophy and background of ideas . . . a world philosophy, a unified and unifying background of thought for the modern world."[1]

When the wider UN project to draft a declaration of human rights was announced, Huxley almost immediately viewed this as an opportunity for UNESCO to play an essential part in the process, since he understood "human rights" to be a potential cornerstone of the world philosophy that was UNESCO's primary concern. To this end, he charged the young first head of UNESCO's philosophy section with organizing a global survey of thinkers, religious figures, political leaders, trade unionists, and many others, on the question of the cross-cultural content and validity of human rights.[2] Jacques Havet, a twenty-six-year-old French philosopher and acolyte of Jean-Paul Sartre, whose once promising academic career had been sidetracked by the war, drafted a questionnaire on human rights that was sent to a long list of the great and the good in what was still very much a colonial world.

This curious and imposing, but nevertheless exclusionary, list included figures such as Aldous Huxley (Julian's brother), W. H. Auden, T. S. Eliot, Alfred Weber (Max's brother), Jawaharlal Nehru, Benedetto Croce, John Dewey, Henry Wallace (the US vice president during the war), Paul Robeson, Richard Wright, and Mahatma Gandhi. In the end, about 180 surveys were received by people around the world, and almost sixty responses of one kind or another were eventually returned to UNESCO at its headquarters in Paris.

Although both Huxley and Havet fully expected that the human rights survey would reveal a global consensus around basic principles and the overriding importance of making the "rights of man" the centerpiece of the postwar settlement, in fact, the survey revealed no such consensus. Instead, it showed to what extent the proposition by the new United Nations to promulgate a declaration of human rights was greeted with various degrees of skepticism, doubt, and outright befuddlement. Among the different responses, the most troubling for the wider effort to privilege human rights as the political, legal, and moral foundation for the new international system were those from the political left, both in colonial or decolonizing countries and at the centers of power in the Global North. Nehru, for example, the architect of independent India who would go on to serve three terms as prime minister, simply refused to write a response to the survey. As a key figure in the socialist Indian National Congress party at the exact moment when it was grappling with the social and economic realities of imminent independence, Nehru felt unmoved by the question of human rights, which he viewed as a collection of mere "pious sentiments."[3]

Yet it was the responses of leading Marxist and socialist intellectuals in the Global North that posed the most fundamental challenges to human rights. For example, E. H. Carr was a polymathic British journalist, international relations scholar, Sovietologist, and diplomat. Earlier in his career, Carr had played an important role in the establishment of the League of Nations after World War I. During the UNESCO human rights survey of 1947–48, Huxley asked him to serve as the chair of a small "committee of experts" that analyzed the results and produced a report that was sent to the CHR in the United States. He also wrote his own response to the survey. He made the point perhaps more clearly than any other that the "rights of man" must be deeply historicized, otherwise the United Nations risked promulgating a declaration that was unfit for the most critical contemporary problems.

As Carr explained, "the conception of the rights of man dates historically from the 18th century when it was particularly . . . associated with the American and French Revolutions."[4] Carr calls this the "political conception" of human rights, in which the rising bourgeoisie in the British colonies and in France proposed the "rights of man" as a new category through which different forms of constraint could be resisted. Human rights was thus an ideological framework for breaking free of two different exploitative structures: in the case of the British colonies, the exploitative political and economic structure of colonialism; and in late eighteenth-century France, it was the semifeudal *ancien régime*, which consisted of divine kingship supported by an all-powerful Church. In both cases, the strategic use of human rights as the foundation for the American and French Revolutions provided the justification for demanding a representative government be established on behalf of a nonaristocratic merchant class.

However, as Carr argues, the circumstances of the mid-twentieth-century postwar period couldn't be more different from those of the late eighteenth century, which were, to be sure, restricted to political and economic conditions in one (important) British colony and one (important) European kingdom. Even more than the two world wars, the most transformative historical change had been the Russian Revolution of 1917, which set in motion a completely different political economic process, one for which, according to Carr, the late eighteenth-century "political conception" of human rights had little relevance.

Instead, Carr points to the 1918 Declaration of Rights of the Toiling and Exploited Peoples and, even more, the Soviet Constitution of 1936—which acquired, over time, the unfortunate moniker as the "Stalin Constitution"—to illustrate how a "modern conception" of human rights should be established. For Carr, the most essential parts of this modern conception were the abolition of structural economic exploitation through the "socialist organization of society in all countries"; the abolition of private property in land within the means of production; the establishment of workers' control of industry and the state nationalization of banks and major financial institutions; and, above all, the guarantee of the right to work through full employment in all countries, which was the first "human right" in the Soviet Constitution of 1936.[5]

Another respondent to the UNESCO human rights survey, John Lewis, went even further than Carr. Lewis, who was a Welsh Marxist philosopher, Unitarian minister, and, at the time of the survey, the editor of the British Marxist journal *Modern Quarterly*, argued that the eighteenth-century conception of human rights simply could not be reconciled with the economic and social realities of the industrialized, colonial, and unequal world of the twentieth century. Indeed, as he puts it, "the conception of absolute, inherent and imprescriptible rights based on man's origins and nature antecedent to society, is not only a myth but involves a misleading conception of the meaning of human rights."[5] Instead, he suggests that the United Nations consider a radically different approach in which "rights [are] based upon human needs and possibilities and the recognition by members of a society of the conditions necessary in order that they may fulfill their common ends."[7]

More specifically, although the eighteenth-century political conception of human rights was—despite its universalist rhetoric—tailored to the "rising industrialist class," a modern approach to human rights should be, according to Lewis, structured around "broad popular demands for social justice and human betterment."[8] Lewis focuses particularly on the fundamental human right to property to make the point that a new vision of human rights must take a completely different form, even if this meant that the existing—that is, late eighteenth-century—conception of human rights had to be "overridden."[9]

As Lewis explains, the human right to property was thought originally to include the right to own people, including the land they cultivated. Although the human right to own people as property was eventually abrogated—though not everywhere in the world—the human right to property, according to Lewis, remained compromised, oppositional, and trapped by its historical origins.[10] The problem, according to Lewis, is that even after slavery was abolished, the human right to property remained at the foundation of social conflict and exploitation, especially when this right was used to justify the development and legal protection of a capitalist mode of production. In "overriding" the eighteenth-century version of human rights—including the right to property—the "gain [would be] infinitely greater than the loss," because the exploitative bourgeois social order would be replaced with one in which the welfare of workers was paramount. As Lewis puts it, a social order based on an alternative conception of human rights would necessarily "exclude not only slavery, but capitalism."[11]

The Scottish mathematician and Imperial College dean Hyman Levy, who was a member of the British Communist Party at the time of the UNESCO human rights survey, rejected the whole UN project to promulgate a declaration of human rights, since the entire approach would be unacceptable to any country that had adopted a Marxist or socialist political and economic system.[12] The problem, according to Levy, was that Marxism had already proved that "expressing abstract ethical principles in a political and social vacuum" was "meaningless in practice." If the UN were to proceed anyway along the lines proposed, the result would be a declaration of human rights that ignored the realities and values of one of the world's major political economic traditions.

The solution, as Levy argues, would require the United Nations to first abandon the search for "a system of human rights as such." Then, the United Nations should begin again by asking, "what are the physical and material conditions that may make the emergence of . . . rights in practice a real possibility?" As Levy acknowledges, to "deal with such things in full would lead [the United Nations] into the realm of controversy from which it would presumably like to steer clear." Nevertheless, such an approach, which must focus on the "material aspects of the problem," might eventually give rise to a very different kind of international declaration, which Levy suggests could be called the "Needs of Man."[13]

Finally, the Marxist economist Maurice Dobb was more sanguine than others about the possible value in a UN declaration of human rights, since "declarations of rights can have a function in summarizing the aspirations of progressively minded persons in a given age, confronted with the given situation and a given group of problems: as pointers to the direction in which efforts at social advance must be turned."[14] Yet Dobb utterly rejected the possibility that such a declaration of aspirations should "point to" the need for a system of human rights anchored in a "group of problems" associated with the rise of bourgeois capitalist economics.[15]

Dobb analyzes the four possible foundations of a new declaration of human rights, one properly directed toward the most critical problems of the time. First, it should guarantee the attainment of (and not just the right to) full employment (here Dobb likewise invokes the 1936 Soviet Constitution). Second, it should guarantee social security against "loss of earning-power from any of the risks to which the wage-earner is prone" and prohibit "any contract of employment which fails to secure a certain minimum standard of earnings." As Dobb emphasizes, this second right/guarantee would require both the pervasive use of planned national economies—as opposed to what he describes as the vicissitudes of "*laissez-faire*"—and an international program of development to allow colonized and other marginalized countries to boost their levels of national production to put them on a level playing field. Third, a new UN declaration of human rights should guarantee the right of workers to organize in order to ensure that their conditions of employment remain fully equal to those of employers. As Dobb puts it, it is "manifestly inconsistent with the dignity of man that labour should be regarded (as hitherto) as a mere hired factor of production, excluded from any voice in the conduct of industrial policy."[16] And fourth, a new declaration of rights must guarantee access to employment without regard to "any considerations of race, creed, opinion or membership of any legal organization."[17]

In considering the far-reaching implications of such a profoundly anticapitalist conception of human rights for the wider global economic system, one that had been significantly reinforced through the 1944 Bretton Woods agreement, Dobb was unequivocal: "It can reasonably be held that ownership of the means of production (including land) by private individuals on such a scale as to imply that independent access to these means of production is barred for a substantial section of the community represents an infringement on the economic rights of man in any full sense of the term."[18]

It should go without saying that these Marxist and socialist critiques and imagined alternatives to the proposal for a UN declaration of human rights were never seriously considered, either by the UNESCO committee of experts or the UN CHR itself. Despite the fact that historical materialist skepticism about a declaration of human rights that appeared to be modeled structurally and normatively on a late eighteenth-century blueprint was strongly represented among the full body of responses to the UNESCO survey, and, even more, among the UNESCO committee of experts, its perspective was suppressed.

Among the eight members of the committee, at least five were highly critical of the UN human rights project. Their resistance seemed to be based less on the findings of the UNESCO survey itself than on their own preexisting understandings of historical and economic conflict. Besides Carr (the chair of the committee), others who expressed strong doubts included French nuclear physicist Pierre Auger, French sociologist Georges Friedmann,[19] Belgian communist and civil servant Luc Somerhausen, and British political theorist and socialist Harold Laski. As Laski put it, in his own response to the UNESCO human rights survey:

> It is of the first importance . . . to remember that the Great Declarations of the past are a quite special heritage of Western civilization, that they are deeply involved in a Protestant bourgeois tradition, which is itself an outstanding aspect of the rise of the middle class to power. . . . "Equality before the law" has not meant very much in the lives of the working-class in most political communities.[20]

For his part, Carr became so disillusioned with the UNESCO human rights survey and the wider drafting process taking place through the UN CHR, that he eventually repudiated both. His reaction was in part the result of a curious development within the UNESCO committee of experts. Despite the fact that its own analysis cast serious doubt on the survey's underlying objectives, which were to reveal a global consensus on human rights and to ensure that this consensus formed the basis for the UN declaration, a committee report was drafted and sent to the UN CHR (in August 1947) that gave no indication of these wide-ranging misgivings. This was because the report, titled "The Grounds of an International Declaration of Human Rights," had been written by the committee's imperious rapporteur, Richard McKeon, dean of humanities and a legendary philosophy professor at the University of Chicago (who later was the basis for the feared character of the "Chairman" in Robert Pirsig's novel *Zen and the Art of Motorcycle Maintenance*).[21]

McKeon understood the task of the UNESCO survey quite differently and strategically: it was to find some support, however tenuous in fact, for a result that everyone knew was predetermined—the promulgation of a declaration of human rights by the new United Nations within an international system in which the United States was the economic and political hegemon. To the extent to which the responses to the UNESCO survey revealed opposition to this predetermined endpoint, let alone opposition to the reality of US economic and political dominance, McKeon believed it was the job of the committee to "facilitat[e] the removal of differences [of opinion]."[22]

To this end, McKeon ensured that "The Grounds of an International Declaration of Human Rights" made no mention of the robust currents of Marxist and socialist critique that had been so powerfully revealed through the UNESCO survey. Indeed, the language and content of "The Grounds of an International Declaration of Human Rights" resemble very closely McKeon's own contribution to the survey, which emphasizes the timeless importance of "natural rights, sacred and inherent in man," as against dangerously contrary approaches based on a "spirit of collectivity" that underpinned a "tyranny of the masses."[23] Carr, having received a copy of McKeon's "The Grounds of an International Declaration of Human Rights," complained in a private letter to Julian Huxley that the UNESCO report reflected all the "hollowness" of the wider project to draft a supposedly "universal" declaration of human rights, a project that was, at its core, "either stupid or intellectually dishonest."[24]

✻   ✻   ✻

There are two main reasons for beginning this chapter on the relationship between economic and social inequality, political economy, and a reinvented human rights with this lengthy recovery of certain key aspects from the 1947–48 UNESCO human rights survey. First, it is important to be reminded of a critical period in relatively recent history in which the end of World War II gave way to profound uncertainty about the future. Against the background of a still deeply colonial global order, the question of how the embryonic international system should respond to the most pressing problems of the day was riven along any number of ideological, national, racial, and regional fault lines.

In particular, the Soviet bloc countries, grounded in an alternative reality of historical materialism and committed to a global revolutionary struggle against capitalism, represented for many a unifying and concrete embodiment of a more advanced and progressive future, one that would be free of the inequalities and socioeconomic forces that had—it was believed—led the world to catastrophic war and untold human suffering twice in only twenty-five years.

Despite the different efforts of communist countries to show that their constitutional foundations were not completely hostile to human rights, in fact, at a broader level, most thinkers and political and social leaders from Marxist and socialist traditions viewed human rights as neither necessary nor sufficient for the realization of this more advanced and progressive future. If anything, the opposite was true, since "human rights" were indelibly associated with the rise of the bourgeoisie as a social class and its political and legal campaigns over the decades to use human rights to justify its exclusionary and exploitative access to productive capital.

From this perspective, the question of whether or not the new United Nations should adopt a declaration of human rights as the normative basis for the postwar settlement was, as the French saying has it, *hors sujet*. Instead, since a more sustainable and just vision for the postwar global order had already been revealed as early as the 1917 Russian Revolution, the real question was how some profoundly reimagined version of human rights, a "modern conception," could serve this vision. As we have seen, most leftist intellectuals in the early postwar period believed a synthesis of this kind was philosophically improbable and politically beside the point.

And second, the relevance of these debates over the relationship between political economy and human rights during this brief, but highly illuminating, postwar (but pre-UDHR) period hovers over our own time like a specter, yet one whose presence is nevertheless denied, ignored, or glossed over. This is in part the result of the course of history, in which the revolutionary program for a world free of capitalist bondage collapsed with the end of the Cold War. As a result, the problem of a fundamental tension between socialism and human rights faded with the political disappearance of socialism itself, which was replaced widely and insistently by the politics of identity as an organizing logic for progressive mobilization.

But what happened to the underlying economic and social conditions for which the Marxist and socialist traditions were supposedly the more just, more "modern," indeed, inevitable, response? Even as the only credible alternative to capitalism and its discontents was swept into the dustbin of history—a turning point that apparently, and conveniently, marked the end of history itself[25]—the most rapaciously productive political economic system in world history was transformed into an unquestionably dominant and unifying global assemblage, one that also became the "truly ambitious and successful moral program of our time" (that is, unlike international human rights).[26]

The remainder of this chapter examines the reality of these economic and social conditions in more detail as well as debates over how existing human rights—especially economic and social rights—have responded to these conditions. As I argue, critics have given heightened prominence to fundamental inquiries that are long overdue, such as, the relationship between human rights and (neoliberal) capitalism. What I suggest is that this relationship is indeed problematic, even in ways that have not been fully acknowledged. Yet what I also argue is that this relationship can and must be transformed through a refashioning of human rights itself as a translocal framework for justice-seeking and collective action. In this, I depart from the more pessimistic account of the future of human rights given by Moyn, who asks, "could a different form of human rights law or movements correct for their coexistence with a crisis of material inequality? There is reason to doubt they can do so by changing radically."[27]

Yet I share his understanding of the source of this serious doubt, which is the daunting power and scope of global capitalism. As he soberly acknowledges, "the truth is that local and global economic justice requires redesigning markets or at least redistributing from the rich to the rest, something that naming and shaming are never likely to achieve, even when supplemented by novel forms of legal activism."[28] Instead of redesigning markets, I argue, we would do better by first redesigning human rights in such a way that the hegemony of global capitalism can be understood and confronted for what it really is: the endemic, pervasive cause of structural immiseration and despoliation (at multiple levels and in multiple senses) and a marker of moral crisis on a global scale.

The Truth about Capitalism

In 2014, the French economist Thomas Piketty published his monumental longitudinal study of the distribution of wealth and income under capitalism. Although Piketty's research in many ways reaffirms a number of central insights from Marx's three-volume *Das Kapital* (1867, 1885, 1894), his study of capital in the twenty-first century also parts ways with Marxist orthodoxy. Yet these divergences nevertheless reinforce a basic truth about capitalism: it is a political economic system that has proven to be even more devastating for global justice and long-term ecological sustainability than imagined.

Among these divergences, the most critical is around Marx's predictions about the inevitable implosion of capitalism, whose internal contradictions, driven by the "principle of infinite accumulation," would bring about the system's demise for one of two reasons: "either the rate of return on capital would steadily diminish (thereby killing the engine of accumulation and leading to violent conflict among capitalists), or capital's share of national income would increase indefinitely (which sooner or later would unite the workers in revolt)."[29] Yet as Piketty observes, "Marx's dark prophecy" never came close to being realized. This was because Marx's critique of capitalism didn't account for the ways in which economic inequality through capital accumulation could be accompanied by "the improvement in the purchasing power of workers," a power that, moreover, "spread everywhere."[30]

And even though the workers did eventually unite in revolt as Marx had predicted, they did so under conditions and through means that limited the extent to which this pivotal revolution could challenge the real long-term dangers of capitalism. First, as is well known, the Russian Revolution took place "in the most backward country of Europe, . . . where the Industrial Revolution had scarcely begun."[31] This meant that the revolt against capitalism as an exploitative and historically destructive mode of production unfolded not amid the squalor of a place like Manchester circa 1844, where the tragedies of early industrial capitalism were embodied in the very toxicity of working-class urban life,[32] but in semifeudal and preindustrial Russia, whose underlying economic and social conditions couldn't be more different.

Second, in the countries that were the driving engines of capitalist development and expansion (primarily in Europe, but later the United States), workers resisted outright rebellion against the capitalist system, preferring, instead, to struggle for better working conditions and workers' rights within—not outside of, or against—capitalism. In this, the workers' movement was already making Faustian bargains with the capitalist Mephistopheles under the banner of "social democracy," a completely pragmatic compromise that allowed global capitalism to flourish throughout the twentieth century and into the twenty-first. And from the beginning, an international system arose to mediate the terms of this Faustian bargain between capitalism and "social democratic" labor, terms that might have improved working conditions from those of Manchester in 1844 but which were really designed to protect capitalism from the existential threat of communist revolution. As historians of the International Labour Organization (ILO) have shown, it was founded in 1919 as a direct response to the Russian Revolution, to provide a means through which the global capitalist system could preserve itself by ameliorating its worst abuses.[33]

And third, even though the revolt against capitalism eventually spread beyond Europe (though never within a major industrialized capitalist country), what resulted was a series of "tragic totalitarian experiments"[34] that became mired in their own humanitarian and moral crises, different from those of capitalism, but corrosive and ultimately calamitous nonetheless. Piketty rightly argues that the tragedy of twentieth-century communism was in part the result of Marx's failure to fully appreciate the difficulty in practically reordering countries politically and economically in which private capital had been abolished. Nevertheless, I think the even more critical historical and ideological failure came with Lenin, whose plans for class war in the early stages of the Russian Revolution planted the seeds for all the violence and mass atrocities that were to follow (in the Soviet Union and elsewhere).

When Lenin announced (in 1919) that the workers would need to organize themselves into a "dictatorship of the proletariat" in order to constitute a collective "weapon" in the class struggle, a "cudgel" with which they would "suppress" and "neutralize" both the bourgeoisie and the mealymouthed "socialists" who were unwilling to "carry the idea of the class struggle to its logical conclusion," he (and the Party) laid the ideological groundwork for every act of revolutionary brutality for the next seventy years, from the purges of Stalin to the killing fields of Cambodia.[35] Although they were more immediately inspired by Maoism, when the Khmer Rouge spoke of "smashing" their enemies—which they did, with genocidal fury[36]—this glorification of revolutionary ultraviolence was connected in a direct ideological line to Lenin's "cudgel."

Yet if orthodox Marxist-Leninism was catastrophically wrong about so much of its blueprint for a postcapitalist world in which private capital and the owning classes had been "suppressed," Marx's underlying critique of capitalism remained paradoxically revelatory. Even if the "principle of infinite accumulation" and its related consequences turned out to be mistaken or grossly overstated, Marx had identified something fundamental about capitalism: the production of wealth, eventually on a vast, global scale, was inevitably, dialectically, connected with the production of economic and social inequality; that is, capitalist wealth and inequality were mutually constitutive.

And here we return to Piketty's historical analysis of wealth and inequality under conditions of global capitalist consolidation. Instead of the problem of infinite accumulation, Piketty's longitudinal research reveals something else, something "terrifying," what he calls the "central contradiction of capitalism." He introduces this finding through a chillingly simple equation: $r > g$. As he explains, r stands for the long-term private rate of return on capital, while g stands for the rate of growth in the real economy, measured by incomes and output. The problem is that capital wealth grows on average between 4 and 5 percent, while the *best* long-term, comparative growth rates in real economies across multiple countries has hovered around 1–1.5 percent. Moreover, there is no way, according to Piketty, for capitalist economies to raise economic growth to come anywhere near that of capital, "no matter what economic policies [internationally or nationally] are adopted."[37]

Even more, because "the return on capital varies directly with the size of the initial stake," and "once constituted, capital reproduces itself [much] faster than output increases," the result is that the "entrepreneur inevitably tends to become a rentier, more and more dominant over those who own nothing but their labor." And this dominance then multiplies and gets reproduced at all scales in which the central contradiction of capitalism is at work, culminating in what Piketty euphemistically describes as "divergence in the wealth distribution . . . on a global scale."[38]

The moral crisis of this global "divergence" is not only the fact that vast, even unimaginable, levels of long-term, structural economic and social inequality are hardwired into the DNA of capitalism; rather, it is also that these inevitable levels of inequality are the result of decisions taken years, decades, and even centuries ago, when the "initial stake" was made. In other words, the moral crisis of capitalism, as Piketty puts it, is that the "past devours the future."[39]

Yet despite having revealed in minute historical and statistical detail the "terrifying" engine of global economic and social inequality, Piketty's proposals for responding to the central crisis of the twenty-first century are almost perversely modest. In the few remaining paragraphs at the end of his six-hundred-page study, Piketty suggests an internationally coordinated "progressive annual tax on capital" that would at least slow the "endless inegalitarian spiral" while making sure to "preserve[ ] competition and incentives for new instances of primitive accumulation." The task, according to Piketty, is not to fundamentally challenge the long-term viability and moral legitimacy of capitalism but simply to try and "regain control" over it. To do so, as he puts it vaguely, "we must bet everything on democracy."[40]

The stark disjuncture between Piketty's landmark critique of capitalism and his essentially reformist prescription for attempting to merely soften its most extreme excesses, did not go unnoticed. As the anthropologist David Graeber ruefully observed, "having demonstrated [that] capitalism is a gigantic vacuum cleaner sucking wealth into the hands of a tiny elite, [Piketty] insists that we do not simply unplug the machine, but try to build a slightly smaller vacuum cleaner sucking in the opposite direction." And more broadly, "the sheer fact that in 2014 a left-leaning French intellectual can safely declare that he does not want to overthrow the capitalist system but only to save it from itself is the reason [fundamental challenges to the system] will never happen."[41]

But why, then, is a frank acknowledgment of these essential truths about capitalism critical for the project to reinvent human rights? First, it is important to remember that the central contradiction of capitalism, $r > g$, does not mean that these two values are inversely correlated. Even as capitalist wealth grows at exponential, explosive, rates, real economies also grow, which means (in the best of circumstances) wages and output do creep up, which might cause workers to experience a measurable improvement in their economic circumstances over time. Yet notice what "growth" really means here: a worker in an advanced capitalist country like the United States, who earns $35,000/year in conditions of optimal long-term growth, will earn $36,597/year after three years, according to Piketty's research. Does this extra $133/month, after three years, represent an improvement in the quality of life sufficient to justify all the social and environmental costs of the underlying system itself?

At the same time, the capitalist, who begins from a dramatically different starting point, and whose wealth is generated from returns on capital (rather than wage labor), would experience these three years quite differently. With an "initial stake" of $10 million, the capitalist would end the same period of time with a return of almost $1.6 million, again, based on average rates of long-term capital growth. And where did this "initial stake" come from in the first place? It came from wealth generated in the same way, perhaps decades or even centuries in the past, growing exponentially—and often passively—across time and space, resulting in an economic and social tragedy in which the four hundred wealthiest Americans control more wealth than the bottom 150 million Americans *combined*.[42]

Second, despite the fact that the tragedy of wealth inequality in the United States, which has had the world's largest economy since the 1870s, crystallizes all the destructive consequences of capitalism more generally, these consequences can only be fully understood as part of a global economic system that is characterized by the same levels of extreme inequality. For example, the $21.5 trillion US economy is larger than the combined economies of the "bottom" 173 national economies. If only one US state out of fifty (California) were its own country, it would have the fifth largest economy in the world, bigger than the economy of India. This also means that California's per capita GDP is about $71,000 while India's is around $2,000. If only one US megacorporation, Walmart, were itself a country, it would have the twenty-fifth largest economy in the world. And so on.

Even more, it is impossible to understand the contemporary global capitalist system without taking account of the history of colonialism in which vast colonized regions of the world didn't even occupy the same structural position as workers in a capitalist enterprise, who are paid wages within a "divergent" and highly unequal mode of production. Instead, colonialism was pure exploitation, since the capitalist system throughout much of its history depended on access to raw materials at the lowest possible costs. This created the underlying incentives for powerful colonial countries to use whatever means were necessary, including ideological means, to compete within this global network of extraction and economic violence. In this way, racism, which justified the transformation of human beings into raw materials, played an essential role in the history of colonialism, which means, by extension, that racism was—and, in many ways, still is—a key ideological pillar of global capitalism.

And finally, if a reinvented human rights is going to confront the full significance and ramifying consequences of capitalism, it is crucial to understand that it is fundamentally a moral project expressed *through*—or, perhaps *as*—an economic system. This was, of course, the central insight of political economy, from Adam Smith to Marx, but it is important to be reminded of just which moral values are being expressed, even celebrated, through capitalism, in order to be in a position to seriously consider alternatives, that is, other economic systems that express different moral values. As Piketty has emphasized, economic systems—at any scale—are not natural, or inevitable, but rather historically contingent, the result of particular choices, or, more important, the absence of choice.[43] In this sense, the actual constraints, even bondage, of capitalism are striking, because it is conceived as a moral project that quintessentially embodies individual liberty through "free" markets.[44]

Moreover, as Jessica Whyte has demonstrated, these older "morals of the market" were mobilized by neoliberals in the decades after World War II not in opposition to the international human rights system that was being created at the same time, but in close alliance with it.[45] Among other things, Whyte's genealogical reconstruction of the intertwined histories of neoliberal capitalism and postwar human rights shows just how little the radically anticapitalist proposals of people like Dobb, Levy, and even Nehru, found expression in the UDHR and the subsequent covenants, the eventual inclusion of economic and social rights notwithstanding.

Chasing the Mirage of Economic and Social Rights

If the multilayered, often obscured, long-term effects of $r > g$ represent one of the gravest threats to global justice and ecological sustainability, a threat that must be a central preoccupation for a reinvented human rights, what about *existing* economic and social rights? In other words, the response might be, why would it be necessary to confront global capitalism through a completely different framework for human rights when a body of international economic and social rights is already well established, in law if not in practice?

The short answer is that economic and social rights have proven to be a mirage with particularly insidious consequences. Because of wider structural factors, economic and social rights have been stripped of any transformative potential that might be found in the norms themselves. Even more, because economic and social rights emerged, especially after the end of the Cold War, as the prevailing aspirational mechanism for socioeconomic justice within the international system, an ideological narrative developed in parallel in which the essential problem was taken to be the failure of states to implement these supposedly far-reaching obligations.

In fact, as the longer answer to the question of the significance of existing economic and social rights reveals, the problems were more fundamental—they were embedded in both the forms through which international human rights were articulated and in the broader historical and political economic contexts in which these rights were set into motion. Regarding form, it is important to recall the debates around human rights and political economy that took place among respondents to the UNESCO human rights survey of 1947–48. When Marxist and socialist thinkers like E. H. Carr or Maurice Dobb considered the possibility of reconciling a historical materialist perspective with a declaration of human rights, they did so because they were asked to do so, not because they agreed that human rights were the best political and legal framework for the postwar international order.

Leaving aside the fact that human rights were fundamentally intertwined with the "Protestant bourgeois tradition," as Harold Laski put it, the real problem, according to Marxist and socialist critics, was that the entire premise was mistaken. Both the normative and historical expression of human rights—civil, political, economic, social—implied a particular approach to the relationship between the individual and the collective, one that was necessarily oppositional, exclusionary, and "egoistic," as Marx himself had put it in his critique of the "rights of man."[46] As Marx explained, in relation to the illustrative "right of man to private property," it is fundamentally the "right to enjoy one's fortune and to dispose of it at one's will; without regard for other men and independently of society. It is the right of self-interest. This individual liberty . . . form[s] the basis of civil society. It leads every man to see in other men, not the *realization*, but rather the *limitation* of his own liberty."[47]

The result, from this perspective, is that human rights—of whatever kind—point to the possibility of forms of economic and social justice that will always be, at best, "partial." Instead, as the Marxist and socialist critics of human rights in the UNESCO survey believed, true economic and social justice will only be possible when "individual man, in his everyday life, in his work, and in his relationships, . . . has become a *species-being*; and when he has recognized and organized his own powers . . . as social powers so that he no longer separates this social power from himself."[48]

And in considering the broader historical and political economic contexts in which economic and social rights were adopted, we can appreciate just how tragically partial these possibilities for justice were fated to be. Once the political conflicts over the UDHR were finally resolved, important struggles that led to the inclusion of economic and social rights into the final document (albeit in a clearly subsidiary way),[49] the real battles began with the process to convert the UDHR into enforceable international law. As Christopher N. J. Roberts has shown, the torturous process through which the International Covenant on Economic, Social and Cultural Rights (ICESCR) was negotiated within the United Nations reflected all of the structural and political weaknesses of the postwar international human rights system. In effect, the well of economic and social rights was poisoned from the very beginning.[50]

What Roberts's reconstruction of the period between 1948 and 1954 demonstrates is the extent to which leading global powers like the United States and Great Britain viewed the question of economic and social rights in particular as toxic, in large part due to domestic political struggles during this critical period of the early Cold War. With the brief Labour interregnum having come to a crashing close with the reelection of Churchill in 1951, the US Democratic Truman administration paralyzed by anticommunist moral panic, and the major colonial powers fearing the growing storms of decolonization, it was a miracle, as Roberts shows, that the UDHR was *ever* transformed into international law through the two covenants. Ironically, even though economic and social rights in the style of "Great Declarations" were panned by actual Marxist and socialist critics before 1948, by the early 1950s, the economic and social rights that eventually did make their way into the UDHR were viewed by many as the very embodiment of communist menace, something to be resisted at all costs.

To give a full sense for just how fierce and pervasive opposition to economic and social rights—and, for many, human rights more generally—was in the United States during this period, Roberts relates the story of William "Fitz" Fitzpatrick, the "seersuckered, bespectacled, and bow-tied" editor of the small *New Orleans States* newspaper. In a series of editorials that quickly got picked up by the national press and widely circulated, Fitzpatrick engaged in a full-throated attack on economic and social rights and the horrifying possibility that a UN covenant would fundamentally alter what he described as the "American way of life."[51]

According to Fitzpatrick, it was obvious that the United Nations had a devious "plan for worldwide socialism" in which the United States, as the world's largest economy, would be forced to financially underwrite its own economic and social downfall. As he put it, economic and social rights meant "social security for all the world, with Uncle Sam . . . footing most of the bill."[52] At the same time, Fitzpatrick linked the proposals for economic and social rights at the United Nations with debates in the United States over the massive Marshall Plan, since its critics charged that this postwar aid program meant that the United States would be funding socialist governments in countries like France and Germany.[53]

In the end, Fitzpatrick's frontal assault on economic and social rights merely crystallized a much broader resistance among a wider segment of the US population. As Roberts explains, "members of Congress embraced his ideas, the legal establishment sought his company, and elite literary circles showered [Fitzpatrick] with praise. After his first series of editorials, the newly anointed plebian prophet stormed onto the conservative lecture circuit and spoke to bar associations around the country about the dangers of human rights treaties."[54] In fact, for his efforts, Fitzpatrick was awarded the 1951 Pulitzer Prize for his harangues against economic and social rights.[55] As for the ICESCR, it wouldn't be until 1976 that it finally entered into force along with its somewhat less ill-fated twin the International Covenant on Civil and Political Rights (ICCPR).

Infamously, the United States never ratified the ICESCR across the decades of both Republican and Democratic presidencies and congresses. The United States, with its $21.5 trillion economy, will likely always remain a "non-party" to the covenant, which is again ironic given how little it ever lived up to the nightmares of anticommunist ideologues like Fitzpatrick. Indeed, in some of her last statements on the process through which the UDHR was transformed into two separate covenants, Eleanor Roosevelt herself seemed to put the last nail in the coffin of economic and social rights almost as they were being born. Not only did she go to great lengths to assure Americans that any trace of "communism, socialism, syndicalism or statism" would be excluded from the covenants; even more, she emphasized that the economic and social rights being "championed by so many non-Western states, though most strongly associated with the communist bloc," were not actually human rights at all but rather a set of vague ambitions that would never be allowed to impinge on American freedoms.[56]

Despite the complete and utter irrelevance of the international economic and social rights regime to either the domestic or global American political economy, one whose disproportionate influence on the broader world economy makes this a significant fact, economic and social rights have shaped history on much smaller scales, including in the resistance narratives of some—though not all—decolonizing countries.[57] However, by any measure, the politically and legally anemic international economic and social rights apparatus has played a very minor role—even viewing it in the best possible light—in either ensuring economic and social justice within particular countries, or, even less, in constraining the global economy to bring it in line with the complicated vision of the ICESCR.[58]

States parties to the covenant are supposed to submit reports every five years to a committee that is based in Geneva. This committee, which is notoriously politicized, can then issue critical comments on national shortcomings in meeting economic and social rights obligations. Although the tone and content of these eventual "concluding observations" are the object of intense sound and fury during the deliberations that take place on the idyllic shores of Lac Léman, they ultimately amount to very little in relation to the functioning of global capitalism as the world's dominant political economy.

China, which unlike the United States, *is* a state party to the economic and social rights covenant, has taken an increasingly active role through its representatives on the ICESCR monitoring committee. And as a communist country, it officially puts economic and social rights at the center of its political ideology. But it would be madness to suggest that China's economic and social rights obligations have any relevance at all, either for understanding the rapid growth of the Chinese economy as an authoritarian capitalist behemoth or in analyzing China's strategic engagement with the international human rights system. The problem, in other words, is not the vaunted failure to implement economic and social rights. The more fundamental problem lies in the form, structure, and history of economic and social rights themselves.

Conclusion: Pulling up the Stakes, Filling in the Ditch

Where ownership of land and productive equipment is concentrated in the hands of a class, the remainder of the community is deprived of the possibility of a livelihood except as hired servants to the former: a situation which involves a substantial inequality of rights *de facto*, and in an important sense involves a deprivation of freedom for the class of non-owners. Such an interpretation of human rights is, of course, incapable of being reconciled with Capitalism as an economic system.

Maurice Dobb, "Economic and Social Rights of Man" (1947)

To conclude, let me summarize the main arguments about the relationship between economic and social inequality, capitalism, and existing human rights before going on to suggest what this relationship *should be* within a reinvented human rights. It is important to be reminded of the extent to which this relationship was fully anticipated by Marxist and socialist intellectuals, political leaders, and trade union activists in the short period after the end of World War II but before the UN CHR managed to present the UDHR to the General Assembly in December 1948. I have focused on the deep skepticism about the transformative potential of human rights, as they were understood at this time among people outside the Soviet Union and the communist bloc, in order to underscore how much "human rights" were associated by the political left *within* Western countries with the rise of bourgeois capitalism in the late eighteenth century.

To the extent to which capitalism was believed to be the central problem to be overcome through a more historically advanced political economy and forms of social organization, the idea that human rights would be a fundamental part of the solution to this problem was greeted with incredulity. Since capitalism was understood to be based on a structurally exploitative relationship between owners and workers, in which workers were forced to alienate their labor as a factor of production within a system over which they had very little control, this mode of production was taken to be incompatible with a "modern" conception of human rights.

Yet this deep skepticism about human rights within a broader theory of conflict and injustice based in historical materialism was soon buried under the weight of Cold War politics, decolonization, and the eventual downfall of revolutionary socialism as a legitimate and radical alternative to the various forms of democratic capitalism that triumphed, including neoliberal capitalism. But if the various historical experiments throughout the twentieth century with political and social organization committed to revolutionary socialism proved to be catastrophic failures marked by varying degrees of brutality and authoritarianism, what about the underlying critique of capitalism that was their justification? As we have seen, long-term quantitative research by political economists such as Piketty not only have reaffirmed Marx's basic insights about the central crisis of capitalism, they have also actually demonstrated empirically, rather than merely ideologically, just how "terrifying" this crisis really is for the current century.

And yet, this crisis is one that is not recognized as such by the most powerful nation-states and institutions in the world, not to mention the hundreds of millions (perhaps even billions) of people who—for one reason or another—view capitalism as the only possible political economic game in town. This, then, becomes the corresponding crisis for a reinvented human rights: how to overcome what is ultimately a ruinous global political economy despite the fact that capitalism is the greatest engine for producing wealth in human history. As Evan Osnos has described, with both historical and ethnographic subtlety, China's fervent embrace of capitalism has completely transformed Chinese social relations. And while China's Gilded Age has produced more economic wealth in a matter of years than was produced during the entire sweep of the Industrial Revolution, it has also produced the most billionaires in the world, also in the shortest amount of time.[59]

And at the same time, as Moyn rightly emphasizes, the stratospheric growth in the (now capitalist) Chinese economy led to much more modest, but still real, growth in incomes and output, lifting hundreds of millions of people out of abject poverty in the process, as the formula $r > g$ would predict.[60] But at what cost? As the formula $r > g$ would also predict, economic and social inequality in China has grown at the same stratospheric rates as capitalist wealth. Whereas wealth distribution was relatively egalitarian in China before the beginning of the shift to a market economy in 1978, by 2015, after years of capitalist transformation, the levels of inequality in China had become similar to those in the United States.[61] And in China, the rural-urban dimension to wealth inequality is particularly stark. By some estimates, the Gini coefficient of inequality between China's urban capitalist powerhouses like Shanghai, Beijing, and Shenzhen and the vast rural hinterlands has reached 0.61, which would place China now among the most unequal countries in the world.[62]

So why does the inevitability of ever-increasing levels of economic and social inequality under a global capitalist political economy represent a profound *moral* crisis, one for which a reinvented human rights must have a response? Because the dominance of global capitalism is anything but inevitable; rather, it is the result of a long-term historical process that was—and remains—fundamentally contingent. Even more, it is the result of a series of consequential choices, taken under highly exclusionary and violent conditions, that were justified on moral grounds. In other words, economic systems are merely means for realizing something more basic, the ends of economic life itself. And there are different, even completely contrasting, visions for the ends of economic life, each of which is supposed to express a distinct set of collective moral values.

The ends of economic life under global capitalism, which have become, by both design and default, the ends of something like a global economic life, have traditionally been conceived as the fulfillment of individual liberty. Although the rise of China as an authoritarian, nonliberal, capitalist juggernaut obviously complicates the analysis of political economic values at the level of state ideology, as Osnos has shown, the "morals of the market" have taken transformative root everywhere else. And beyond China, it goes without saying, the Hayekian vision remains as hegemonic as ever, perhaps even more so. On this view, capitalism is the only economic system in which individual freedom is both guaranteed and expanded, the only economic system that guarantees a wider society free of the enslaving bonds of government intrusion and the evils of redistribution.[63]

But can the world of the twenty-first century and beyond (if we collectively make it that far) afford economic and social systems that are anchored in these values, that are dominated by these ends of economic life? Knowing that vast levels of economic and social inequality are inevitable under conditions of capitalism, it would be ecologically catastrophic (as it now is) and morally suicidal not to see this global political economy for what it really is. And if it is true, as Herder once put it, that we live in a world that we ourselves create, who would want, in the end, to live in a world in which the consequences of long-term, structural inequality are everywhere, and getting exponentially worse by the year? The answer, unfortunately, for the moment, is many, perhaps a majority of people in the world, but only because other political economic systems of our own creation are so difficult to conceive.

Nevertheless, as a start, a reinvented human rights should be taken as a framework for confronting the political economic world that we've created; a catalyst for resisting and eventually rejecting its entire structure—ideological, distributional, relational; and as the basis on which we can visualize the contours of what we must create to replace it. A reinvented human rights, in other words, would demand that we finally listen to the admonitions of Rousseau, that we look to the future by reinterpreting the past, that we recognize the moral imposturings of capitalism for what they are, and that we pull up the stakes and fill in the ditch with courage, against all odds, before it's too late.

CHAPTER 3

Remaking Sovereignty in the Image of Human Rights

TO UNDERSTAND HOW THE CENTRALITY of the nation-state within the existing system of international law and politics has created any number of structural tensions, negative incentives, and the pervasiveness of bad faith, a useful place to start is with the curious framework of treaty monitoring. Within the UN human rights system, individual states sign and ratify human rights treaties, whose terms are then supposed to be incorporated into a state's domestic law. Once this is done, however, special committees of experts called "treaty bodies" are charged with overseeing compliance with a state's treaty obligations, evidence for which comes from a process of self-reporting—for example, every four years—in the form of "country reports."

These reports are then ceremoniously presented by a varied ensemble of representatives from each reporting country during meetings in Geneva,[1] where the reports become the basis for public hearings in which the experts take a wide range of approaches—praise, skepticism, condemnation, chastisement, recommendations for improvement—depending on the country, the treaty body, and the content of the reports. As might be imagined, these sessions are infused with politicking and diplomatic machinations both within and beyond the walls of the Palais des Nations, where government officials, human rights activists, and NGO workers jostle for one another's attention on the streets and in the cafés of "International Geneva."

The anthropologist Sally Engle Merry conducted extended and multisited research on the monitoring of one important human rights treaty: the Convention on the Elimination of All Forms of Discrimination against Women (CEDAW).[2]

For perhaps the most revealing case study in her comparative ethnography, Merry spent several years tracking the highly fraught process through which Fiji presented its first-ever country report to the CEDAW committee. The country report itself opened a window onto a spectrum of cultural, legal, and political conflicts in Fiji, including the struggle between women's rights activists and politicians, who feared the UN would attack the Fijian cultural traditions described in the report.

To complicate matters even further, Fiji's first report to the CEDAW committee took place against a tense political climate in the country, in which Indigenous Fijian nationalists sought to subvert a postcolonial power structure that had been dominated by Indo-Fijians, descendants of Indian laborers who had been brought to Fiji by British colonial authorities in the late nineteenth century. Key to the nationalist cause was the revendication of Fijian cultural values, which centered on traditional village life, modes of production, and kinship structures.

Despite the feelings of pride and commitment to international participation that accompanied the Fijian delegation, its country report presentation quickly descended into a spectacle in which aspects of Fijian culture were held up to skepticism bordering on ridicule. The particular object of scorn by the CEDAW experts was a practice called *bulubulu*, a type of exchange in which "a person apologizes for an offense and offers a whale's tooth (*tabua*) and a gift and asks for forgiveness."[3] In this sense, bulubulu had much in common with many kinship-based frameworks for conflict resolution in other parts of the world, which similarly privilege reconciliation as the dominant normative principle, even in cases of serious violation.[4] The linchpin of the criticism during the hearings, however, was the fact that the Fiji country report acknowledged that bulubulu was widely used in cases of sexual violence, including rape. The victim, in these cases, was not understood to be the girl or woman who had suffered the attack, but her father, and, more specifically, the wider kin group of which the father acted as representative. To comply with the expectations of bulubulu, the accused rapist issued an apology to the victimized kin group, accompanied by significant material prestations.

The CEDAW committee members grilled Fiji's assistant minister for women, social welfare, and poverty alleviation: what had the country done to eliminate bulubulu, "a very old and very patriarchal custom"?; shouldn't the country consider making the practice illegal under domestic law?; how can Fiji comply with its obligations under international human rights law if it allowed reconciliation to be used in cases of rape?[5] From the perspective of the CEDAW committee, the

use of bulubulu to resolve conflicts over rape and sexual violence in Fiji represented a paradigmatic example of the kind of discriminatory cultural practices
that CEDAW was intended to undermine. Even worse, according to the CEDAW
committee, was the fact that national courts in Fiji would decline to issue prison
sentences to perpetrators of sexual crimes if the procedures for bulubulu had
been followed, a completely unacceptable legal practice that had the effect of
"providing legitimacy to rape."[6]

In the end, Fiji's first country report under its CEDAW treaty obligations
resulted in a "concluding comment" by the CEDAW committee that was scath-
ingly critical of the continuing influence of traditional conflict resolution
procedures. Even more, the concluding comment specifically instructed Fiji
to ban reconciliation in all cases of rape and sexual assault. The harshness of
the critical spotlight—turned unexpectedly on a fundamental pillar of Fijian
culture during what was hoped would be a historic moment of international
validation—provoked an indignant and defensive backlash. Set against the background of continuing political instability and nationalist mobilization in the
country, it was simply impossible for the Fijian representatives to remain passive
in the face of such harsh condemnation by the international human rights system.

According to Merry, the Fijian assistant minister believed that the rebuke
by the CEDAW committee went directly to the heart of Fijian cultural integrity,
something especially egregious given the legacy of colonialism and the ongoing
conflict between Indigenous Fijians and Indo-Fijians, the latter of whom were
much more likely to embrace international human rights discourse, in part as a
way of resisting the claims of their Indigenous Fijian adversaries. As a response,
she explained, Fiji was considering withdrawing not only from CEDAW but also
from other international human rights treaties.

In an unfortunate coincidence, Fiji was at the same moment in the midst of
being put through the critical international wringer in front of yet another treaty
body, the one that monitors the Convention on Racial Discrimination.[7] In that
case, the object of criticism was not bulubulu or other cultural practices but something quite different: affirmative action legislation in Fiji that gave preference to
Indigenous Fijians over Indo-Fijians, legislation that represented—according to
the concluding comment issued by the second treaty body—a "failure to promote
a multiethnic society" in the country.[8]

In the end, Fiji didn't follow through on the threat to turn its back on the
international human rights system, but the lingering implications of its experiences within the human rights monitoring apparatus shed light on a much wider

range of systemic problems. As Merry explains, the entire treaty body system is marked by confusion and incommensurabilities that dramatically limit the extent to which it can function as a practical mechanism with any correspondence at all with actual human rights protections for people living within diverse cultural, political, and economic realities.

In her analysis, the monitoring process—which is the key interface between states and the international human rights system—operates as a kind of self-contained bubble in which the "detailed knowledge of the social conditions in each country" has no place.[9] Instead, the grand institutional and ideological ambitions of the international human rights system become trapped within bureaucratic procedures, boilerplate legal and political language, and even debates over the form of documents, something that Annelise Riles memorably described as a game of trying to contain "infinity within the brackets."[10]

And yet, the critical failures of the UN human rights monitoring process are not the result of factors limited to treaty implementation and enforcement. On the contrary, the particular history of Fiji's travails as a "state party" to CEDAW is illustrative of something much more consequential: the fundamentally misbegotten fact that the state is both the normative and practical anchor of the existing international human rights system. And by "the state" I mean both the particular model of the nation-state that forms the institutional core of the postwar international order, and specific states themselves. In considering a reinvented human rights for the future, a reformulation that leaves no component of the existing human rights system unexamined, I argue that the paramountcy of the state is a taken-for-granted part of the existing foundation that must be left behind.[11]

First, because the existing international human rights system is built on and through nation-states, its genetic makeup is both institutionalist and bureaucratic. What this means is that the underlying moral or normative bases of human rights become completely obscured and even transformed in practice, as states strive to fulfill—or, more likely, not—their treaty obligations within the postwar human rights framework. In addition, the institutional and bureaucratic capture of human rights takes place at multiple levels, all of which amplify the basic problem.

State human rights bureaucracies organize and manage human rights implementation and reporting at the subnational and national levels; these bureaucracies then interact, often in oppositional ways, with the UN's human rights agencies and bureaucracies; and finally, different kinds of parastate human rights NGOs mimic the institutional and bureaucratic posture of states, since "seeing like a state" is essential to organizational legitimacy and confers on NGOs the right to participate alongside states during UN deliberations.[12] The institutionalization and bureaucratization of human rights denude it of most of its emancipatory potential and converts "human rights" into just another logic of state governance, one, moreover, that is most often utterly marginal in relation to others.

Second, the state-centricity of the existing international human rights system sets up a structural conflict of interest in which states occupy the roles of perpetrator, judge, and "savoir."[13] States are charged by the international human rights system with implementing social, political, and economic reforms in response to enduring inequalities and ongoing legacies of violence for which the state typically bears significant responsibility. Yet this structural conflict of interest was not an unintended consequence of the effort to establish a postwar world order that would supposedly serve as a powerful check on individual states.

On the contrary, from the UN Security Council to the international treaty ratification process, the state was given priority in all matters, with certain states establishing themselves as global guardians of sovereign hegemony. In relation to human rights, the objective of dominant states like the United States and the Soviet Union was to shield themselves from the "dangers" of international oversight and censure.[14] The anti-human-rights principle of state-centricity was therefore adopted to ensure that states would remain immune from any *real* consequences of future claims (let alone direct action) by meddlesome visionaries or international critics.

Third, because the state is both the principal protagonist *and* antagonist of the existing international human rights system, the status of people's "human rights"—defined and thus circumscribed by international law, as problematic as this is—depends almost entirely on the whims of internal state politics. These whims can take a wide range; indeed, there is no question that some states have put in place domestic regulations that reflect earnest national interest in complying with human rights treaty obligations.

But for every comparatively rare case of Country *X*, there are many more cases of Countries *A*, *B*, *C*, and so on, in which the whims of state responsibility for human rights take the form of neglect, politicization, incapacity, or sheer bad faith, that is, when state leaders are not actively engaged in destroying subversive populations or otherwise making a complete mockery of the proposition that their citizens "have" human rights. Regardless of the particular state in question, or where it might be placed on something like a spectrum of internal human rights compliance or violation, the underlying problem remains the same: the human rights of people within the existing international system are fundamentally limited by the often-violent caprices of national politics and the domestic histories of discrimination that national politics can embody.

And finally, from the perspective of a reinvented human rights, state-centricity runs directly counter to the most important aspects of a logic of translocal collective action based in solidarity and directed, in practice, toward the most serious and endemic of contemporary crises. Among the many categories of difference that are the basis for conflict, dehumanization, and the structural incapacity to act collectively in ways that are equal to the scope of our regional and global problems, *national* differences have proven to be the most catastrophic. This is not to say that other categories of difference are not also barriers to human rights in this alternative register. But national differences, which define the architecture of the international system, are the most insidious.

As with other "schemes to improve the human condition," here, too, we see how doctrines of sovereignty, nationalism, and the "rights of citizens" were originally conceived as progressive responses to existing problems: feudal and ecclesiastical governance, imperial domination, and political and social inequality. Yet over time, national identity and its political forms proved to be equally destructive, equally deleterious to the cause of long-term global sustainability, albeit in different ways and justified on different ideological grounds. Despite all the problems with the hollow pretensions of "all members of the human family," the orthodox formulation of existing human rights at least has the virtue of extending beyond the boundaries of national belonging, even if this universal framing is contradicted or undermined by every other facet of the international system in which it is awkwardly rooted.

Nevertheless, in conceiving of human rights as a logic of translocal collective action, it is clear that the most imposing and difficult categories of difference are those defined and circumscribed by the state, regardless of *which* state (Country *X*, Country *Y*, Country *Z*) or regardless of *what kind* of state (democratic, authoritarian, monarchical, theocratic, and so on). Yet almost all of the most urgent contemporary crises, those that demand collective action on a large scale, are caused by processes and systems that transcend the boundaries of individual nation-states: climate change, economic inequality, resource depletion, environmental degradation, pandemics. Although categories of difference also shape conflict and thwart the expression of translocal solidarity and purposive action at much smaller scales, it is the national scale, defined and symbolized by the state, that remains the most structurally pernicious.

The rest of this chapter examines in more detail why and how the state is such a formidable obstacle, both for the realization of existing human rights and, more important, for a future vision of human rights that seeks to overcome the dominance of state-centricity. In the next section, I begin by considering the elemental principle that undergirds the history and the ideological legitimacy of the modern state: the principle of sovereignty. In a remarkable way, the fatal weaknesses of sovereignty parallel those of the "human" in human rights. Much as the historically and culturally particular concept of humanity was presented as an ontological fact of universal scope, so too with the principle of sovereignty. As will be seen, sovereignty emerges within a highly specific historical and political context, one intimately linked to widespread conflict and to idealist philosophy. Yet as a long-term proposition, the principle of sovereignty has come into fundamental contradiction with its original purposes, a contradiction that must be overcome if the future of human rights has any meaning at all.

The chapter then returns to the problem of the nation-state as the lodestar of the existing international human rights system. Leaving aside the more abstract question of a structural conflict of interest, the comparative ethnography of state power reveals a wide variation, from earnest state actors like New Zealand to bad faith state actors like Russia, with a range other cases and categories in between. As will be seen, in many instances, the real problem is not internal state repression but various forms of state disregard or indifference. As a case study from my own research demonstrates, hundreds of millions of people around the world live not in fear of state violence but in vast zones of neglect marked by the absence of the state and its instrumentalities. This means that even if the state, in the best of circumstances, might function as an ally of a reinvented human rights in the future, it must still be kept—when possible—at a distance, something to be regarded warily, that is, when it is not being actively confronted.

The chapter then examines one of the odder institutional creatures within the existing international human rights system: the National Human Rights Institution, or NHRI. These are hybrid and often compromised state institutions that are created and funded by states in order to hold these same states and their officials accountable for human rights violations within state boundaries. Although most NHRIs lead precarious institutional lives under the constant threat of defunding or delegitimization by the same state officials they are called upon to name and shame, their peculiar position within the wider international human rights system is emblematic. As will be seen, the largely failed effort by the international community to encourage the establishment of state human rights institutions that purport to be independent of the states that created them provides yet further evidence that a reinvented human rights must be essentially detached—conceptually, institutionally, politically—from the state in order to stand any chance of flourishing.

The chapter concludes by returning to the principle of sovereignty. If sovereignty itself, like human rights, was invented through a particular historical and political trajectory, then it, too, can be reinvented. I argue that the principle of sovereignty can and must be remade in ways that support an alternative conception of human rights, one in which sovereign legitimacy is located in translocal collective belonging and action, not in states. This is not a conception of sovereignty that readily lends itself to the formation of political associations, even traditional political parties. Rather, sovereignty becomes the justification for the mobilization of social power necessary for transformative action, even—or, especially—action that demands upheaval, resistance, and confrontation with existing social, political, and economic institutions.

Human Rights and the Sovereign Contradiction

I remember well the revelatory first encounter with the history and philosophy of so-called social contract theory. As a university student in political science (with a declared specialization in political theory), the road through the iconic European theorists of the sixteenth, seventeenth, and eighteenth centuries was an intellectual rite de passage. The road could take brief detours, depending on the teacher, but the direction was usually the same: a beginning with Jean Bodin's *De Republica* (1576), followed by the ritualistic succession of Thomas Hobbes's *Leviathan* (1651), John Locke's *Second Treatise of Government* (1689), and, finally, Jean-Jacques Rousseau's *The Social Contract* (1762).

Along the way, the discussions took forms that would be immediately familiar to anyone with even a passing knowledge of the issues: what was the "state of nature" in relation to which social contracts were deemed necessary?; what was the relationship between individuals and the political entities created through the social contract?; are rulers created through a social contract subject to its terms?; what happens when rulers fail in their obligations under the social contract?; and so on. We learned that the American and French Revolutions were, in part, attempts to put the insights of social contract theory into practice for the first time in history, signal moments in which values like consent and propositions like natural rights were given social and political expression.

However, despite the many months spent trying to understand the nuances of the social contract master narrative, at least in order to be able to recount it during an exam, I became bizarrely fixated on something else. Long before the age of ebooks and even the internet, we were assigned one of the Penguin Classics copies of Hobbes's *Leviathan*. I stared for long stretches at the cover, fascinated by what it represented and what its meanings were for contemporary political theory. We were told that the principles of *Leviathan* remained at the core of modern democracies, including the United States. Although certain of its propositions had been replaced by those of Locke, according to the master narrative, Hobbes's masterpiece remained fundamental to both contemporary political theory and political organization, at least in the "West" (this was at the end of the Cold War, when "West" and "East" were still used to discuss differences between the NATO and Warsaw Pact countries).

But what, then, to make of the frightening, if mesmerizing, image on the cover of *Leviathan*? This is the iconic etching by the French Huguenot printmaker Abraham Bosse, in which an idealized provincial seaside town is depicted, surrounded by gentle rolling hills and dotted with numerous churches, their spires rising up in the distance. Yet over this serene landscape, from beyond the hills, a massive figure looms with outstretched arms: in his right hand, he wields a sword; in his left, he clutches a crosier. The figure appears to be a man, since he also wears a crown and sports long, curly hair and a Van Dyke beard that made him look—to my late 1980s Californian eyes, at least—like a lead guitarist for a rock-and-roll band. The figure looks directly at the viewer with an expression that seems to be just on the brink of a smile; despite its imposing size and its aggressive, almost warlike, posture, the figure is placid and assured, yet also dominating.

However, on closer inspection, something else comes into focus. Although a regal male figure, its body is actually composed of hundreds of human beings, all tightly packed together and looking upward toward the figure's calm visage. As it turns out, the figure is not a giant human being at all, let alone a rock star from the 1980s, but some kind of humanoid monster with unimaginable powers and unknown designs on the small seaside town. The disturbing scene is only magnified by the quote in Latin above its head, taken from the book of Job: "There is no power on earth to be compared to him."

So what, then, is this surreal figure chosen by Bosse and Hobbes to adorn one of the pillars of social contract theory, a choice that was meant to symbolize its most fundamental propositions? It is, of course, the sovereign, the ruler who is the repository of the rights that have been voluntarily ceded by the collective—in this case, the residents of the seaside town, one imagines—over which the sovereign exercises power. Although Hobbes actually argued that a monarchical sovereign, as opposed to democratic or aristocratic variations, was the best possible among the three ideal types, the central claim about the sovereign remained the same: a sovereign's power and legitimacy were derived from the consent of the governed, rather than from, for example, the divine right of kings or the will of God.

As J. L. Brierly explains, in his classic study of the origins of international law, although this "doctrine of sovereignty" was already being developed by theorists such as Jean Bodin, it reached its culmination with Hobbes's *Leviathan*.[15] Even more, the argument for sovereignty as a new principle of governance took place against the backdrop of different conflicts in Europe, from the French civil wars of Bodin's time to the English Civil War of Hobbes's. Yet it was the resolution to the catastrophic Thirty Years' War that would prove the most lasting and problematic turning point for the future of human rights. During the same period in which *Leviathan* was published, the multigenerational religious wars in the heart of Europe were brought to a close through a series of peace treaties that came to be known as the Peace of Westphalia (1648).

As Brierly puts it, the Peace of Westphalia sounded the death knell to the existing political order in Europe, which was based on governance divided between feudal social and political regimes and ecclesiastical authorities. In its place, the Peace of Westphalia ushered in an era that "abandoned the medieval idea of a world-state" in favor of the modern state: "secular, national, and territorial," but above all, marked by the conceptual primacy of sovereignty, in which each state was conceived as a billiard ball on a vast playing table, part of the same game, but fundamentally autonomous.[16]

Without having to trace the genealogy of sovereignty from the mid-seventeenth century to the present, it is enough to say that the sovereign Westphalian state would become the international standard, a model for both national and international politics whose pervasiveness and deterministic inevitability would come to rival the "human" in human rights. And yet, therein lies both the problem and the paradox. If the "human" in human rights is founded in claims of universal sameness—however dubious—the sovereign state is based in equally problematic claims of political and social separateness. Moreover, despite the fact that sovereignty and the modern state were imagined as *merely* a principle and form of governance that followed from the establishment of a social contract, the humanoid monster on the cover of Hobbes's *Leviathan* reveals something else.

Long before ideologies of nation and nationalism were conceived as a means of drawing hostile distinctions with "foreigners, liberals and socialists" and justifying the "aggressive expansion of . . . [the] state,"[17] the doctrine of sovereignty was evolving into what might be thought of as a protonationalist ideology. In this register, as Bosse's 1651 engraving anticipates so vividly, sovereignty becomes an ideology of embodiment, a doctrine in which political power and autonomy are literally embodied in the distinct—and ontologically incommensurable—collectivities whose consent is sovereignty's lifeblood.

Yet over the course of time, the originary fact of consent faded as a key constituent of sovereignty, leaving political embodiment as the defining value, a value that formed the basis on which later doctrines of racial and cultural nationalism could be built. This explains how the doctrine of the sovereign state could be so easily adapted to a wide range of national political systems and eventually the international system itself, in which international relations are organized around national autonomy and embodied separateness rather than around international respect for the consent of the governed.[18]

Given this, the enduring and fatal contradictions between state sovereignty and human rights come into sharper focus. As Christopher N. J. Roberts describes, in his study of the "contentious history" of the struggle to transform the UDHR into binding international law, the reality of this fatal contradiction—fatal, to be clear, for the cause of human rights—was accepted and even embraced from the very beginning. Far from a moment of global reckoning, the creation of the United Nations was viewed as a security measure by the victorious "wartime alliance," which then promptly established the permanent Security Council, allocating to each of its five members the "sovereign right to overrule" resolutions and otherwise put national interests above any others.[19]

Within its first two years, the United Nations had already become an institution wracked by "competing geopolitical interests and conflicting visions of international security," an institution in which tensions among members of the exclusive Security Council overwhelmed other concerns. Roberts quotes the US senator, Harry Byrd, who complained as early as 1947 that Cold War politics within the United Nations were marked by "selfish and obstructive tactics," which had "virtually stymied and made impotent the United Nations."[20]

Against this background of "sovereign right" translated into postwar Realpolitik conflict, the development of a full-blown international system animated by the "inherent dignity and . . . the equal and inalienable rights of all members of the human family" was rendered impossible even before the UDHR was ratified in December 1948. And indeed, as Roberts shows, the powerful countries that formed the unequal financial and institutional backbone of the United Nations did nothing during the succeeding years to weaken the crippling supremacy of sovereignty. By the time the UDHR *had* been finally converted into a legal form that could be adopted by states and implemented domestically, almost three momentous decades had passed.

During these same decades, the anticolonial fight for self-determination had only strengthened the doctrine of sovereignty. What is more, despite the fact that a number of decolonizing and postcolonial states took a radically different approach to the possibilities of human rights,[21] superpower states like China, the Soviet Union, and the United States considered human rights—when they were considered at all—as an ongoing threat to sovereignty, albeit a toothless threat that could be easily brushed aside.[22]

Even during the decade of the Age of Human Rights, the relatively brief period of real florescence and liminal possibility after the end of the Cold War, the primacy of sovereignty was never seriously questioned; if human rights remained a "danger" to state sovereignty, it was only when this danger was conceived as an arid abstraction, one conjured in the fantasies of cosmopolitan political philosophy. In reality, however, as the post–Cold War gave way to our troubled present, were entered a period of *hypersovereignty*, in which the devasting consequences of political embodiment were manifested in crises as diverse as climate change, state-sponsored homophobia, and the unthinkable fact of lifeless migrant children washing up on the shores of sovereign Europe.

In an era of hypersovereignty, therefore, the state will remain in structural opposition to human rights—existing, as we have seen, but even more, in opposition to a reinvented human rights conceived as a logic of translocal collective action detached from both its orthodox legal and philosophical foundations. As long as the doctrine of sovereignty not only constitutes the bedrock of states, but, in a meaningful sense, actually defines them, the state—*any* state—will remain the most consequential and formidable political barrier that a reinvented human rights must overcome.

State Power, State Neglect, State Impotence

If the global monopoly of state sovereignty represents the greatest political threat to the future of human rights, there is yet another enduring problem with state-centricity that must be considered, another reason why the essentially Westphalian structure of the existing international human rights system should be regarded as obsolete. So much of contemporary human rights scholarship and activism are rightly concerned with the manifold ways in which different states are engaged in ongoing projects of violence and discrimination against marginalized groups within their own national populations. Yet the shocking nature of these cases, and the ways in which they funnel international outrage and focus the levers of naming-and-shaming, obscure other means through which state power works as an obstacle to human rights.

For every lamentable and justly condemned incident in which a state brutalizes people within its own national boundaries, hundreds of other cases of what could be considered state violence go unnoticed and unacknowledged, in large part because they do not constitute violations of human rights per se. Instead, states in many parts of the world—well beyond the facile Global North/Global South dichotomy—engage in a form of violence that is defined by absence, neglect, and apathy. Because states are charged with ensuring compliance with international human rights norms—political, civil, socioeconomic—within their sovereign borders, this narrows the power of obligation to political and institutional actors who are often least able, or inclined, to act on it.

State bureaucracies are obviously complicated and heterogenous entities, and even in cases of state absence or neglect, one can usually identify well-meaning governmental agencies and officials—usually based in national capitals—who take this power of obligation seriously. But in practice, the power of obligation for ensuring substantive compliance with human rights norms remains largely a negative power, one whose force is felt through its absence. If, as the phrase has it, "silence is violence," so, too, is neglect, indifference, incapacity. As long as the power of human rights is fused with the power of the state, it will remain crippled by the vicissitudes of political prerogative and trapped within glacial structures of institutional inertia. To paraphrase one of the early critics of bureaucratic organization (Trotsky): bureaucracy and human rights are inversely proportional to each other.[23]

Yet beyond the ways in which state bureaucracies confine the potential of human rights to its state-managed institutional forms, the negative power of obligation expresses itself at the same time through what might be described as the banality of insufficiency. This is without question the more obscure form through which state-centricity suppresses the latent possibilities for human rights. To give empirical shape to the banality of insufficiency, I draw from research on human rights conducted in Bolivia in the late 1990s.

Despite the fact that the later Movement to Socialism (MAS) government of Evo Morales (2006–19) would seek to demonize the "neoliberal" Bolivian administrations of the 1990s, this was also the period in which human and Indigenous rights politics were embraced for the first time by the Bolivian state. The different neoliberal governments during this decade oversaw a remarkably robust process through which new human rights institutions were created at the national level to much fanfare from human rights activists within and beyond Bolivia.

For example, Bolivia ratified CEDAW in 1990, a move that was eagerly welcomed by numerous women's rights organizations in La Paz, which had been mobilizing since the mid-1980s against the endemic problem of violence against women in the country. In 1993, the government created a new office of "ethnic and gender issues" to oversee the implementation of CEDAW. In 1995, as part of this initiative, the new office launched a hybrid institution called the "integrated legal service center," which was conceived as a sort of one-stop mechanism for the implementation of CEDAW. Women could use these centers to seek legal advice, medical treatment, and psychological counseling, and even as temporary lodging to escape abusive relationships.

The actual establishment of these innovative centers, however, took place on a limited scale, and—with few exceptions—only within Bolivia's major cities: La Paz, Cochabamba, Santa Cruz. On the one hand, this was a function of deep ambivalence by the Bolivian state about how much to actually invest in human rights promotion—despite official narratives and frenzied legislative activity—an ambivalence that was only amplified by a chronic budgetary crisis in what was then the second poorest country in the Western Hemisphere.

But on the other hand, the minimal rollout of the CEDAW centers, restricted to a few urban centers, reflected something much broader and more systemic: the fact that the Bolivian state and its institutions were present only within tightly circumscribed political, social, and, especially, geographical spaces. This phenomenon, so common across different countries and regions in the world, is not the same thing as the "withdrawal" of the state, which has been critiqued as an intentional strategy characteristic of neoliberal governance.[24] Instead, the near absence of Bolivian state institutions and provision beyond these tightly circumscribed boundaries was the result of a tradition of neglect in which vast swaths of the country were ignored, forgotten, or otherwise dismissed as part of a sociopolitical wasteland that is described in Bolivian Spanish as simply *el campo*, "the countryside."

Despite this, my research happened to take place in one small corner of the neglected campo in which a CEDAW center had actually been established, like a lonely outpost set up far beyond the fortress walls of state indifference. The reasons this particular center was established in the town of Sacaca are not as relevant as its tenuous and short-lived existence, which merely underscores the broader point: the presence of state institutions in places like Sacaca is almost a category error, a violation of an implicit understanding that people outside the narrow spaces of state presence might technically be part of the sovereign collectivity that is "Bolivia," but, in reality, lead their lives completely apart from it.[25]

The two years in which the CEDAW center was open in Sacaca were marked by curiosity, confusion, and, ultimately, neglect, yet neglect by people in the province as much as by the two functionaries of the center itself, a surprising dynamic that sheds light on how the banality of insufficiency is experienced and even reinforced by those living far beyond the care of the state. Despite the best of intentions by the center's director, a local lawyer who had received training in human rights, the grand ideological ambitions that the center channeled were greeted with widespread ambivalence bordering on hostility. This was not because gender relations in this part of rural Bolivia are fundamentally patriarchal, although violence against women and children—especially during fiestas and periods of heavy social drinking—was a real and enduring problem throughout the province.

Rather, resistance to the CEDAW center, which eventually fell into disuse and was then closed, was based on the fact that social relations were embedded within cultural and productive networks that were completely closed to the Bolivian state—that is, the effects of the banality of insufficiency were felt in both directions. The fact that a new state institution suddenly appeared in *el campo*, with ambitions to transform the most intimate of social relations—those between men and women—represented an extraordinary reversal of the ongoing reality of state absence, one that was neither understood nor tolerated.

Thus, if state-centricity has doomed the cause of existing human rights as much through state neglect and incapacity as through the prevalence of state-mediated violence and internal repression, this is not to suggest that the argument for a reinvented human rights is also, by extension, an argument against the state as such—Westphalian or otherwise. Leaving aside the decaying condition of traditional political parties in many countries, the need for some organizational structure remains essential, especially when considering how future forms of collective action might be directed toward the most significant and widespread of global crises. Yet the evidence of the last eight decades should leave little doubt that the future of human rights must be imagined and then built beyond the control of state institutions.

Neither Fish nor Fowl: The Strange Case of the NHRIs

If state sovereignty and state-centricity have proven to be disastrous for existing human rights—normative and political barriers that were intentionally hard-baked into the postwar international system to protect against the "dangers" of world government and transnational collaboration—these structural weaknesses have been acknowledged in a peculiar way by the international human rights system itself.

In 1991, an event called the "International Workshop on National Institutions for the Promotion and Protection of Human Rights" was held in Paris. Anticipating the coming explosion in human rights advocacy as the Cold War order came to an end, and understanding the ways in which the future of human rights would be held captive to the capriciousness of state compliance, workshop participants attempted to ward off the inevitable by drafting a blueprint for National Human Rights Institutions, or NHRIs.

This blueprint, which came to be known as the "Paris Principles," provides a set of ideal functions and characteristics for institutions that would be created by states, yet charged with the mandate to monitor and, if necessary, criticize the state for failing to fulfill its human rights obligations to its own citizens. Nevertheless, according to the Paris Principles, the most important feature of NHRIs was their supposed independence. In other words, although NHRIs were state institutions, created through state legislative or executive processes, financed by state budgets, and (as history would show) led and staffed by state officials or even political appointees, they were supposed to function as completely independent entities committed to naming-and-shaming the very same states to which they owed their ongoing existence.

Although various kinds of national human rights institutions appeared from time to time during the decades of the Cold War, it was during the early period of the 1990s when the NHRI came into its own as a potential mechanism for translating the burst of enthusiasm for human rights into national institutional action. Indeed, the benchmark international charter for the coming Age of Human Rights, the 1993 Vienna Declaration, draws explicit attention to the role of NHRIs (in action item 36), and the Paris Principles themselves were adopted by the UN General Assembly later that year.

Yet even in the Vienna Declaration, which remains the most expansive statement of confidence in the power of existing human rights ever articulated, state sovereignty rears its menacing head. In the same action item in which NHRIs are given such prominence as national wardens of universal human rights, the

Vienna Declaration asserts an entirely countervailing principle: "it is the right of each State to choose the framework which is best suited to its particular needs at the national level."

And as Julie Mertus has shown, in her comparative and historical study of NHRIs, the subsequent years would reveal just how much "the right of each State" would render the mandate of NHRIs fragile at best, contradictory and even impossible at worst.[26] Her research documents the ways in which these chimerical institutional creatures are forced to inhabit an "imagined space somewhere between the state and civil society," while necessarily "operating in a highly charged and deeply politicized atmosphere" in which they are "subject to manipulation by governmental actors" who are responsible for authorizing the NHRIs and ensuring their continued financial support.[27]

Nevertheless, perhaps specifically because of these constraints and contradictions, NHRIs proliferated throughout the 1990s and 2000s, becoming, as Mertus puts it, a "worldwide phenomenon."[28] In fact, NHRIs became arguably the most prolific human rights institutions in the world, both during and after the Age of Human Rights, despite the fact that their capacity to shape structural change through human rights compliance from within, as it were, was demonstrably negligible, even in the best of circumstances. More commonly, as Mertus shows, the willingness of states to create NHRIs in their midst was part of a "disingenuous" strategy to use the existence of the NHRI as a symbolic "badge of human rights observance," a shield to deflect international attention away from ongoing abuses and neglect.[29]

Even more, the promotion of NHRIs was transformed into yet another form of sovereign soft power in which powerful countries insisted on the creation of NHRIs abroad as a precondition for foreign aid or political support, while either refusing to establish their own national human rights institutions or exercising their "right . . . to choose the framework which is best suited to . . . particular needs at the national level" by undermining the legitimacy of their own existing NHRIs. Although Mertus cites the unsurprising case of the United States, so notorious for its human rights "exceptionalism and exemptionism,"[30] it is the example of the Danish NHRI that carries the most far-reaching implications for the position of the state within a reinvented human rights.

As Mertus describes, the place of the Danish NHRI (known as the DIHR) is highly charged, but for a set of reasons that are astonishing, given the common image of Denmark as one of the few states whose domestic and foreign policy is suffused with a commitment to the postwar human rights project. In fact, as

Mertus's research reveals, Danes draw a rigid distinction between internal Danish politics, social programs, and even Danish culture, and international relations and foreign aid obligations.

Within Denmark, cultural norms have traditionally been based on obligation and the importance of social equality, which "reward egalitarian behavior, support [the] peaceful resolution of conflict, and encourage advancement of the collective over the individual. This contrasts sharply with the human rights framework, which empowers citizen rights holders to make their own particular rights claims [against the state]."[31] As Mertus explains, the belief among Danes is that "the good life in Denmark has been the product of the solidarity principle, not the result of any kind of rights-based advocacy."[32]

The stunning—and, likely, extremely rare—consequence of the pervasiveness of the "solidarity principle" in Denmark is that many Danes reject the idea that human rights should be applied within domestic law and politics, not because human rights are associated with the unwanted impositions of internationalism, but because Danish society has evolved beyond the need for human rights. As a prominent human rights researcher in Denmark put it, "it is almost like we are too good for human rights, . . . the notion [is] that sophisticated people like us . . . are above the fray of human rights."[33]

Indeed, the mere suggestion that Danes would be reduced to using the language of human rights within domestic policy making would be "upsetting" to many people. The invocation of human rights would represent an "aggressive" assault on Danish values of consensus building and social action, and would be seen to violate a national ethics called *janteloven*, a set of commonly held "ten commandments" that have been criticized by some as promoting an "extreme egalitarianism that goes beyond modesty to [become] enforced commonality."[34]

Against this background, the DIHR has struggled to fulfill its mandate as an NHRI, but not because the Danish state has viewed it as a meddlesome and easily delegitimized critic of internal repression and corruption, which is the fate of so many NHRIs in different parts of the world. Rather, the DIHR has struggled because it is viewed as an advocate for an approach to claims-making and individual rights that has little relevance to either local Danish politics or the country's vaunted social welfare system.

Nevertheless, the marginality of the DIHR within Denmark has not offered it protection from the shifting currents of domestic politics. At one point, the Danish government submitted a proposal to merge a number of human rights organizations into a new single institution as a cost-cutting measure, to be called the Danish Academy for International Affairs. This move not only would have scrubbed "human rights" from the title of the new institution, it would also have folded the DIHR into the Ministry for Foreign Affairs, ending its nominal independence from the Danish state and effectively dissolving the country's NHRI.

Although this proposal was greeted with indifference within Denmark, the "international human rights community was horrified."[35] Given that Denmark was angling to take over the European Union's rotating presidency at the time, the government was particularly sensitive to the "groundswell of international criticism," which included a forceful rebuke from Mary Robinson, the UN High Commissioner for Human Rights. Although the DIHR was eventually saved, it was reorganized in a highly unusual way. Despite its legal status as a *national* human rights institution under the terms of the Paris Principles, it adopted a mandate that concentrated most of its activities and human resources into *international* human rights activism.

In particular, the DIHR became the world's leading advocate for the establishment of NHRIs—that is, in other countries, typically those in the "developing" world in which the Danish International Development Agency was heavily invested through humanitarian aid and development assistance. At the same time, the DIHR became a major center for interdisciplinary scientific research on human rights, research that, again, concerned human rights problems largely beyond Denmark.

In fact, given its precarious status before the reorganization, the DIHR later thrived precisely because it evolved into a human rights institution that neither focused its activities at the national level nor was substantively independent of the Danish state. Instead, its members conducted research on human rights around the world while its support for NHRIs abroad made it an important extension of Danish foreign affairs.[36]

Although I remain largely agnostic on the question of the future of NHRIs within a reinvented human rights, much more important is what they reveal, or, rather, confirm—even in unexpected ways, in unexpected places, as with the DIHR—about the debilitating position of the state. The saga of the DIHR should be taken as a limiting case that definitively settles the point that state-centricity is the kiss of death for the future of human rights.

When even social- and economic-index topping Denmark can't be trusted to prioritize its domestic human rights obligations because of competing national interests or cultural values[37]—however progressive in their own terms—is it any surprise that the "organized hypocrisy"[38] of state-centricity has proven to be the greatest *political* obstacle to the cause of existing human rights, the single most important driver of "disregard and contempt"?[39]

Conclusion: Remaking Sovereignty in the Image of Human Rights

> Imperial power whispers the names of the struggles in order to charm them into passivity, to construct a mystified image of them, but most important to discover which processes of globalization are possible and which are not.
>
> Hardt and Negri, *Empire*

In a reassessment of the relationship between human rights law and the state, the Finnish international legal scholar Martti Koskenniemi poses the question, "what use for sovereignty today?"[40] By way of response, he devotes most of his answer to a long list of the ways in which Westphalian sovereignty has formed a baseline barrier against which international lawyers like him have spent their careers struggling. He makes the insightful observation that despite this barrier, state sovereignty is not the only international logic that counts. As he argues, the doctrine of sovereignty is challenged from various directions, including from different transnational networks of capital and expertise as well as through the formation of supranational regimes such as the European Union, which affect the expression of sovereign prerogative within member states. Nevertheless, as he acknowledges, although "we longer see any magic in sovereignty,"[41] it still constitutes both the normative and historic foundation of the international system, the glue that holds it together and which justifies its inherent limitations.

And yet, instead of the expected lament about the impossibility of resolving what I have described as the sovereign contradiction, Koskenniemi's analysis takes an unexpected turn. Rather than imagining new ways in which sovereignty could be undermined on behalf of existing human rights, an approach that is the international lawyer's stock and trade, he argues that sovereignty should be stripped of its Westphalian meanings and reinvested with a set of values and associations that would allow it to be reappropriated and, in a sense, rehabilitated. Interestingly, his primary concern is not that conventional state sovereignty works to block the development of human rights by giving states free rein to prioritize national security or domestic politics. According to Koskenniemi, the more critical problem is the way in which sovereign state bureaucracies concentrate decision-making power over people's lives, often at the service of "transnational networks of private interest."[42]

In making the case for an alternative, Koskenniemi argues that the doctrine of sovereignty—even in its original Westphalian framing—contains the seeds of its own reformulation. At its core, he proposes, sovereignty can be reconceptualized to emphasize a particular way of understanding collective life, as the assemblage of "rules, institutions, and practices through which the forms of collective life are constantly imagined, debated, criticized, and reformed, over and again."[43] Even more, sovereignty—in this contrasting register—points to the necessity for social action since it is an expression of "frustration and anger about the diminishing spaces of collective re-imagining, creation, and transformation," whether imposed by the state or broader forces of "global power and expert rule."[44]

In returning to the wider project to reinvent human rights, I would build on Koskenniemi's central insight: the doctrine of sovereignty, so essential in its Westphalian forms to the existing international system, can and must be recreated to serve other functions. From this perspective, sovereignty is reinserted as the basis for "collective self-formation" directed against problems such as "war, economic collapse, and environmental destruction."[45]

Among other things, the reappropriation of sovereignty in these terms gives structure to the concept of translocality, yet without making the ill-fated leap to the cosmopolitan fantasy realm of global citizenship. In other words, sovereignty gives meaning to the "collective" in "collective action"—the purpose of a reinvented human rights—yet without having to adhere to existing and reified categories of collective life, since these must remain fluid, indeterminate, and subject to "collective re-imagining."[46]

As we have seen, as a matter of both intellectual and political history, the doctrine of state sovereignty preceded the full development of philosophical and moral systems that would be grounded in universal rights. By the time of the rights-based revolutions of the late eighteenth century, the Westphalian firmament had been well-settled for almost 150 years. If the conventional doctrine of state sovereignty expresses a particular account of political embodiment and national separateness, this means that the sovereign contradiction has always been at the center of the history of human rights, exerting pressure and ultimately undermining the ambition to privilege universal human rights over much more limited and exclusionary categories of belonging.

Indeed, this countervailing pressure has taken surprising forms over the history of human rights. In conceiving a postaristocratic and postecclesiastical French state, key revolutionary thinkers went to great lengths to ensure that the categories of "man" and "citizen" in the foundational Declaration of the Rights of

Man and of the Citizen were as constrained as possible. The influential Girondin lawyer and revolutionary leader Jacques-Guillaume Thouret, who later fell victim to the guillotine during the Reign of Terror, was responsible for introducing the concept of "active citizenship." This category restricted the "rights of man" to property-owning male citizens who could demonstrate that they had paid "direct taxes at a rate equal to the local value of three days of work," and were not "in personal relationships that are all too incompatible with the independence necessary to the exercise of political rights."[47] This is the doctrine of sovereignty working not only to define state boundaries—in the language of rights—but also to define discriminatory social and political boundaries *within* the state.

And as we have also seen, the sovereign contradiction was given full effect during the creation of the postwar international system, in which the great powers took an elaborate series of political and institutional steps to ensure that national autonomy would be protected from the dangers of human rights. As a result, international human rights were made in the image of sovereignty.

Yet in considering the ways and means of a reinvented human rights for the future, something like the opposite becomes a necessity: sovereignty must be (re-)made in the image of human rights. In reimagining sovereignty as the justification for "collective self-formation" in which the state is neither referent nor arbiter, sovereignty becomes the means through which social power can be directed toward emancipatory, egalitarian, and ecologically sustainable ends. In this way, remade in the image of human rights, sovereignty is reinfused with magic of a different kind.

CHAPTER 4

Human Rights beyond the Rule of Law

I FIRST BECAME SENSITIZED to the unexpected dilemmas of law in a remote region of the Bolivian Andes during the late 1990s. As was seen in the last chapter, I conducted extended ethnographic research on conflict resolution and gender relations among Indigenous and mestizo populations in the north of Potosí Department, which was famous in the anthropological literature for the existence of Indigenous social and land tenure systems called *ayllus*, which linked land use and communal life between less fertile highland and more fertile lowland zones through a conceptual—rather than geographical—cultural map based on noncontiguity and ritual guardianship.[1]

But ayllus were also the basis for local Indigenous leadership within a wider authority system that included positions that were derived from the colonial period and those that were created much more recently, in the wake of the 1952 National Revolution, and were influenced by the rural syndicalist movement. These three separate, but tightly interwoven, lines of local authority—ayllu, colonial, syndicalist—provided the authority figures and the normative and procedural bases on which conflicts of all kinds were mediated and ideally resolved for people living in widely dispersed settlements in which the basic mode of production was agro-pastoralism.

To complicate what I later came to conceptualize as a multilayered and polyvalent legal assemblage, this sociolegal world in rural Bolivia also included a state legal institution in the region's administrative capital, a court of first instance called a *juzgado de instrucción*. The courthouse itself was an unassuming building on the plaza in a small town that was one among hundreds of such towns throughout the Andes designed by Spanish colonial officials in the mid-sixteenth century. These ubiquitous *reducciones* were intended to replicate the model of provincial Spanish legal, political, and religious organization, and to "reduce" the Indigenous population, which meant to force them to leave their traditional ayllus and move to a "civilized" colonial space where they could be better governed under the watchful eyes of church and civic officials. Although the effort to reduce the Andean populations in this way proved to be an unmitigated failure, one of the legacies of this early colonial period was the persistence of isolated state institutions—including these small courts of first instance in the Bolivian judicial system—throughout vast swaths of the highlands in which, as we have seen, the presence of the Bolivian state is otherwise minimal.

This particular *juzgado de instrucción* was a modest institution, staffed by just three people: a judge, who had both adjudicative and investigatory functions; a notary, who took minutes on a typewriter during court sessions; and a secretary, who kept the court calendar at the desk outside the judge's "chambers," which consisted of a small room adjacent to the court's dusty archives, where case files that began in the mid-nineteenth century were stacked on metal shelves.[2] The entrance to the judge's chambers was flanked by the standard portraits of Simón Bolívar and Antonio José de Sucre, founders of republican Bolivia (1825), while the court's extremely light docket was posted on a wall. Indeed, entire weeks would pass without any judicial activity. In addition, the court was shuttered for long periods around Christmas and during the festival season known as "Carnival," when the judge (who was not a local) would disappear from the town, sometimes without providing a fixed date on which the court would reopen.

Yet when the court *was* in session, it became a remote microcosm of a distinct conception of the rule of law in which legal norms are combined with legal procedures to create the illusion that social life is being regulated in ways that are orderly, transparent, and, above all, just. The judge himself viewed his role in precisely this way: as a conduit for and representative of the rule of law in a region populated by Indigenous Bolivians whose languages (Aymara and Quechua) he didn't speak, whose spiritual lives he didn't understand, and whose social conflicts remained largely opaque to his judicial sensibilities.

In order to enforce a rigid adherence to procedure in the court, the judge would begin each hearing in the same way. Everyone would be required to stand while the judge held an oversized crucifix in one hand while pressing his thumb and pointer figure together with the other hand, which was kept away from his body at eye level, a gesture used for oath-taking throughout Bolivian officialdom.

When everyone present was duly focused and appropriately solemn, the judge would utter the incantation with which he began every session: *Será justicia*, there will be justice.

The problem, however, was that the court, while formally one of first instance, was actually one of last resort for the thousands of people in the region. The reason that the court's docket was so light was not that social conflicts were so uncommon within the hundreds of settlements throughout the province; indeed, as I found out, the opposite was true. Conflicts of different kinds were endemic in this part of rural Bolivia, from fights to property damage to defamation to homicide.[3] With the exception of the most serious cases (such as homicide, including infanticide), almost all conflicts were resolved within the surrounding nonstate structure, which included its own rough jurisdictional boundaries, its own levels of appeal, and even a highly elaborate culture of forum-shopping, in which claimants moved strategically between different politico-legal authorities based on the type of conflict, likelihood of desired outcome, and even the person who occupied the relevant authority position at the time, since the "cargo" usually rotated every two years.

The result was that from the perspective of the provincial court, the rule of law was strictly limited to what took place within the crumbling walls of the *juzgado de instrucción*, while at the same time the judge and his two staff members viewed themselves as the embodiment of the law itself, symbolic actors whose very presence in such a far-flung place ensured that, despite it all, there would be justice. Yet in fact, within the vast webs of legality in the region, the provincial court was only one node, one institution among hundreds, in a part of rural Bolivia that was saturated with conflict, conflict resolution processes, and cultures of legal ordering, none of which would be considered part of the "rule of law" by either the Bolivian state or the numerous NGOs that worked in the region, including human rights NGOs.

I begin this chapter with a legal anthropological anecdote from rural Bolivia because the broader relationship between human rights and the rule of law has likewise been marked by similar histories and practices of legal-ideological posturing, actually existing legal pluralism, and what might be thought of as cases of mistaken normative identity. Even more, as a form of regulation, as a logic of moral ordering, and as a framework for political legitimacy, the law has dominated the postwar history of human rights in multiple ways and at multiple levels. Therefore, in considering an alternative approach to human rights, one that critically reconsiders every dimension of the existing international system, it is absolutely essential to reexamine the place of law as the principal form of human rights and the rule of law as the prevailing global ideology that justifies this form.

In so doing, I argue that the central place of law and legal institutions, including international criminal tribunals, has proven to be at best ambiguous for human rights and, at worst, an institutional and normative straitjacket that has kept existing human rights tightly confined in ways that have dramatically limited their wider potential as a framework for transformative social and political action. At the same time, the close bundling of human rights with wider processes of neoliberal humanitarianism—which typically includes the Holy Trinity of democratization, market reforms, and rule of law initiatives—has meant that the relationship between human rights and law also has a geopolitical dimension, one that prominent postcolonial scholars have claimed privileges a "state-centric enforcement paradigm" and a Euro-American model of the nation-state.[4]

Even in the aftermath of mass atrocity, the role of law and the "enforcement paradigm" have long been shown to be highly problematic as the fundamental modes through which human rights are expressed and given practical force. If this is true, then a reinvented human rights must be conceptualized and developed largely beyond the reach of what the Irish legal scholar Kieran McEvoy has called the "seduction of legalism," even beyond a conventional understanding of the rule of law itself.[5]

To this end, the chapter is organized in the following way. In the next section, I examine different factors that are structural to law itself in order to show how and why even the most well-intentioned legal forms impose limits on the extent to which human rights might flourish in a broader and more compelling register. I then turn to the question of the relationship between human rights and law. As will be seen, this relationship underwent important changes during the roughly decade-long Age of Human Rights, when many forms of political, social, and moral life were reinterpreted within legal categories. This was as much an ideological as a normative shift, one that accompanied the rapid expansion of human rights law during a period in which progressive politics was also being repurposed as a basis for recognition rather than a mechanism for structural economic and social change.

The chapter then examines the ambiguous history of the institutions and doctrines committed to legal accountability for mass human rights violations, including the processes associated with transitional justice.[6] Some scholars who take a "pragmatic" approach to the value of existing human rights often point to the apparent empirical links between human rights tribunals and positive outcomes, such as a reduction in state-sponsored violence.[7] Although this might be true in specific instances, I argue that this does not mean that law—let alone international criminal law—should retain its privileged status as the cornerstone of a reinvented human rights. The chapter then concludes by returning to broader questions of justice, cultural diversity, and the possibilities for preserving a reformulated conception of the rule of law as one among several principles on which human rights might be based.

E. P. Thompson and the Janus-Faced Logics of Law

In the course of reexamining one of the most perplexing moments in English legal history, the passage and implementation of the Black Act of 1723, E. P. Thompson—admittedly despite his own Marxist sensibilities—also discovered a number of surprising aspects about the law itself, transcendent structural elements that characterized diverse forms of English common law across the centuries.[8] Thompson, the great New Left historian who wrote an incomparable study of the English working class,[9] wanted to understand one of the most notorious periods in English legal and social history: the passage of a major law by the House of Commons that dramatically expanded the use of capital punishment for an extraordinary array of crimes against property.

The "Black" in the law's title was the colloquial way to refer to legislation that, in part, made the mere blacking of faces as camouflage by poachers on private—including royal—estates a crime punishable by death. Other capital property crimes within the act included "breaking down the head or mound of any fish-pond," "sending anonymous letters demanding 'money, venison, or other valuable thing,'" and even "cutting down trees 'planted in any avenue, or growing in any garden, orchard or plantation.'"[10]

Although the passage of the Black Act came several decades before the centuries-long enclosure movement in England finally extinguished almost all common rights in land, the first part of the eighteenth century was the period in which the power of private property was transformed into the moral and material foundation for early English capitalism. In this sense, the Black Act both crystallized a long-term transition and was a signpost pointing toward the future, in which thousands of landless laborers would be forced to leave the countryside and migrate to cities, where they would form the pool of workers that made the Industrial Revolution possible.[11] Yet by 1723, this transformation was far enough along that English law had been reduced almost to a single-purpose tool for the protection of the new private property regime, a tool that the state was expected to wield with singular focus. As Thompson puts it, "the British state, all eighteenth-century legislators agreed, existed to preserve the property and, incidentally, the lives and liberties, of the propertied."[12]

Even more, the use of the Black Act of 1723 to eliminate any challenges to England's emerging political economy was cloaked in a moral narrative that would anticipate the more elaborated justifications for capitalism a century later. Yet at this embryonic stage in the long-term process that would ultimately culminate in the triumph of neoliberal capitalism as the "truly ambitious and successful moral program of our time,"[13] the protection of private property through law was not based in doctrines of individual liberty.

Instead, the economic and social lines that divided the landed gentry from the landless rural masses were those that divided different moral orders altogether: one (the propertied), which represented progress and ethical rectitude; and the other (the landless), which represented reactionary tradition and ethical darkness. Thompson quotes from a newspaper article from 1723, which imagines the landless targets of the Black Act as inhabitants of a different world entirely, one that threatened the economic and social order of England: " 'Tis said this lawless band are firmly subjected by the most solemn oaths to a blind obedience to their Mock Monarch . . . whose wicked agents have lately bid so fair for involving this nation in blood and confusion. An army of Blacks would be proper instruments for establishing the Kingdom of Darkness."[14] It is not surprising, therefore, that Thompson's study shows the Black Act being used for precisely its intended purposes: poachers and petty property criminals were duly convicted and executed, while the very existence of the act itself loomed as a juridical symbol of the irreversible transformation of English economic and social life.[15]

Nevertheless, Thompson's research did uncover something quite unexpected, even shocking: in a number of cases, defendants were actually found not guilty by the courts, to the horror of the landed claimants who fully expected a rigid and instrumental application of the law on their behalf. These not guilty verdicts were the result of a range of factors: procedural technicalities, problems with evidence, the death of witnesses, mistaken identifications. In short, despite the broader context in which the Black Act was meant to forge a new political economic order through legal terror, it made a difference that this terror was instantiated through *law* and not through other means.

Thompson argues that although these not guilty verdicts paled in comparison with the many applications of the Black Act as a tool of class oppression, these outliers were nevertheless highly significant for what they revealed about what he calls the "forms and rhetoric of law." As he puts it, in a classic passage in which he also confronts the limitations of his own ideological predispositions:

> We reach, then, not a simple conclusion (law = class power) but a complex and contradictory one. On the one hand, it is true that the law did mediate existent class relations to the advantage of the rulers. . . . On the other hand, the law mediated these class relations through legal forms, which imposed, again and again, inhibitions upon the actions of the rulers. For there is a very large difference, which twentieth-century experience ought to have made clear even to the most exalted thinker, between arbitrary extra-legal power and the rule of law. . . . The rhetoric and the [laws] of a society are something a great deal more than sham. In the same moment they may modify, in profound ways, the behavior of the powerful, and mystify the powerless.[16]

Yet if the forms and rhetoric of law mediate its use as an instrument of class power, the same must also be true of its use as an instrument of social change. In thinking about how, for example, human rights law is expected to be a progressive tool for pursuing accountability in the aftermath of mass human rights violations, for protecting marginalized populations from discrimination, and for promoting economic and social rights, Thompson's formula still applies, only in reverse. The forms and rhetoric of law "modify"—that is, constrain—the radical potential of human rights at the same time they might, at best, "mystify" the powerful interests against whom human rights are turned.

The implications of the Janus-faced logics of law for reimagining human rights are profound. Even though the forms and rhetoric of law "mediate" in the same way in both directions, both the contexts and consequences are completely different. When law mediates—or, in a Weberian sense, rationalizes—potentially destructive realities, from what Thompson calls the "exercise of unmediated force" to the destabilizing effects of social conflict more generally, we view these effects as salutary. The problem is not that the forms and rhetoric of law mediate in these ways; the problem is that it is usually not enough.

But with the use of human rights law as an instrument of potentially far-reaching change, the objective is not to mediate, or rationalize, let alone to limit, this potential. On the contrary, the objective, one might say, is to unleash the power of human rights. Yet the forms and rhetoric of law act as a barrier to this power, just as they do to the exercise of power by the ruling classes in Thompson's study. These structural limitations can, under certain circumstances, become insidious. As the American legal scholar Richard Thompson Ford has argued, among other consequences, "law corrupts the struggle for equality."[17]

The Apotheosis of Law: Juristocracy

If these Janus-faced logics lead to structural and largely internal arguments against the place of law within a reinvented human rights, we must also consider the wider ideological and historical contexts in which law and legal institutions became powerful in new ways, especially after the end of the Cold War. At both international and national levels, law expanded dramatically at the same time in which existing traditions of political mobilization and resistance were denuded of effectiveness and legitimacy. The legal philosopher Ran Hirschl has described the ascendency and eventual apotheosis of law during this period as "juristocracy"—the rule not *of* law, but *by* law.[18]

In the early years after the Cold War system collapsed, the coming of juristocracy was signaled by the renewed prominence given to national constitutions, especially within turbulent processes of democratic transition and social reckoning. Even more, constitutions and constitution-making quickly became the juridical means through which human rights were given form in widely disparate political and historical contexts. For example, as Heinz Klug has shown, the postapartheid transition in South Africa was viewed as a laboratory for testing an idea that soon became widespread globally: a national constitution shaped by international human rights was not merely a statement of national principles, it was an instrument for forging democracy.[19]

Yet even before the South African transition, the countries that were created from the former Yugoslavia had embraced a fraught approach to human rights constitutionalism as the foundation for their independent political futures. Through ethnographic research conducted in the early days of the Age of Human Rights, the legal anthropologist Robert Hayden documented the ways in which the newly independent states were able to use the language of rights to juridically launder what later became a virulent ethnonationalism. Far from promoting inclusive social practices based on concepts like dignity or equality, the early post-Yugoslav constitutions legalized an exclusionary vision of the nation, "defined in terms of race, language and culture."[20]

If the human-rights-infused constitution of the new South Africa made bold claims to remake democracy in the image of an inclusive "Rainbow Nation," the equally rights-infused post-Yugoslav constitutions represented, in Hayden's analysis, something quite different: an *attack* on democratic principles. Among other implications, that existing human rights can be put to such diametrically opposed constitutional ends should raise serious questions about the future viability of what I have described elsewhere as "revolution by constitution."[21]

Yet taking an even broader geopolitical and historical perspective, the endemic problems of law as the central framework for the promotion of human rights come into even sharper focus. Although the end of the Cold War made a particular kind of legal ascendency possible, even inevitable, the apotheosis of human rights *as* law was long prefigured within histories of legal subjugation through colonialism. Indeed, as the Sudanese American human rights scholar and former political prisoner Abdullahi Ahmed An-Na'im has argued, powerful Euro-American states in the postwar period were inspired by well-established ideological models in which "state-centric legality" was the primary mechanism for the diffusion of an ethnocentric vision of Western civilization.[22] For An-Na'im, this legal-historical legacy taints the entire structure of international human rights, which relies on the twin juridical pillars of international treaties and "state-centric enforcement." As a critical response, An-Na'im gestures toward his own proposal for an alternative future for human rights, one in which these legal pillars are replaced with "cultural transformation" and "political mobilization" guided by "consensus-based" human rights norms.

But if juristocracy has enclosed existing human rights in institutional forms that pose both normative and historical dilemmas, an even more far-reaching problem is the way in which the unprecedented expansion of law and legal forms has severely limited the scope of political and social alternatives for advancing human rights as the basis for transformative change. Scholars have described this broader effect as "juridification," which often takes the more specific form of "judicialization" when the grounds for political activism are reduced at the same time in which courts become the key—sometimes the only—sites in which social and political claims can be made. The juridification-to-judicialization nexus is obviously highly variable depending on a number of factors, but it is revealing that its effects have been most prominent—and most prominently documented—in regions of the world like Latin America, where the post–Cold War diffusion of human rights was accompanied by the almost total collapse of revolutionary politics.[23]

The long-term consequences of juridification for the future of human rights are twofold. First, juridification represents a form of what might be called social capture, in which social relations are co-opted by legal-bureaucratic imperatives, logics, and expectations. In a more abstract sense, this process of co-optation can be understood as a type of colonization in which the capacious moral potential of human rights is reified, or hardened, into legal categories.[24] More concretely, the juridification of social life can cause people to overestimate the progressive power of law in their lives, something Sally Engle Merry has described as the "paradox of legal entitlement."[25] This is particularly problematic for people from vulnerable or historically marginalized populations, including those from Indigenous communities.[26]

And second, juridification has created a new and much more consequential version of what James Ferguson described as an "anti-politics machine."[27] Ferguson conducted ethnographic research on the large-scale Canadian-funded Thaba-Tseka development project in Lesotho during the waning years of the Cold War. As he shows, despite the fact that the project ultimately failed to meet its stated development objectives, it did lead to widespread changes in the way Lesothans viewed political and social change.

Structural poverty and social powerlessness came to be reinterpreted through the course of the project as technical problems that could be solved through the intervention of international development experts in collaboration with their state counterparts. This took place against a wider background of political instability in the country and in the region, in which a strongman regime in Lesotho and the apartheid government of South Africa (which completely surrounds Lesotho) viewed organized political and social mobilization as a grave threat to the existing order, something to be resisted at all costs.

Yet a similar, and much more global, dynamic has characterized juridification, especially juridification through international human rights. Social and political movements were first encouraged, and then obligated, to reinterpret long-standing claims in the language of human rights and then turn exclusively to state or international institutions to mediate these claims. A poignant example is the way in which marginalized Indigenous communities are forced to narrow their resistance to resource plunder and land-grabbing to legal procedures outlined in state or regional rights frameworks. As a broad range of research has shown, from supposed victories at the Inter-American Court of Human Rights, to national legal interventions that are hailed by states and transnational NGOs as signs of human rights compliance, juridification through rights has done very little to stem the tide of economic and environmental violence throughout much of the Global South.[28]

Even worse, at least in certain regions like Southeast Asia, juridification through rights has been eagerly embraced by major transnational corporations as a means to legalize the massive expropriation of land as part of wider risk-management strategies. As Saturnino Borras and Jennifer Franco have put it, national rights frameworks throughout the region have become a "one-stop-shop" for resource corporations. These corporations support national titling processes of communal land to ensure access, reduce the possibility of conflict, and even to take advantage of the common requirement in rights legislation for communities to develop "resource management" plans that companies can immediately adopt for purposes of intensive resource extraction.[29]

But the de-politicizing effects of juridification are not limited to the Global South. Beginning with the end of the Cold War, the pervasive legal ascendency was accompanied by the equally pervasive disappearance of forms of politics that depended on sustained mobilization and direct action, often against economic and national institutions. Despite exceptions, such as the 2011–12 Occupy Wall Street protests against economic inequality, most attempts at organized social resistance have confronted what Nancy Fraser called the "dilemma of justice in a 'post-socialist' age," in which the methodologies and objectives of revolutionary politics were widely abandoned without being replaced by a similarly robust or coherent framework.[30]

Needless to say, human rights law failed to constitute such a framework. Instead, like the development project Ferguson examined, human rights law has functioned as an "anti-politics machine" in which legal experts reinterpret economic and social problems as rights violations, which then come within the exclusive purview of courts and legal officials. These agents and institutions of human rights law then deform and elide the underlying economic and social problems even further, guided by the dictates of legal procedure, trapped within the vicissitudes of institutional idleness, and inspired, if at all, mostly by what James Boyd White described as the uncertain "rhetoric and poetics of the law."[31]

Legal Accountability: An Ambiguous History

A final category through which the relationship between human rights and law must be interrogated is the sacrosanct category of legal accountability, one whose practical expression takes forms such as legal enforcement and legal monitoring. At a more abstract and jurisprudential level, the importance of legal accountability can be traced back to orthodox accounts of the nature of law itself, in which law, properly understood, must include the combination of what H. L. A. Hart called "primary rules" and a corresponding set of sanctions that follow from the violation of these rules.[32] Even early legal anthropologists emphasized the fundamental importance of punishment or sanctions in distinguishing law from other forms of social obligation. As Bronislaw Malinowski put it, "rules of law stand out from the rest in that . . . they are sanctioned . . . by a definite social machinery of binding force."[33]

But beyond jurisprudence, legal accountability has played a fundamental political role in the postwar history of human rights, beginning with the Nuremberg and Tokyo trials. Leaving aside the debates around the organization of the postwar trials and questions about legal doctrine and due process, the prosecutions of Nazi and Imperial Japanese political, military, ideological, and industrial leaders created an important international precedent: those responsible for organizing the worst human rights violations, including crimes against humanity and genocide, will be held legally accountable and duly punished.[34]

This precedent lay dormant, however, until the waning years of the Cold War, when a newly democratic Argentina prosecuted those responsible for the violence of the Dirty War (1976–83). This was followed by the establishment of a number of "special" (time or region-limited) courts to hold accountable those responsible for paroxysms of mass human rights violations in different places and times, from the Cambodia Tribunal to the International Criminal Tribunal for the former Yugoslavia (ICTY).

The international legal accountability movement culminated with the adoption of the Rome Statute by the UN General Assembly in 1998, which authorized the creation of the first permanent international criminal court. The political legitimacy of the ICC, which issued its first international arrest warrants in 2005 and convicted its first defendant of human rights violations in 2012, has nevertheless been attacked with varying degrees of vehemence by a number of powerful nation-states, including the United States, China, Russia, India, Turkey, and Indonesia.[35]

Yet in considering the importance of the principle of legal accountability within the history of the international human rights system (including its short postwar, but pre-UDHR, history), three major problems become evident, problems that lend additional weight to the argument that the place of law must be dramatically reduced within a reinvented human rights. First, it is worth reconsidering the entire premise behind legal accountability for human rights violations. One of the most consistent proponents of legal accountability as a central pillar of existing human rights has been Kathryn Sikkink and her colleagues, who have conducted large-scale quantitative studies in order to demonstrate the relationship between legal accountability, improvements in human rights compliance, and global justice.[36]

According to Sikkink, this research establishes a number of empirical findings: "countries using [human rights] trials see improvements [meaning reductions] in levels of repression compared with countries that do not use trials"; human rights trials are "concrete, focused, and relatively inexpensive compared to . . . massive structural changes"; "accountability is important because it can help build rule of law, thus strengthening democracy"; and human rights prosecutions "lead to improvements in human rights practices through a combination of deterrence and normative communication."[37] Sikkink argues that a proliferation in human rights prosecutions around the world during the 1990s, the same decade of the Age of Human Rights more generally, set in motion what she has described as a "justice cascade," a kind of global suffusion of demands for justice that Sikkink believes heralds "good news for human rights worldwide."[38]

Without entering into an important, although ultimately limited, discussion of the methodological controversies around the production and use of the "indicators" that form the basis for quantitative claims like these,[39] what concerns me here is the way in which statistical studies are used as the foundation for making improbable judgments about the global power of human rights law in general and human rights prosecutions (whether national or international) in particular. The idea that human rights prosecutions—or the threat of such prosecutions—are "changing world politics" in ways that have made human rights a kind of controlling check on state and corporate power seems to me both counterfactual and counterintuitive.

Indeed, when the rose-colored quantitative glasses are removed, the global justice cascade either dries up or appears as something quite different: a simulated cascade, like one might find in an amusement park, a superficial structure that one scholar has described as a "justice facade."[40] The anthropologist Alexander Hinton has been conducting landmark ethnographic and historical research around the Cambodian genocide for decades, a record that has made him a distinct voice on questions of international law in practice, collective memory, mass violence, and transitional justice processes.[41] Working primarily in the Khmer language with interlocuters from a wide range of Cambodian social, political, and religious backgrounds, including many who participated at different levels in the genocidal violence, Hinton has demonstrated in thick ethnographic detail the ways in which the international hybrid tribunal took place in a kind of parallel universe that had very little relevance to the everyday lives of Cambodians.

As he argues, the so-called justice cascade is a way of imagining a global movement based on human rights in which the mechanisms of legal accountability are conceived as universal tools that can be readily adapted to all histories of mass violence and their aftermath, since what is being redressed through law in each instance is a corresponding harm of universal scope—violations of human rights. Yet far below the radar of this global imaginary, Hinton's longitudinal ethnography in Cambodia reveals how this vision of justice masks the complicated cultural and socioeconomic realities of each specific history of mass violence, each specific trajectory of transition. Even more, Hinton's research challenges the ideological framework of the wider global legal accountability movement, which is deeply embedded in what he describes as "teleological and transformative assumptions."[42] A very different approach to human rights and its meanings in practice, therefore, would be one that breaks free from what Hinton calls the "webs of the transitional justice imaginary."[43]

A second problem with the centrality of legal accountability within the existing international human rights system is the fact that it has taken both institutional and discursive forms that have perpetuated a number of colonial and neocolonial tropes. For example, although prominent human rights activists like Kenneth Roth have made a convincing case that at least some of the state-level resistance in Africa to the ICC is based in bad faith by authoritarian politicians,[44] researchers who have studied the institutional legacy of the ICC against the background of Africa's diverse economic and political realities have documented a much more ambiguous history.

Kamari Maxine Clarke has emphasized the ways in which the ICC's "all-African indictments"[45] have created a powerful institutional culture of illegibility based on the exclusionary enforcement of what she describes as "fictions of justice."[46] With reference to much older histories of colonial legal imposition justified by doctrines of evolutionary progress and the civilizing mission, Clarke argues that the ICC seeks to render illegible existing conflict resolution mechanisms in Africa and to co-opt responsibility for confronting the consequences of violence from local religious and political communities. What results, according to Clarke, is a destabilizing politics of elision in which the imperatives of international legal accountability mediate—but do not overturn—unequal relations of power.[47]

And discursively, the international legal accountability movement has too often relied on what the Kenyan legal scholar Makau Mutua has called the "metaphor of human rights," in which the deep economic, political, and social origins of violence have been obscured by an orientalizing narrative in which the "saviors" of human rights protect "victims" from the inhumane atrocities perpetrated by "savages."[48] Beyond contemporary human rights prosecutions, Antony Anghie has gone even further in arguing that international law has always depended on metaphors of civilizational confrontation through which non-European peoples must be governed and transformed at the same time.[49]

A third and final problem with legal accountability and the so-called enforcement paradigm as key pillars of existing human rights has been the inability of human rights tribunals and transitional justice mechanisms to account for cultural diversity and legal pluralism. As the first extended, interdisciplinary study of the "intersections of law and culture" at the ICC demonstrates, the entire jurisprudential and institutional framework of the court is hostile to the realities of cultural and religious difference, either as the basis for making claims or as the grounds on which a defendant might mount a defense.[50] In addition, the court's regard toward the concept of "culture" is shaped by a reified and antiquated approach that could be described as "spurious,"[51] an approach that utterly fails to account for the nuanced development over time of what another study has described as "multicultural jurisprudence."[52]

Yet even when hybrid or local justice procedures have been proposed in an effort to accommodate cultural diversity, the results have still been problematic. As Thania Paffenholz has argued,[53] the "local turn" in human rights enforcement, transitional justice, and broader peacebuilding embodies its own essentializing orientation toward culture, one that ignores the reality of asymmetric and often violent power relations *within* communities, asymmetries that are also commonly gendered.[54] As the anthropologist Mariane Ferme has put it, the "underneath of things" should not be romanticized;[55] that is, there is no immediate "communal fix" to the problems of legal accountability,[56] no obvious means through which the mechanisms of legal enforcement can or should be refashioned as a privileged framework for a reinvented human rights.[57]

Conclusion: Human Rights and the Siren Song of Themis

To conclude this chapter on the fraught relationship between human rights and the rule of law, let me return to the place at which I began: the rural court in the Bolivian Andes. I spent more than a year attending every session on the sparse docket and then following the course of conflicts before, during, and after their passage through the *juzgado de instrucción*. The nature of conflicts spanned a wide range, from multigenerational struggles over shifting land boundaries to domestic abuse to defamation (*calumnia*), an "offense against honor" that was considered grave enough to require the intervention of the state court in the provincial capital.

For the judge, the court was only partly an extension of the Bolivian judiciary, a lone institutional post at the very "capillary ends" of state power.[58] Even more, he saw the court as the embodiment of "the law" itself, a juridical citadel surrounded by a sea of unknowable cultures of conflict resolution, a guardian of a legal tradition that was connected—as he explained—in an unbroken historical line to the great doctrinal monuments of Roman jurisprudence. Above all, the court in the town of Sacaca was the guarantor of justice; indeed, for the judge, the court was the *only* means through which people in the province could legitimately seek justice. Each time he intoned solemnly, *Será justicia*, there will be justice, the judge made this exclusionary claim, one wrapped within "teleological and transformative assumptions" marked by the simple future verb tense.

But beyond the court, no one ever invoked the concept of "justice," let alone the Spanish word. Depending on the region in the province, the first languages were either Quechua and Aymara; most of my research was conducted in a combination of Quechua and Spanish. During conflict resolution sessions in the hamlets, people would use the Quechua verb *pajtachay*, which has the meaning of putting things in their proper order, but must be understood as part of a broader social ontology about the organization of communal space. Hinton makes a similar point about the ultimate incommensurability of "justice": "it is difficult to even translate the word 'justice' in Khmer, a term that has Buddhist resonances and is understood by many Cambodians in terms of ideas like karma."[59]

Yet instead of trying to make the forced cultural and normative argument that *pajtachay* is just a local variation on the universal category of "justice-seeking," a local form that underscores the importance of preserving law as the basis for human rights, I would rather use this illustrative example to make a much more paradigm-shifting argument. In reframing human rights as a logic of collective action that demands the formation of lines of alliance beyond existing cultural, linguistic, and religious categories (among others), the question becomes: what should be the role of law—in its different institutional and doctrinal forms—in facilitating and protecting human rights conceived in this radically different way?

Since the recourse to law might very well be one among various expressions of collective action that are animated by this different understanding of human rights, the law and even traditional legal accountability might return as practical tools, depending on the particular historical, political, and social context. But given the different structural limitations examined in this chapter, there is no question that the relationship between a reinvented human rights and law will always remain tenuous.

Even more, in reimagining human rights in this way, the roles of legal accountability and enforcement take on very different meanings and possibilities. If human rights are not legal or even moral entitlements guaranteed by international treaties and national laws, then the kinds of economic and social violence that must be confronted should not be understood, in the strict sense, as *violations* of human rights. The law, in other words, might prove useful in certain cases in amplifying translocal collective action, but not because human rights have been violated.

In making this admittedly provocative argument, I am not, by extension, seeking to undermine the importance of the rule of law. There are some who have indeed questioned the apparently neutral value of the rule of law as yet another Western imposition that has been used to justify imperial governance, and, even worse, the plunder of global resources.[60] Although I am sympathetic to this critique, especially when so-called rule of law initiatives become bound up with what David Kennedy described as the "dark sides" of international humanitarianism,[61] here I must side with Thompson: as between "arbitrary extra-legal power and the rule of law," the "notion of the regulation and reconciliation of conflicts through the rule of law—and the elaboration of rules and procedures which, on occasion, ma[k]e some approximate approach towards the ideal—seems . . . a cultural achievement of universal significance."[62]

Nevertheless, in reimagining human rights as a logic of translocal collective action through which we can and must respond to the greatest challenges of our time, the orthodox primacy of law must necessarily be abandoned. To cast human rights free from its juridical moorings is to recognize that the logics of law—however necessary for the "regulation and reconciliation of conflicts"—are particularly ill-suited to the broader tasks of economic and social transformation toward which a reinvented human rights must be directed. And at the same time, to place the center of human rights *beyond* the rule of law is to resist the siren song of "justice," conventionally and revealingly represented by the Greek goddess Themis, and thereby open human rights to stunningly plural and generatively diverse forms of confrontation, obligation, and redress.

CHAPTER 5

Decolonizing Human Rights

The settler makes history; his life is an epoch, an Odyssey. He is the absolute beginning: "This land was created by us"; he is the unceasing cause. . . . Over against him torpid creatures, wasted by fever, obsessed with ancestral customs, form an almost inorganic background for the innovating dynamism of colonial mercantilism. . . . Thus the history which he writes is not the history of the country which he plunders but the history of his own nation in regard to all that she skims off, all that she violates and starves.

Frantz Fanon, *The Wretched of the Earth* (1961)

IF IT IS TRUE, as the Spanish legal scholar Javier Malagón Barceló once aphoristically put it, that "America was born beneath the juridical sign," then something analogous can be said about human rights: they were born and then reborn beneath the colonial sign.[1] The late eighteenth-century American revolution was a landmark revolt against colonial exploitation and the debasements of a society indelibly marked by "patriarchal dependence," a revolt instigated by colonial subjects who drew from the languages of natural rights and social contract theory to justify their economic, political, and social independence. Despite the fact that "men" in the signal phrase "all men are created equal, . . . they are endowed by their Creator with certain unalienable rights" appears to us now as an intolerably exclusionary framing, there is no gainsaying the fact that the American revolutionaries wielded human rights as a weapon against the colonial order. Indeed, this must be taken as a fundamental lesson within the history of human rights more generally: in turning a doctrine of radical equality against systems of exploitation and violence, such radicalism has never been fully inclusive or without contradiction.[2]

Yet if the early history of human rights and colonialism reveals ambiguities of economic exploitation, revolutionary mobilization, and legacies of racial violence, later periods in the trajectory through which human rights were invented are no less critical for understanding this fundamental relationship. In the short period between the end of World War II and the ratification of the UDHR in 1948, the different processes through which the "Magna Carta for all mankind" was conceived, debated, and eventually drafted took place within a deeply colonial world in which vast swaths of territory (including most of the continent of Africa and Southeast Asia) were under the control of a handful of largely European countries.

Even more, of the five permanent members of the UN Security Council, whose status rendered the postwar international system unequal at its political and institutional core, two (the United Kingdom and France) were still in the full flush of colonial domination; one (the United States) exercised colonialist control through the threat of military intervention, financial power, and a self-proclaimed hemispheric hegemony justified by the Monroe Doctrine; and one (the Soviet Union) was arguably created through a process of internal Russian colonialism that then extended to colonial control of so-called satellite countries, whose nominal independence could be violently and decisively undermined (as in Hungary in 1956, Czechoslovakia in 1968, and Afghanistan in 1980).

The colonial background to the promulgation of international human rights in this early postwar period crystallized the relationship between human rights and colonialism more generally in two principal ways. First, the dominant actors went to great pains to ensure that the "Magna Carta for all mankind" could do nothing to threaten a global colonial order in which hundreds of millions of people were not full members of the category "all mankind," but were rather captive subjects of a parallel economic and political system whose raison d'être was exploitation. During the drafting of the UDHR, the "colonial problem" was how this potential threat was described by countries such as the United Kingdom, France, and Belgium, that is, how to *prevent* the doctrine of universal human rights from being taken up as the basis for anticolonial mobilization throughout the colonial world.

As Christopher N. J. Roberts has demonstrated, the British, in particular, were not assuaged by arguments that as a mere declaration, the UDHR—if adopted—would not undermine the legal or political structure of its empire. To cover itself, the British pushed vigorously behind the scenes to have a "colonial clause" inserted into the UDHR and the subsequent covenants through which colonial powers would retain a veto over whether the human rights documents would apply to what was described in international law as "non-self-governing territories."[3]

Although the eventual inclusion of Article 2 in the UDHR—which explicitly rejected a colonial clause—represented a victory of sorts for the Soviet Union's supposed anti-imperialist human rights diplomacy, the colonial system would remain intact for almost two more decades as the movement to transform the declaration into binding international law became bogged down almost immediately by Cold War geopolitics and colonial reentrenchment.

Indeed, in a memorable section titled "The Day After," Roberts describes something like a colonial sigh of relief that the adoption of the UDHR, the passage of a "revolutionary, international statement on the human condition," could be so easily and unobjectionably relegated to the back pages of metropolitan consciousness:

> The global news in the December 11th edition of *The Times* of London revealed nothing out of the ordinary—there was certainly no mention of an imminent global transformation. As Londoners glanced through their papers on this day, the headlines were relatively mundane. On page 2 there was an article about the ongoing debate surrounding the creation of a permanent settlement in Palestine—a parcel of desert land recently in conflict following two decades of British rule. In cricket news, the West Indies beat the Indian national team on its own soil in Delhi. On page 3 there was alarming news out of Uganda about profit skimming in His Majesty's cotton trade. And on the final column of the fourth page, just after a timely piece on the preservation of historic houses, there appeared a short article about the UDHR. The lead-in grumbled that the General Assembly's desire to address the problems in Palestine "had been frustrated by yesterday's discussion on the Declaration," which itself, the article added, was mired in Cold War controversy.[4]

As Roberts adds, "as much as the UDHR was a ground-breaking text, it was entirely clear that the colonial powers had little immediate intent to allow human rights to level the relationships of inequality upon which their empires were built."[5]

And second, the colonial context from which the contemporary international human rights system emerged posed problems beyond the protection of imperial economic stability. As the parallel history of the 1947–48 UNESCO human rights survey shows, the implacable reality of colonialism was seen to create problems of what might be described as cultural legitimacy: how could a universal declaration of human rights be adopted that so manifestly excluded the voices and perspectives of so many people, nations, religions, and cultural traditions? Even by the standards of the time, no one seriously believed that the country representatives of the United Kingdom, France, or Belgium, for example, had any interest in ensuring that the enormous cultural diversity among the peoples under their colonial control would somehow be taken into consideration during the deliberations over the UDHR.

The UNESCO survey, by contrast, was meant to bypass the state-level, highly restrictive, nature of the multiyear UDHR drafting process in order to elicit perspectives from a wider range of people and cultures. Although it ultimately failed to achieve its grand ambitions, the ways in which the UNESCO survey failed, and the perspectives on human rights it did manage to elicit, are important markers of the colonial origins of human rights. Yet despite the fact that many of the respondents to the UNESCO human rights survey invoked the underlying problem of colonialism to one degree or another, remarkably, only one actually made the realities of colonialism the formal basis for a response.

In his reflections on what he calls "The Rights of Dependent Peoples," Leonard Barnes argues that all historic declarations of human rights have been—and should be—the expression of demands of people who are relatively powerless, "politically disabled," and oppressed. As he puts it, in language that rises to the occasion:

> Liberty is the cry of the bond, equality the cry of the victim of discrimination, fraternity the cry of the outcast, progress and humanity are the cry of those whom their fellows use as a means instead of respecting as ends, full employment is the cry of the worker whose daily job or lack of job stunts his soul and mocks his capabilities, social planning is the cry of those who are trampled underfoot when privilege and power strive to make the world safe for themselves. That is why declarations of rights of man are strong allies of social progress, at least when they are first promulgated. For social progress *is* reorganization in the interests of the unprivileged.[6]

For Barnes—who was a British anticolonial activist, foreign service officer, journalist, and farmer, and also the author of the curious study *Caliban in Africa: An Impression of Colour Madness* (1931)—colonized peoples were the paradigmatic class of "unprivileged," since they suffered from the dual violence of being forced to labor within an "equity-less economy" and having to live with the "psychological effects of absolute powerlessness."[7]

Nevertheless, according to Barnes, the long-term usefulness of the UDHR for colonized peoples would ultimately be limited to both symbolic and critical functions. Given that it would likely be saturated with "traditional democratic slogans," these would continue to have little meaning for people living under political economic subjugation. Yet under the right circumstances, the universalist principles of the UDHR might prove useful as a critical mirror into which the hypocrisies and contradictions of the colonial powers would be reflected, since "such slogans are handy for embarrassing the metropolitan authorities."[8] Instead of a declaration of universal human rights, Barnes argues, what the "dependent peoples" of the world seek to wield is the double-barreled weapon of liberation and national autonomy: economic, social, and psychological liberation from the crushing bonds of "foreign domination"; and national sovereignty as the sine qua non for equality within the international system.[9]

One of the two anthropologists to respond to the UNESCO survey, the Boasian Melville Herskovits, took a very different approach to the problem of human rights and colonialism.[10] His "Statement on Human Rights" later gained some notoriety, since it was published by the American Anthropological Association (AAA) as its own response to the survey in which the world's largest association of professional anthropologists appeared to thoroughly reject the UN's proposal to adopt a declaration of human rights.[11]

Yet in relation to colonized peoples, Herskovits did not even view such a declaration as a "strong," if merely symbolic, "all[y] of social progress"; indeed, quite the opposite. On the one hand, Herskovits argued that the history of anthropological research on moral values and cultural conceptions of the person made it impossible to propose a set of truly universal human rights that would not, in fact, bear the heavy imprint of "values prevalent in the countries of Western Europe and America." And, on the other hand, the entire project to assert, a priori, such universal and transcendent human rights would inevitably devolve into yet another form of colonialism in which "economic expansion, control of armaments, and an evangelical religious tradition" had been justified historically by "philosophical systems that have stressed absolutes in the realm of values and ends."[12]

From Herskovits's perspective,[13] the instrumental use of "absolutes" as the ideological foundation for colonial expansion had been "disastrous for mankind," leading inevitably to the development of racist doctrines such as the "white man's burden," which barred the "right to control their own affairs to millions of peoples [sic] over the world, where the expansion of Europe and America has not meant the literal extermination of whole populations."[14] Instead of seeking to liberate colonized peoples by adopting a so-called universal declaration of human rights as part of a centuries-long "civilizing mission," the United Nations would do much better to put in place systems that are based on "respect for the cultures of differing human groups" and that recognize the "principle that man is free only when he lives as his society defines freedom, that his rights are those he recognizes as a member of his society." Liberation, on these terms, is not something that can be meaningfully realized on a universal or international scale. Rather, from Herskovits's anthropological perspective, liberation must be, at its core, cultural—not liberation *from* culture, but liberation *through* culture.[15]

It perhaps goes without saying that Herskovits's critical analysis of the relationship between human rights and colonialism, and his opposition to the cultural validity of human rights more generally, were not considered welcome contributions by UNESCO. On the contrary, the fact that one of the world's leading anthropologists had raised serious and extensive doubts about the emancipatory pretensions of the UN human rights project was actively suppressed during the UNESCO committee's internal deliberations; silenced in the report that was sent in August 1947 to the UN Commission on Human Rights; and, perhaps most revealingly, completely elided in public characterizations of the UNESCO human rights survey and its "global" scope.

For example, in order to rebut charges that the UN human rights project might actually be an extension of colonial power, the imposition of "values prevalent in the countries of Western Europe and America" masquerading as a "revolutionary, international statement on the human condition," UNESCO went out of its way to describe the survey in sweeping, hyperbolic terms that it knew, internally, to be highly misleading. In an August 1948 *UNESCO Courier* article, published just months before the United Nations adopted the UDHR, Jacques Havet, who led the day-to-day management of the survey, described its findings in a way that precluded the possibility that the UDHR could be considered an imposition of Western values. This is because the results of the survey, which supposedly revealed a global consensus on the universality of human rights, "represented nearly all the world's national groups and nearly all ideological approaches," including those associated with the hundreds of millions of people living at that very moment under the yoke of colonialism.[16] Except that the UNESCO survey did not, in fact, reveal such a consensus, and nor did it achieve anything like such a global reach. Instead, the question of the relationship between human rights and colonialism would remain unanswered—normatively, politically, and ethically.

✳   ✳   ✳

With these various colonial legacies of human rights as a starting point, this chapter examines the ways in which colonial and neocolonial structures shaped the meanings of human rights within later anticolonial political movements and, later still, within arguments for decolonizing human rights as a necessary precondition for their reappropriation and renewal. The wider proposal to reinvent human rights is shaped by these histories and understandings of decolonization. On the one hand, the strategic use of the language and ideology of human rights within various political histories of decolonization provides a resource that can be used to reconsider the future possibilities of human rights more generally. As I argued in chapter 1, part of the project to reinvent human rights is based on recovery—the reinterpretation of human rights histories and practices that have remained largely hidden from the main currents of scholarship and institutional mobilization. In recovering the role of human rights within decolonization in this first sense, we see that parallel, and often subversive, histories were unfolding during the years and decades in which the international human rights system was confined within the debilitating boundaries of Cold War geopolitics.

But on the other hand, there is another important meaning to decolonization, one that is equally vital to the project to reinvent human rights for the future. Here, "decolonization" demands the critical interrogation of even the most apparently progressive doctrines and ideologies, in order to identify—and, ideally, strip away—hidden or unacknowledged assumptions that work to undermine radical potential. The importance of decolonization as a mode of intellectual liberation has taken surprising forms, including political and institutional forms. For example, before the Movement to Socialism (MAS) government in Bolivia, led by Evo Morales, was ousted in November 2019 in a revanchist right-wing coup d'état—one that was eagerly embraced by the US Trump administration, which had been actively, if unsuccessfully, fomenting regime change in Venezuela—it had established the world's only vice-ministry for decolonization.[17] The vice-ministry's portfolio was to oversee a long-term national process through which both social and psychological structures of colonialism were revealed and then eliminated: through legislation, government support, and reform of educational curricula.

Yet more broadly, as a methodology of intellectual and cultural liberation, decolonization works by peeling back layers of meaning that have accumulated by a process of historical and discursive accretion, a process that inevitably smothers the original progressive core of the idea, the doctrine, the political objective. From this deeper perspective, decolonization shares much with the critical theory of the early Frankfurt School, which made the so-called enlightenment of the Enlightenment one of its most important collective projects.

For scholars like Max Horkheimer and Theodor Adorno, this meant the recovery of the progressive potential of eighteenth-century reason, which had, in the intervening centuries, become deformed by numerous political and social appropriations, including colonialism. Apropos of existing human rights, the "regression" of reason into forms that could be destructive was a "fate which has always been reserved for triumphant thought. If it voluntarily leaves behind its critical element to become a mere means in the service of an existing order, it involuntarily tends to transform the positive cause it has espoused into something negative and destructive."[18]

And yet, in working to decolonize human rights in this second, critical sense, we must be careful not to replace one set of potentially regressive accretions with another. As will be seen, much of the influential literature on decolonizing human rights relies on a set of binaries, such as Global North/Global South, that obscure as much as they reveal about the possibilities for alternative or counterhegemonic formulations. Although I am sympathetic to the effort to invest decolonization with a kind of general spirit of anticolonial resistance and nonmetropolitan intellectual and political creativity, I don't believe the undoing and redoing of human rights will be well served by retaining essentialist categories and merely reversing the relations of power between them.

After examining in greater depth the meanings and importance of decolonization for the project to reinvent human rights, the chapter concludes by considering the role that education must play in this process. Drawing on innovative work in the field of human rights education (HRE) and from the critical pedagogy of theorists such as Paulo Freire, I show how education must mediate the transformation of existing human rights from its legal and institutional forms into a logic of translocal collective action. If decolonization (in its dual senses) can be thought of as the ideology that grounds the proposal to reinvent human rights, then education—broadly conceived—is the social mechanism through which this transformation must take place.

Recovering the Decolonial Histories of Human Rights

By the time the UN Charter was being devised at the end of World War II, several of the leading colonial and postwar powers had decades of experience behind them in ensuring that the international system was consistent with colonial prerogatives.[19] The British, in particular, had mastered the political art of playing both sides of the colonial coin. The British had been working as far back as the Covenant of the League of Nations (1920) to guarantee that international law and politics protected imperial structures and ideology, for example, the need to maintain colonial domination as a supposedly benevolent "sacred trust of civilization." As Article 22 of the covenant puts it:

> To those colonies . . . which as a consequence of the late war have ceased to be under the sovereignty of the States which formerly governed them and which are inhabited by peoples not yet able to stand by themselves under the strenuous conditions of the modern world, there should be applied the principle that the well-being and development of such peoples form a sacred trust of civilization and that securities for the performance of this trust should be embodied in this Covenant.

This "colonial trusteeship" system was carried over directly into the negotiations around the UN Charter, where it formed the core of chapters XI–XIII. Article 73 reaffirms the colonial ideology of the "sacred trust" and confers on colonial powers—which are euphemistically described as "Members of the United Nations which have or assume responsibilities for the administration of territories whose peoples have not yet attained a full measure of self-government"—the right to continue to rule their colonial territories with the full blessing of international law, subject only to the obligation to report back "regularly" to the United Nations on how such colonial rule was being exercised "for the well-being" of the colonized peoples.

Nevertheless, the major colonial powers understood that victory over Nazism and Japanese imperial militarism did not bring full closure to the far-reaching upheavals of World War II. On the contrary, the war had provided an important spark for anticolonial mobilization, which might have been catalyzed by war against Nazism and Japanese militarism but was soon being redirected toward the victorious colonial powers themselves. As Roberts puts it:

> As a beleaguered Great Britain limped to Potsdam to mark the end of a world war and a prelude to the Cold War, it was already part of another large-scale historical transformation—colonial recession. Like that of Great Britain, the strength of the other colonial powers such as France, Belgium, and the Netherlands had been greatly depleted during the war. For these nations, postwar uncertainty extended well beyond their own European borders. Riots and instability in colonial territories such as Algeria, Madagascar, India, and Indonesia made the future of their respective empires all the more uncertain.[20]

Yet beleaguered or not, the colonial powers could make gestures, some of them significant (like the partition of India), toward this coming large-scale historical transformation, while using the colonial ideology of trusteeship in order to try and postpone it as long as possible. In the end, despite support within Great Britain, especially within the ascendant Labour Party, for the eventual end to colonialism, no prime minister really wanted to be the one to bring the final curtain down on what remained of Pax Britannica, the unparalleled imperial system the British had "attained over the past several centuries through . . . naval superiority, military strength, and a rapacious appetite for land, labor, and resources"[21] The doctrine of the sacred trust provided the ideological flexibility to try and keep the colonial curtain up indefinitely. Colonial powers could commit to eventual independence, while at the same time reserving for themselves the international right to decide when their colonial subjects were finally "able to stand by themselves under the strenuous conditions of the modern world."

But as a growing body of revisionist history has revealed, anticolonial movements were not willing to wait to be declared able to stand by themselves by colonial overlords who had such deeply entrenched reasons for maintaining the violent fiction that colonial rule was being exercised for the well-being of the colonized.[22] Instead, potent and highly contextual hybrid discourses were developed that combined demands for self-determination and human rights in ways that have important consequences for how human rights more generally can and should be understood.

As an initial point, however, it is important to remember that the plural decolonial histories of human rights unfolded both in relation and opposition to the colonial histories already described. In other words, it is not the case that the *real* locus of human rights agency during these decades was the Global South or its various country representatives in the United Nations rather than the power centers and political leaders of the Global North.[23] As Mary Ann Heiss has argued, the various frameworks of human rights history must be seen for what they are: historical accounts that tend to mirror underlying ideological positions rather than undermine them.[24]

It does no good to continue searching for the El Dorado of human rights history, whether by insisting that it is a particular decade that should be given priority in our collective understanding, or a region of the world, or a specific philosophical or political tradition. Instead, it is much more fruitful to recover human rights history by viewing it as a complicated cultural, social, and political matrix in which many nonlinear and often fragmented histories cohere at a global level only in the starkest of chronological terms. Although some of these historical fragments obviously deserve much more emphasis than others, the sheer fact of reimagining human rights history through its matrices provides compelling reasons for shifting these emphases or for tracing the lines of influence in different directions.

In so doing, four broader lessons emerge from the decolonial histories of human rights, all of which bear importantly on the project to reinvent human rights for the future. The first is that anticolonial movements harnessed the language of human rights in ways that underscored what might be thought of as lived practices instead of normative principles. Even if the critical importance of lived practices was eventually translated into legal and political categories that required a certain amount of abstraction, the central point is that the turn to human rights within anticolonial struggles was always grounded in the concrete structural violence of colonialism itself.

For example, as we have seen, there were good reasons for the fact that the UDHR makes no mention of the right of self-determination, but merely acknowledges (in Article 2) that colonized peoples, who live under what it describes (again, euphemistically) as a "limitation of sovereignty," are entitled to the UDHR's "rights and freedoms." Yet between 1948 and December 1966, when the International Covenant on Civil and Political Rights (ICCPR) was adopted, it became increasingly difficult for a small group of colonial powers to preserve human rights in part as a form of ideological bondage.

During these intervening eighteen years, the wider colonial system gradually imploded as the leading colonial powers on the UN Security Council became locked in the epochal geopolitical conflicts of the Cold War. At the same time, anticolonial movements in Africa, Asia, the Middle East, and the Caribbean fought for cultural, political, and economic freedom, and (as in South Africa) racial equality, struggles marked by tremendous hardship, violence, and eventual liberation.

Moreover, as the colonial system was increasingly and decisively driven back by the dozens of distinct anticolonial movements, the representatives of the newly independent nation-states engaged in an equally transformative confrontation with the international human rights system. In fact, as revisionist historians have argued, it would be more accurate to say that the anti- and then postcolonial countries of the United Nations helped build the international human rights system throughout the 1950s and 1960s, even if, as Roland Burke has shown, the dominance of the so-called Afro-Asian bloc has also been used at times to protect the interests of authoritarian postcolonial regimes.[25] Yet what concerns me here is not the critical evolution of the international human rights system in ways that show agency beyond the narrative of "Global North" hegemony; rather, it is that decolonial struggles—in all their heterogeneity—were translated into terms that reflected the lived realities of both colonialism itself and the difficult struggles to end colonialism.

The importance of anchoring human rights in concrete realities instead of abstract principles is epitomized by the right of self-determination, which was forged by anticolonial diplomats, intellectuals, and social leaders as a way to give unifying legal form to the core of the anticolonial struggle across its ideological, regional, and political multiplicities. Representatives of countries as diverse as Jamaica, Liberia, Ghana, and the Philippines fought for the idea that grassroots struggles for freedom throughout the colonial world could be crystallized into a human right of all "peoples" to determine the course of their collective lives.[26] Thus, very local, and often explosive, anticolonial struggles for freedom could be given broader collective form. In this sense, the historical importance of Article 1 of the ICCPR cannot be overstated: instead of a recitation of the classically liberal, late eighteenth-century, individualistic, "natural" rights of life, liberty, or property, the covenant foregrounds the collectivist right of self-determination, a right, moreover, that bears the heavy emancipatory imprint of the recent anticolonial struggles from which it emerges.[27]

A second lesson to be found in the decolonial histories of human rights is partly related to the first. By insisting on the profoundly anticolonial right of self-determination as the first right articulated in the all-important ICCPR, bedrock of the "International Bill of Human Rights," the leaders in the struggle for decolonization showed how *subversion* could be interwoven with human rights at its very core. On one level, subversion meant upending the essentially colonial foundations of human rights, which were built around the economic and geopolitical interests of a small number of colonial and colonialist powers. But on another level, histories of decolonization reveal subversion in the creativity through which human rights were, at least for a period of time, "rekindled" as a language of confrontation with global power, a language that was used to try and unmake and remake the modern world that the colonial order had bequeathed.[28] If the subversive potential of human rights was eventually suppressed during a post–Cold War era in which the idea of subversion became illegitimate, even unthinkable, it will be absolutely necessary to recover this potential for a reinvented human rights.

A third lesson from the plural histories of decolonization is the fact that the language and categories of human rights were deployed in ways that revealed what would be described now as their intersectional capacities. In other words, it was never a question of anticolonial movements adopting human rights as a monolithic framework for resistance or as a replacement for preexisting discourses shaped by nationalism, liberation theology, Marxism, antiracism, or any number of other ideological categories through which the anticolonial struggle was waged. Instead, what we see are numerous cases in which human rights were appropriated strategically and combined innovatively—and sometimes episodically—with other currents as a reflection of the deep historical and political complexities of particular movements in the face of particular expressions of colonial and structural violence.

For example, the Nigerian scholar Bonny Ibhawoh shows how leading African anticolonialists engaged in highly creative discursive refashioning in which human rights was fused with other social categories through which people could be mobilized under dangerous and uncertain conditions. He cites the Ghanaian nationalist politician Kwame Nkrumah, who later went on to become the first prime minister of independent Ghana, as he built the case during the 1950s for the right to self-determination in combination with existing Christian dogma: "Seek ye first the political kingdom and all other things shall be added unto you."[29] As Ibhawoh explains, along with the language of human rights and religious injunctions, African nationalists drew from socialism, antiracism, and local cultural values in forging what he describes as a "lexicon of liberation."[30]

The intersectional capacities of human rights during the era of decolonization were perhaps most dramatically on display during the highly charged 1964 Rivonia Trial, in which the African National Congress (ANC) leader Nelson Mandela, among others, was sentenced to life imprisonment for the crime of sabotage (he served twenty-seven years of the sentence and was released in 1990). Assuming that a death sentence was inevitable, Mandela stood in the dock to deliver what has come to be known as the "I Am Prepared to Die" speech, which he concludes by telling the court that he was prepared to die for his militancy against South Africa's neocolonial apartheid regime.[31]

Mandela's speech is a masterpiece of intersectional power. Although he devotes much of his oration to the attempt to distinguish the ANC's anti-apartheid resistance from Marxist insurgency, of which the ANC had been accused, he goes on to construct a highly elaborate image of the ANC movement that manages to combine African nationalism, redistributive (though non-Marxist) economics, egalitarianism, republicanism, parliamentary democracy, *and* human rights. He even goes so far as to pay homage to both the British system of justice and the classical liberal human rights with which it was associated. As Mandela puts it, the "Magna Carta, the Petition of Rights, and the Bill of Rights are documents which are held in veneration by democrats throughout the world."[32]

A fourth and final lesson to be found in the decolonial histories of human rights bears directly on a central pillar of the project to reinvent human rights—that it must be reconstructed as a logic of translocal collective action that demands the formation of enduring alliances beyond existing boundaries of class, nation, race, and political ideology. As Meredith Terretta has argued, human rights language and categories coalesced into a powerful framework within which African anticolonial activists confronted the violence of colonial rule and created alliances with transnational NGOs and Pan-African social movements.[33] As she shows, well beyond questions of political independence within colonial Africa, grassroots activists and social and political leaders used the full suite of rights discourse as a logic of mobilization and the basis for what she describes as "collaborative political agency."[34]

As Terretta's research establishes, the use of human rights as a logic of translocal collective action during decolonization was most vital *beyond* debates in the United Nations and the human rights petitions that were sent from Africa's UN Trust Territories, although, as Terretta observes, hundreds of thousands of petitions were sent during this period, including nearly 45,000 from the French and British Cameroons in a single year (1956).[35] Instead, the potential of human rights in this alternative register must be understood as a form of social practice that extended beyond political and institutional boundaries as part of a wider, if diverse, liberation strategy that was being formulated by a vast constellation of actors and movements. These included Tanganyikan coffee planters, exiled African anticolonialists, British and American anticolonial lawyers,[36] and some of the earliest human rights NGOs, including the New York–based International League of the Rights of Man (ILRM), whose leader, Roger Baldwin, viewed alliances with anticolonial activists to be essential to the wider project to promote human rights as the basis for new forms of global justice.[37]

Yet as Terretta's critical revaluation of human rights within the histories of decolonization also reveals, the development of human rights as a logic of collective action beyond law and institutional politics did not last, something that must also be analyzed when considering the lessons of these histories for the future of human rights. Focusing on the transition to independence in Cameroon,

Terretta argues that anticolonial activists who worked to harness human rights in innovative ways outside of official channels were largely excluded from playing an important role in the country's postcolonial development.

The most obvious reason for the end of innovative mobilization through human rights—at least for Cameroon—was the fact that the country's first post-colonial political leaders had formed an alliance with France, which guaranteed France's continuing interventions in Cameroonian affairs for decades.[38] In this sense, the capacity to harness human rights as a logic of collective action was as much a threat to the new regime, which outlawed opposition political parties in 1966, as it had been to the French colonial order.

But Terretta also suggests that there was another reason that the creativity of anticolonial human rights activism did not survive independence: the fact that human rights discourse was often assimilated to calls for revolutionary violence. Indeed, evoking the essential place of violence in the human rights revolutions of late eighteenth-century France and the United States, African anticolonial activists drew a distinction between legitimate and illegitimate violence, with legitimate violence being reframed as a form of human rights activism by other means. As Terretta puts it, quoting from the Afro-Caribbean anticolonial intel-lectual Aimé Césaire, for many, "anti-colonial revolution was the only means to undo the hypocritical, 'sordidly racist,' pseudo-humanism of colonialism that 'diminished the rights of man.'"[39]

Decolonizing Human Rights beyond Binaries

If the recovery of the decolonial histories of human rights offers critical resources for reimagining the future of human rights, there is a second, distinct sense of decolonization that must also be considered. To return to the 1947–48 UNESCO human rights survey, there was already an embryonic concern with the ways in which an international declaration of human rights would embody Western values and therefore wittingly or unwittingly serve as a conduit for continued colonial imposition. Although the concept of decolonization was not used during the survey, the idea was to break out of a colonial ideological and philosophical ori-entation by discovering universal principles that necessarily transcend particular traditions, including those associated with the "Great Declarations" that were a "quite special heritage of Western civilization."[40]

From the leaders of the UNESCO survey to many of the respondents, there was a concern to, in effect, *pre-decolonize* human rights, that is, to work col-lectively to strip particularistic—including colonial—values from the project before it was even codified. These efforts were mixed, yet revealing. For example, of the few respondents to participate in the survey who actually were colonial subjects at the time, all made the question of the relationship between colonial ideologies and human rights, in one way or another, central to their responses.

Humayun Kabir, a Muslim Bengali intellectual and future minister of education in independent India, assumed that the proposal being developed by the United Nations for a "universal" declaration of human rights would be yet another mechanism of Western ideological control. For Kabir, a decolonized version of human rights, by contrast, would be one "based on the recognition of the equal claims of all individuals within one common world." As he explains,

> It is necessary to emphasize this because of one fundamental flaw in the western conception of human rights. Whatever the theory, in practice they often applied only to Europeans and sometimes to only some among the Europeans. In fact, the western conception has to a large extent receded from the theory and practice set up by early Islam, which did succeed in overcoming the distinction of race and color to an extent experienced neither before nor since.[41]

The Hindu nationalist S. V. Puntambekar was even more skeptical that a UN declaration of human rights could overcome its colonial roots, which he associated with violence, dispossession, and intellectual coercion, colonial practices that were often reproduced by British India's colonial subjects themselves. His response is full of desperation:

> To talk of human rights in India is no doubt very necessary and desirable, but hardly possible in view of the socio-cultural and religio-political complexes which are so predominant today. . . . Our intelligentsia and masses are mad after racial privileges, religion [sic] bigotry and social exclusiveness. . . . Our classes and communities think in terms of conquest and subjugation, not of common association and citizenship.[42]

Even those responding to the UNESCO survey from within the heart of countries or institutions most closely associated with the "special heritage of Western civilization" underscored the need to pre-decolonize human rights before the UN process got too far along. In making a version of this argument, the Yale philosophy and law professor F. S. C. Northrop rejected the very concept of "universal" human rights. As he explained, the idea of universal human rights was itself colonial, reflecting, as it did, the values of what he called "pro-Kantian" European philosophy. Yet more generally,

The usual approach to the Bill of Rights . . . [is] to assume that the traditional modern French and Anglo-American concept of freedom . . . exhausts the meaning of the concept. Precisely this assumption operates when anyone proposes to extend the governmental forms of the United States of America to a United States of Europe or a United States of the World. Such proposals have always left their recipients cold.[43]

For Northrop, the better way to keep human rights uncolonized from the beginning was to abandon what I have called elsewhere the "myth of universality" altogether.[44] Instead, what Northrop proposed was a surprisingly provocative conception of human rights pluralism through which even contradictory ideologies must be allowed to flourish without violence or suppression. Otherwise, a colonial "culture of laissez-faire businessman's values" will inevitably predominate, "with all the other values and aspirations of mankind left anemic and spiritually and ideologically unsustained."[45]

Yet in the event, neither the decolonized-in-practice vision for human rights of Kabir, nor the culturally pluralist alternative of Northrop, nor the many other proposals elicited by the UNESCO human rights survey, were ever considered by the UN CHR, or later by the UN General Assembly, which adopted a "universal" declaration of human rights that was not just closely associated with the "special heritage of Western civilization." In fact, it bore the heavy influence of *just one person*, John P. Humphrey, the Gale Professor of Roman Law at McGill University, whose hurried work on the first draft of the UDHR in late February 1947 led one historian to conclude that the "baby was [already] born" before the UN CHR even began its work in earnest.[46]

In light of these complicated histories, what would it really mean to decolonize human rights as part of the project to reinvent human rights for the future? Although I would not argue that international human rights law and the vast international system that exists to enforce it—at least theoretically—through national ratifications and implementation should be eliminated, its value for a reinvented human rights should perhaps be thought of as symbolic, a historical legacy from which critical insights might be gleaned. It makes little sense, therefore, to waste undue effort in considering ways to decolonize *existing* human rights.

Nevertheless, as a logic of translocal collective action, a reinvented human rights must be developed in such a way that it remains noncolonial at its very core. In this, insights from the literature on decolonizing human rights as an intellectual and ethical project are useful.[47] Yet in reimagining the noncolonial possibilities for human rights, we must be wary of hewing too closely to the various received binaries, even in an effort to reverse the power relations between them.

On the one hand, although binaries like East-West[48] and Global North–Global South might serve important functions as heuristic categories that clarify the global stakes and reinforce the ways in which legacies of colonialism are perpetuated through existing inequalities, the categories themselves bear little relation to actual regions, social or cultural spaces, or zones of political economic demarcation. Moreover, as decolonial theorists are acutely aware, constructed categories like "Global North" and "Global South" have long formed the basis for what Étienne Balibar describes as *inclusion exclusive*, the act of excluding through inclusion.[49] To privilege epistemologies of the "Global South," even as part of an argument for "cognitive justice," is still inescapably to engage in a process of exclusionary inclusion.

And, on the other hand, if a reinvented human rights is to flourish beyond, and against, "cognitive empire,"[50] it will have to be on the basis of what might be considered an anthropological—rather than a critical theoretical—conception of epistemological diversity, interconnection, and solidarity. In other words, a decolonized and eventually noncolonial conception of human rights must be one that does not reproduce categories of exclusion, that does not depend on even emancipatory narratives about categories like humanity, which, ultimately, "cannot be found."[51] Rather, I believe that a reinvented human rights must depend on a quite different epistemology, one that foregrounds the translocal value of an anthropological, *inclusionary* ethics. But where and how to nurture such an alternative approach to decolonizing human rights?

Conclusion: Decolonizing Human Rights through Pedagogies of Inclusion

In April 1948, elated but also weary, Eleanor Roosevelt, chair of the UN CHR, published a revealing essay titled "The Promise of Human Rights" in *Foreign Affairs*.[52] Realizing that the adoption later that year of the UDHR would have a minimal immediate impact on global politics and international affairs, Roosevelt struck a wistful and restrained tone. Although the UN CHR had managed, despite it all, to "put into words some inherent rights," the real importance of the process was that it represented an aspirational mirror into which the violence, insecurity, and inequalities of the contemporary world would be clearly—and critically—reflected.

Yet beyond this, Roosevelt made a surprising claim about the future of human rights: instead of a system of law or politics, she imagined the project of human rights to be pedagogical, a proposition for a new form of education in which people were taught to view and, more importantly, treat others, differently—that is, in ways that fostered an intriguing fusion of equality and collective security.[53] For Roosevelt, the UDHR was less an international statement of rights soon to be adopted by the nascent—and colonialist—UN General Assembly; instead, she understood it much more as a primer, a text that would "forward very largely the education of the peoples of the world."

Nevertheless, as we have seen, this pedagogical vision for postwar human rights was realized only sparingly, marginally, and certainly never in ways that added up to a global transformation of the kind Roosevelt and others imagined. After the end of the Cold War, when international human rights were loosened—though not freed—from the shackles of great power Realpolitik, cultures of human rights emerged in different parts of the world through pedagogical as much as legal or political means.[54] Yet precisely what was being taught and the lessons that were ultimately learned were highly variable and capable of being put into practice in unexpected and often creative ways.

For example, Bolivian peasants attended human rights "workshops" in the late 1990s organized by European-based NGOs in which *derechos humanos* were introduced in quite general terms as a moral system that would, if adopted, improve social and family relations in the region. One local peasant leader, who was also the only licensed lawyer in a province of 23,000 people, adopted this pedagogical approach to human rights when he officiated at weddings, explaining to the young and wide-eyed couples that "human rights" meant that men and women should distribute the load equally as they traveled across the area's mountainous footpaths.[55]

Yet examples like this—multiplied thousands of times, particularly during the first decade of the post–Cold War, the Age of Human Rights—did not, in the end, add up to a parallel conception of human rights, one that came to challenge the dominant approaches of international human rights from which these local appropriations were necessarily derived. Instead, the practice of human rights in this pedagogical and moral register took place—and continues to take place—in the shadows of treaties, tribunals, and compliance monitoring.

By contrast, a reinvented human rights, which is formulated beyond the boundaries of law and political institutions, especially those circumscribed by the state, must be developed and diffused *largely* as an educational project. If a reinvented human rights is to take root as a logic of translocal collective action that demands the creation of enduring alliances that transcend categories of difference, this logic must be taught, explored, and modeled across widely diverse social, economic, and political contexts. The precedent I have in mind for such a widespread pedagogical shift, one that was itself closely linked to decolonization, is what the Brazilian educator and philosopher Paulo Freire described as a "pedagogy of the oppressed," which offers a deeply critical approach to education that is based on practical experience, solidarity, rehumanization, coteaching, and the capacity to act against structures of oppression.[56]

Yet instead of a pedagogy of the oppressed, what I would propose is what might be called "pedagogies of inclusion" as the educational grounding for the development of a reinvented human rights. Given that so many contemporary crises are either caused or worsened by categories of exclusion, even those animated by righteous demands for change, the fundamental task will be to refashion our pedagogies so that we, collectively, yet plurally, will learn to privilege the value of translocality and come to understand the transformative implications of forging alliances *beyond* categories of difference in the renewed name of human rights.

A pedagogical orientation, in this sense, to a reinvented human rights would give the broadest scope to the principle of decolonization, the imperative to cast off the last vestiges of colonial ideology and to replace it with a logic that foregrounds "inclusive inclusion," what Santos has described as "non-abyssal thinking,"[57] and the willingness to live in the present through the future, instead of through the past.

CHAPTER 6

Human Rights Otherwise

A boy of fourteen, nephew of Adela, confided to me his fears of the
gruesome journey [a person's two souls make after death]: "If a gimokud
[the right-hand, or good, soul] is not brave, he waits for a companion to die.
I am afraid to go alone to the Great City. When I am dead, my spirit will wait
near my friend, Karlos, and will say to his spirit: 'I want you to go with me to
the One City.' Then my friend will get a sickness and die, and I shall have a
companion; but if he does not want to go with me, I do not force him, but I
ask other friends—many."

Laura Watson Benedict, "People Who Have Two Souls" (1916)

IN 1996, TWENTY-ONE YEARS into his retirement from Oxford University, and
only one year before his death at age eighty-eight, the Russian Jewish philosopher and intellectual historian Isaiah Berlin was asked by a Chinese scholar
named Ouyang Kang to provide an overview to his thought for Chinese read-
ers.[1] Although suffering from a long-term illness, Berlin nevertheless took the
opportunity to offer a final account of many of the historical and philosophical
problems to which he had devoted his intellectual life over much of the twentieth century, including the legacies of Vico and Herder, the enduring impact
of "Romanticism and its offspring," determinism, idealism, and the distinction
between negative and positive forms of liberty.

For example, regarding the distinction between negative and positive forms
of liberty, Berlin, after decades of reticence, finally lays his cards on the table.
As between negative liberty—"freedom from"—and positive liberty—"freedom
to"—it is positive liberty that holds the greatest danger of being transformed
into the "vilest oppression" in the name of a wide range of political doctrines
and ideologies, "whether the tyranny issues from a Marxist leader, a king, a
Fascist dictator, the masters of an authoritarian Church or class or State."[2] If the

classically liberal value of negative liberty "could be interpreted as economic laissez-faire, whereby in the name of freedom owners are allowed to destroy the lives of children in mines, or factory owners to destroy the health and character of workers in industry," this paled in comparison to the "frightful perversions" of positive liberty, in which progressive elites and righteous warriors for justice committed terrible acts of violence as "engineers of human souls" on a mission to shape the course of the future to a particular, and always exclusionary, vision of social and moral truth.[3]

However, it is Berlin's final thoughts on the concept for which he was most celebrated as a theorist, value pluralism, that hold the most interest for the project to reinvent human rights. On the one hand, Berlin's greatest contribution—across a vast corpus of intellectual history, essays, speeches, and collected writings—was to show how most of the great and terrible conflicts in history could be traced to inexorable clashes over what he calls "monism," the "ancient belief that there is a single harmony of truths into which everything, if it is genuine, in the end must fit."[4]

The problem with monadic thinking, according to Berlin, is that it is based, ultimately, on a tragic fallacy: that a grand synthesis—religious, political, national, moral—is both necessary and inevitable, if only enough time is allowed to pass, or competing ideas sufficiently suppressed, or enough people sacrificed to the cause. Instead, Berlin argued that it was the search for the one, exclusionary truth that was the great evil to be avoided. In its place, he proposed an approach to value pluralism that would have to accommodate a range of what he called "ultimate human ends," plural social visions that were equally legitimate yet, at some level, necessarily incompatible.

But on the other hand, Berlin went to great pains to distinguish value pluralism from relativism, the view—as he characterized it—that human values were the "arbitrary creations of [people's] subjective fancies" and therefore liable to be twisted into forms and systems that could justify any action, however grotesque. As Berlin put it, the fact that there was a "plurality of ideals" in the world, a "plurality of cultures and temperaments," did not imply the inevitable descent into mutual incomprehension, mistrust, and nationalist violence, because human values were "objective" and therefore the potential bridges to understanding and cooperation within a plural world. As he explained this critical distinction between pluralism and relativism:

> I am not a relativist; I do not say "I like my coffee with milk and you like it without; I am in favor of kindness and you prefer concentration camps"—each of us with his own values, which cannot be overcome or integrated. This I believe to

be false. But I do believe that there is a plurality of values which [people] can and do seek, and that these values differ. There is not an infinity of them: the number of human values, of values which I can pursue while maintaining my human semblance, my human character, is finite—let us say 74, or perhaps 122, or 26, but finite, whatever it may be. And the difference this makes is that if a [person] pursues one of these values, I, who do not, am able to understand why he pursues it or what it would be like, in his circumstances, for me to be induced to pursue it. Hence the possibility of human understanding.[5]

Despite his stated intention to spell out his thoughts in the clearest possible way, as a sort of living intellectual last will and testament, Berlin was not, in the end, able to go beyond this, to offer any further guidance about how to draw a line between values that maintained a "human semblance," and those that did not, between values that expressed "human character," however detestable in practice, and those that were beyond the pale. Indeed, although Berlin doesn't hazard a draft list of these plural, yet objective, human values, he strongly suggests that its range is surprisingly, even shockingly, wide: despite the fact that they were "wickedly wrong," the ardent, lifelong Zionist Berlin acknowledges that "Nazi values" must be considered "human values," since he understood how "given enough misinformation, enough false belief about reality, one could come to believe that [Nazism was] . . . the only salvation."[6]

Yet just because "Nazi values"—used here by Berlin, one imagines, as the extreme, barely conscionable, limiting case—cannot, despite it all, be cast into the realm of the inhuman as values that were either created by, or created, people whose human semblance had been destroyed, this does not mean that these "human" values must be passively tolerated; indeed, quite the contrary. As Berlin explains, although they must be understood, values such as these must also be attacked because they are so catastrophically misguided, so "wickedly wrong." The line between values that retain the human semblance yet are disastrously false and those that spiral beyond the boundaries of human semblance into incomprehensibility, pathology, and collective insanity, is the line, according to Berlin, that defines the boundaries of humanity.[7]

Of course, it is not at the extreme limits of human values, at the boundaries between the human and inhuman, where Berlin's value pluralism shows its real ambitions. Instead, it is at the points of overlap, actual or potential, the places at which what he calls "common values" converge.[8] It is here, among the points of congruence that render intercultural dialogue both possible and generative, where the grounds for solidarity and collaborative action are to be found. Without wanting to go any further, Berlin, at the end of his life, at least pointed the way toward a future in which multiplicity and diversity were at the very core of our systems—social, political, moral—yet multiplicity and diversity within limits. But how are these limits to be demarcated? Who has the right or obligation to draw these boundaries? And how are the inevitable conflicts over these limits to be resolved?

With the central insights of Berlin's value pluralism as a point of departure, this chapter examines these and other questions. In developing a reinvented human rights, the problems of pluralism, universalism, and cultural diversity must be addressed from a different perspective, in light of alternative assumptions about the relationship between cultural difference and the potential for translocal collective action. In the next section, I explore the problematic legacy of the "universal" in universal human rights, the complicated historical, legal, and philosophical heritage of the Enlightenment in which claims of ahistorical, immanent, "natural" rights became, over the succeeding centuries, quintessentially—and paradoxically—associated with a deeply contingent history and *particular* set of cultural values. As I argue, when "universal human rights" becomes a "universalism," that is, a system that asserts its singular wisdom and synthetic truth, its relationship to the world's actually existing "plurality of ideals" changes significantly: it becomes exclusionary and structurally hostile to any "cultures and temperaments" that show any signs at all of divergence.

Next, the chapter returns to the fundamental importance of pluralism as the basis for a new conception of human rights. Here, the anthropology of human rights is critical, since researchers have documented the many ways in which existing human rights have been creatively adapted and even transformed through processes that Sally Engle Merry described as "vernacularization."[9] Although the ethnographic record of vernacularization around the world is largely based on the "travel, translation, and transformation" of existing international human rights norms derived from international treaties and human rights policy documents, this research provides a window into how a pluralistic reorientation toward human rights might look in practice.[10]

The chapter then concludes by considering the grounds of a reinvented human rights beyond questions of economic, political, and social change. Apart from its other objectives, explicit or implicit, the UDHR was seen by at least some leading visionaries to represent a profoundly different framework through which people around the world would relate to each other. Given that widespread destruction, military conquest, and genocide were the result of political divisions based on national and racial difference taken to their logical and murderous conclusion, the new world order would be organized on diametrically opposed grounds. Instead of categories of cultural, political, or national difference, the UDHR proposed a new category, the most ambitious and capacious possible: "all members of the human family." It would be this fictive kinship group—that is, all of us—that would be responsible for ensuring "freedom, justice and peace in the world."

Yet as the social basis for existing human rights, the "human family" has proven over the succeeding decades to be barely recognizable, a figment of the early postwar moral imagination kept alive mostly by well-meaning human rights advocates, nostalgic intellectuals, and international diplomats. The universalist urge—like its cognate, the cosmopolitan—is an understandable and historically common response to the manifold evils of human difference translated into political, social, and ideological terms. But as a basis for actual belonging in a world of salutary diversity, it has proven to be no match for what it seeks to replace, with devastating consequences.

It is in this sense that I envision a reinvented human rights to propose a new way of belonging, one that does not merely replace one unlived abstraction with another, for example, the idea that pluralism can only constitute the basis for social and political community if it is structured by something like a Rawlsian "overlapping consensus."[11] Instead, human rights should become a well-traveled relational bridge, one that is built with materials that cannot be specified a priori. Rather, in mediating the fraught passage between existing differences and the call to collective action *beyond* these differences, human rights should provide the means through which our "pluriversal" realities are given both emancipatory and unifying form.[12]

The Dark Sides of Universalism

To return to the debates that took place in the short period of time between the end of World War II and the adoption of the UDHR in December 1948, it is helpful to first draw a distinction between two senses of "universal" or "universality"— which are conceptually the same for my purposes—and then to draw a distinction between universal/universality and "universalism." Regarding the first, both history and philosophy show that there is a key difference between what I would call the "empirical" and the "aspirational" senses of universal/universality. By "empirical" I mean the ontological claim that all human beings—from the beginning to the end of time, indeed, from the birth of the first member of our species—have been, are, and will be, endowed with a particular set of rights simply by virtue of being human. Notice that this quasi-biological claim rests on the assumption that all humans *have* rights, not that we are entitled to them by virtue of something else.

This sense of universal/universality is empirical in that it is asserted as a moral-ontological fact, something that can be denied, ignored, or acted on, but nevertheless remains objectively true. All human beings *have* human rights. This claim to universality, importantly, does not depend at all on a particular moment in history, or the general consensus of many "cultures and temperaments," or the need to create an international legal and political system to enforce it. If human rights are "natural in the sense that their source is human nature,"[13] then it is only a curiosity of history that this way of understanding human beings—as bearers of rights that are naturally entailed by a common human nature—has waxed only rarely, for relatively limited periods of time, and within the currents of a narrow (if powerful) segment of intellectual and moral traditions.

Although what has often been described as the deontological orientation toward human rights universality has dominated debates over natural/human rights at least since the late eighteenth century, there is another approach to the question that has also been proposed from time to time. The "sociological" perspective on universal/universality is one that treats the axiomatic truth that all human beings have human rights as something like a hypothesis and then seeks to "prove" this hypothesis through sociological or other forms of qualitative inquiry.

Indeed, the most important example of the sociological approach to the question of human rights universality was the UNESCO human rights survey of 1947–48.[14] As we have seen at different places throughout this book, this nascent "specialized agency," under the direction of its controversial and charismatic inaugural director-general Julian Huxley, charged itself with the task of discovering the universal principles that would form the basis of the world's first declaration of human rights. The importance of establishing the universality of human rights was front and center in the process, during which the problem took both philosophical and political forms.

Philosophically, Huxley and Jacques Havet, the young head of UNESCO's philosophy section, believed it was necessary to reaffirm empirically what was already believed to be true, especially by Havet: that all human beings *had* human rights as the most fundamental fact of human existence. And politically, the proponents of the UNESCO human rights survey went to great lengths to emphasize the ways in which a reaffirmed universality of human rights would blunt any criticism that the UN project was actually a reflection of "Western" values.[15]

Yet beyond the empirical, there is another quite distinct sense of universal/universality that has played an important role in the history of human rights. It is a sense that is more subtle, less clearly articulated, but nevertheless has been influential at least since Eleanor Roosevelt declared in 1948 that human rights must be understood as a long-term educational project, a process that would unfold, gradually, with great resistance, over the decades.[16] This is the "aspirational" sense of human rights universality, the hope that, over time, human rights will *become* universal.

The meaning of this becoming can and does take different forms. Aspirational universality could mean widespread national legal ratification, implementation, and compliance. It could describe something more limited, like numbers of states parties to an important international human rights treaty. Or, more broadly, it could mean the global diffusion of a pervasive "culture of human rights," in which norms, practices, and "particular constructions of self and sociality" shaped by international human rights eventually come to replace existing alternatives.[17]

Obviously, the conceptual differences between the empirical and aspirational senses of universal/universality are enormous, but the two relate to each other in practice in important ways. For example, human rights activists might privately express doubts about the universality of human rights—all human beings *have* human rights—but nevertheless continue to promote this account of human rights through their interventions, written materials, and funding applications.[18] The hope is that by insisting on the a priori ontological truth about human rights (though not in these terms), that human rights will eventually come to form the bedrock of political, social, and moral life everywhere—universality ex post facto.

But note that the path to aspirational universality is also laid by what might be thought of as strategic uses of the proposition that all human beings *have* human rights, its truth value, its self-evidence. In other words, within these "diverse conjunctions,"[19] the power of human rights is believed to flow from their transcendence, from their unassailable objectivity, and, above all else, from their detachment from anything that would render them essentially contingent.

Yet if universal/universality refers to a set of empirical or aspirational claims about human rights, how do these claims relate to "universalism"? Here, I use the latter to describe the ways in which claims to human rights universality, to transcendence, to self-evidence, to immanence ("inherent dignity"), to natural endowment, whether explicit or implicit, are transformed into an ideology that is meant to structure action in carefully controlled ways. Although human rights universalism is interpreted in different ways depending on a range of national, political, and cultural contexts, the entire point of the postwar human rights project was to limit this variation as much as possible. This is in part how human rights universality is tightly connected to human rights *universalism*: if all human beings *have* human rights, and if acquiescence to this fact is the "foundation of freedom, justice and peace in the world," then the struggle becomes one of harmonization, of narrowing the range of permissible conduct at all levels so that it fits within brackets that can be defined, monitored, and defended from what lies outside.

In reimagining the future of human rights, there are several aspects of human rights universalism that have proven to be problematic. It is important to remember that claims about human rights are both ontological and moral. They are ontological in that they are truth claims about the nature of things (in this case, of human beings). But it is the moral dimension of human rights that is of most concern. From the perspective of human rights universalism, the truth value of human rights universality makes it possible—indeed, imperative—to judge different practices and systems around the world to the extent to which they fit, or not, within the brackets.

It then becomes possible to establish a global moral metric that allows the social complexity of human life to be reduced and then sorted into categories of good or bad, just or unjust, compliant or noncompliant. There is nothing that should be controversial in this description of the moral dimension of human rights universalism: this reduction and sorting, based on specific normative bright-lines, is the only way to ensure that human rights become *the* foundation of freedom, justice, and peace in the world.

Yet in working to reduce and sort in practice, human rights universalism is inevitably conflictual, since the application of the moral metric is meant to disrupt, to replace, to suppress. In this, the history of human rights universalism, particularly during the ascendant Age of Human Rights, came to resemble the histories of other universalisms that were likewise based on moral-ontological claims to universality, such as those of the proselytizing "world" religions. And given that the great powers like the United States, China, and Russia have always been insulated from any real consequences of having the moral metric of human rights turned against them, the conflictual reduction and sorting process was left to become yet another tool of international control to be used well beyond the centers of global power. When significant foreign aid is at stake at a national level, or the possibility of development collaboration at much smaller scales, the consequences of being judged to be outside the human rights brackets are usually quite harsh.[20]

Beyond the problems of global political inequality and the socioeconomic implications of moral sorting, the workings of human rights universalism also have serious repercussions for social and political change. After observing—as an insider—the emergence during the post–Cold War of what he describes as "humanitarian power," David Kennedy shows how human rights universalism leads to a pervasive "corrosion of practical reason," the increasing inability by those *within* the human rights brackets to consider "emancipatory possibilities" that clearly come from other directions or traditions.[21]

But if the problematic consequences of human rights universalism—for both human rights advocates and those whose lifeways have been decried and suppressed—are now well-established, there is another aspect that leads me to propose abandoning human rights universalism altogether in favor of what might be called human rights pluralism. This is the fact that existing human rights, human rights that derive from the international human rights system, function in practice as a discourse of exclusion within a world of tremendous cultural, political, and moral (if not necessarily economic) diversity.

This is obviously paradoxical, since at its very core, universal human rights are meant to be maximally inclusive, indeed, coextensive with another imagined universal category—"human nature."[22] Thus, in proposing a reinvented human rights as a logic of translocal collective action that depends on the formation of alliances beyond categories of difference, an alternative grounding is needed, an alternative conceptual and moral framework that would replace the brackets of universalism with the bridges of pluralism.

Pluralism, Vernacularization, Generativity

Yet if pluralism is to replace universalism as the foundation of human rights for the future, if the fiction of "all members of the human family" is to be put aside for a much more variegated and even open-ended vision of belonging, then it is important to go beyond the critique of existing limitations and examine in detail what such an alternative grounding would entail. What would it mean to place cultural, moral, and political diversity at the center of human rights? What would it mean to convert the centripetal impulse of human rights into one that is explicitly centrifugal, so that human rights can work as a polyvalent rationale for creative social action, resistance, and solidarity rather than as a framework for constraint?

Fortunately, such a task is not entirely speculative, since the practice of human rights over the last thirty years has provided important evidence for how human rights pluralism might take shape, despite the fact that this documentary record is based on reformulations and adaptations of existing human rights. Nevertheless, the study of human rights practices in widely diverse contexts provides a window into the breadth of socio-moral life and shows how a full-spectrum human rights pluralism would resolve the tension between cultural specificity and translocality. Yet before considering lessons from the practice of human rights in more detail, it is necessary to take stock of different background problems.

To begin, it is important to draw a distinction between pluralism as a basis for mapping diversity and various assimilationist alternatives, such as multiculturalism. Although multiculturalism has taken different forms, it emerged as a distinct ideology in the early years of the post–Cold War, as the politics of identity accelerated the impetus behind the promotion of various cultural or collective rights regimes, for example, the international Indigenous rights system based on International Labour Organization Convention (ILO) 169 (1989). As Charles Hale has shown, the codification of multiculturalism—particularly in states in which cultural difference had historically been the basis for social and political marginalization—was initially resisted by state officials, who viewed the legal and political protection of cultural diversity as a threat to state narratives of national identity.[23]

Yet as it turned out, multiculturalism never offered a serious alternative to culturally homogenizing approaches to state governance, or a transformative response to demands by marginalized populations to be granted real cultural independence within the sovereign structure of what could be highly centralized political systems. Instead, officials across a wide range of states developed remarkably consistent approaches to incorporating multiculturalism into the very heart of neoliberal governance, which allowed states to concede to "soft" markers of justice such as cultural heritage protections and bilingual education programs while violently resisting all claims for "hard" markers of justice, such as extensive land redistribution or territorial self-determination.[24] If the earlier postwar approach to cultural diversity had been formally assimilationist—represented by the heavily criticized 1957 ILO Convention 107—neoliberal multiculturalism became something more insidious: an ideology of assimilationism that dare not speak its name.[25]

Human rights pluralism, by contrast, is framed by a fundamentally different orientation toward diversity as the basis for forging alliances that reach *beyond* cultural and other categories of difference. Curiously, this alternative approach to pluralism is not entirely absent from the international system. Under extraordinary and indeed desperate circumstances, the 2001 General Conference of UNESCO adopted a remarkable document that subsequently played almost no role of importance in either international or national law: the UNESCO Universal Declaration on Cultural Diversity (UDCD). In the wake of the attacks of September 11, UNESCO officials and state representatives gathered in Paris to consider how to respond to what was being presented as a Huntingtonian nightmare of civilizations clashing violently and uncompromisingly: on the one side, apocalyptic death cults masquerading as religious movements; on the other side, righteous neoconservative warriors preparing to unleash the dogs of war; and all taking place with the Age of Human Rights going precipitously up in flames.

Although UNESCO's "Universal Declaration" bears all the marks of having been rushed into existence, including the standard clauses that unconvincingly try and square various circles—such as the lawyerly idea that "no one may invoke cultural diversity to infringe upon human rights guaranteed by international law, nor to limit their scope" (Art. 4)—its twelve articles express a surprisingly innovative account of pluralism.

"Aspiring to greater solidarity on the basis of recognition of cultural diversity," as the preamble puts it, the UDCD makes the argument that cultural flourishing is a precondition for global sustainability on the same terms as biodiversity. And although the UDCD contains the typically flaccid qualification that "it is for each State . . . to define its cultural policy and to implement it through the means it considers fit" (Art. 9), it nevertheless underscores the fact that cultural pluralism is a "catalyst[ ] of creativity," that public life itself depends on the social creativity made possible by pluralism.

Although the UDCD was conceived at the time as a pillar of what the UNESCO director-general, Kōichirō Matsuura, described as the "new ethics promoted by UNESCO in the early twenty-first century," there is no evidence that it ever lived up to Matsuura's "hope that one day it may acquire the same force as the Universal Declaration of Human Rights."[26] Even so, this strange and even plaintive text is a reminder that the proposal to meet the manifold limitations of human rights universalism with the creative potentiality of human rights pluralism is one that is not as heretical as it might seem.

And in considering human rights pluralism as the basis for a reinvented human rights, something must be said about the nature of culture itself. There are, in fact, two questions of importance here: first, what is meant by the category of "culture"; and second, how to apply this concept to differentiate among and within particular cultures. In other words, if we agree to adopt a version of the classic anthropological definition of culture, the one proposed by A. L. Kroeber and Clyde Kluckhohn in 1952—"Culture consists of patterns, explicit and implicit, of and for behavior acquired and transmitted by symbols, constituting the distinctive achievements of human groups, including their embodiments in artifacts"[27]—the question then becomes: how to agree on the boundaries that separate one group's patterns, behavior, and symbols from another.

The problem is that the difficulties multiply very quickly. In fact, the classic anthropological approach to the concept of culture, an approach that finds expression across a wide range, is treated with skepticism bordering on contempt by many intellectuals and undermined by the entire thrust of international human rights law, which considers the concept of culture an obstacle to the globalization of human rights norms.[28] In addition, even if a rough consensus is achieved regarding the concept of culture—for example, by preserving the core of the classical anthropological approach but allowing for cultural hybridity and change—the questions of how to understand the contextual realities of particular cultures, and who has the power to define and articulate such complex understandings, remain. Indeed, struggles over these questions lie at the heart of many enduring social and political conflicts, struggles over cultural boundaries, symbols, and authenticity that can become extremely destructive.

But despite this matrix of interconnected and unresolvable problems, the stubborn facts of culture remain, which makes it all the more necessary to reorient our understanding of the relationship between culture and human rights. Beyond the more practical reasons why cultural diversity must form the pluralist and open-ended foundations of a reinvented human rights, there is another aspect to the unresolvable problem of culture, one that could be thought of as ethical.

This is the way in which the realties and potential of cultural diversity have been filtered for decades through different elite lenses that darken the fact of cultural differences, politicize them, and pronounce them relics of a preglobalized and tribalist past. This enduring cosmopolitan hostility toward culture—except, of course, toward the culture of cosmopolitanism—can be explained in part by the fact that cultural difference has proven to be an enormously difficult basis on which to build theories of transformative social and political change, that is, change that is not directed toward exclusionary, persecutory, or ethnonationalist ends.

But at subtler levels, there is something in the cosmopolitan experience—academic, diplomatic, humanitarian—that leads those who exercise an outsized role in defining and responding to the realities of cultural difference at a global level to minimize their quotidian importance for the vast majority of people whose lives are shaped by these realties. The end result has been the dominance of a prevalent regard toward cultural difference in law, international politics, and social theory that resonates and is self-confirming within a cosmopolitan bubble, but that completely fails to comprehend the actually existing nature of cultural difference beyond this bubble.

Yet what is so revealing is the fact that despite these dominant orientations toward the relationship between human rights and cultural difference, the practice of human rights has taken place largely beyond these elite bubbles of ideology and affiliation, within culturally nuanced contexts that provide a glimpse into how pluralism and human rights might be reconciled on different grounds. Instead of examining the full documentary record of the practice of human rights here, I draw from three illustrative examples that provide evidence for how the vernacularization of human rights is more than simply an act of translation.[29] Rather, the creation of a logic of translocal collective action from diverse normative sources can and should be, by definition, generative, culturally and politically nonhierarchical, and recursive, in the sense that a reinvented human rights must remain conceptually dynamic and discursively malleable.

As a first indication of what human rights generativity might look like in the future, I turn to the groundbreaking work of Sarah E. Holcombe, who spent years as part of an interdisciplinary and intercultural team that worked to translate the UDHR for the first time into an Aboriginal Australian language, the Luritja language spoken by the Pintupi-Luritja people of the Western Desert Lands.[30] Although initially a more limited—yet still enormously complicated—project to translate the actual text of the UDHR into Luritja, it developed into a much more ambitious attempt by Holcombe to understand what she calls the "ethno-epistemological" implications of rendering, that is, the effort to forge linkages between thoroughly distinct moral and social worlds.[31]

What became clear was the extent to which many of the "key words" in the English text of the UDHR were actually portals into globally pervasive but still historically and culturally specific genealogies, in which terms like "dignity," "freedom," and, most important, "human rights"—despite their universal pretensions—were the building blocks of a particular "secular modern" world. This is a world that depends on an "intentional agentic citizen"; that views the individual as an "egocentric subject," ontologically distinct from all others; that draws a rigid line of separation between individual and society; and that celebrates the right to remain independent from society, free from interference or social engagement, as the highest normative ideal.[32]

Yet the Pintupi-Luritja people with whom Holcombe collaborated in the translation of the UDHR live within social worlds that are organized around very different logics of belonging and action. As Holcombe argues, the Pintupi-Luritja people have developed a highly elaborate social identity system that she describes as "relational-spiritual."[33] People are born into an everlasting continuum that is anchored in the eternal ideoscape of the Dreaming, or *Tjukurrpa*. This is a lifeworld that would seem to be nearly the opposite of the one associated with the "secular modern": it is "sociocentric," expressed through multigenerational kinship ties, and marked by multilayered interconnection, in which persons, objects, places, and chronology are "fundamentally coextensive."[34]

Given these elemental incommensurabilities, the process of "translating" the UDHR into the Luritja language became much more a project of eliciting and organizing Pintupi-Luritja values into categories that, at best, alluded to the corresponding article or human rights concept. As Holcombe explains, these incommensurabilities were even expressed through stark differences in what she describes as the "metaphorical organ of thought." For the Pintupi-Luritja, the locus of thinking is the ears, rather than the head. Indeed, they do not draw a distinction between thinking, understanding, or hearing, all of which are described with the same word. This is not surprising, since sociocentricity—as opposed to egocentricity—is a form of organization that is produced and reproduced through dialogue; to understand something, in this sense, is not to apply "reason" to a question or problem, but to "hear well" among others who are also "listening and talking together."

In the end, Holcombe's team found that the concept of "human rights," given its historical, philosophical, and cultural particularities, simply could not be translated into Luritja in any meaningful sense. Instead, vernacularization required the creation of allusive normative linkages between the "secular modern" world of human rights and the Pintupi-Luritja lifeworld, linkages that suggested entirely new possibilities for "human rights" amid deep pluralism. This is how "human rights" was given form as just such a linkage: "All of us should be equal. Being peaceful, reconciled and without spite we should be living together all as a family. We should be kind to people with respect and understanding."[35]

A second illustrative example that provides an equally suggestive signpost to different ways of imagining the relationship between human rights and cultural difference comes from the long-term ethnographic research of Arzoo Osanloo, an Iranian American sociolegal scholar who studies the politics, discourses, and practices of justice in Iran.[36] As Osanloo shows, the framework of international human rights has not been completely rejected by the Islamic Republic, in which the organization of justice around Qur'anic principles is viewed by the state and many citizens as an expression of cultural and religious independence and a symbol of liberation from the degrading values of the secular West.[37] On the contrary, Osanloo's research—which focuses on a number of social, legal, and political institutions in Tehran—reveals the ways in which rights practices from both religious and international sources are brought together syncretistically in ways that produce new frameworks within which people negotiate social and moral conflicts.

In Osanloo's earlier work, she documents the creative ways in which pluralistic rights talk is mobilized by Iranian women as a complex dialogical tool that gives women space to maneuver within otherwise restrictive social conditions, provides a discursive resource to confront and even challenge social and familial wrongs, and reinforces their privileged status as women within a distinct cultural and religious conception of gender relations.[38] Far from a case study of culture clash, or of the confrontation between a liberal international human rights order and an intentionally isolated anti-Western Islamic counterorder, Osanloo's ethnography offers a window into how people—even in a highly regulated state—are able to generate novel normative frames that are essentially hybrid and rooted in everyday conflicts and ambitions, yet susceptible to being mobilized for wider social purposes.

In her later research, Osanloo studies the development of a culture of rights in Iran that is centered on practices of mercy, despite the fact that mercy is neither a right under international criminal law nor part of the sharia codes that govern the Iranian criminal justice system. On the contrary, as Osanloo acknowledges, Iran has one of the highest per capita rates of capital punishment in the world, in addition to its use of a range of devastating forms of corporal punishment such as public floggings, amputations, and blinding. Yet against the background of such a deeply embedded system of retributive and spectacular criminal justice, a parallel system of "forgiveness work" has emerged in Iran in which a wide spectrum of social actors and institutions—lawyers, social workers, artists, intellectuals—foster what she describes as an "affective lifeworld" that encourages victims of crimes to show mercy.[39]

Instead of the right to have justice done by the state as an instrument of divine retribution, Iranians work together to craft and then put into practice a quite different right, whose meanings and consequences are interwoven throughout Iran's cultural, political, and religious history: the right to forgive. As Osanloo's research documents, the practice of the culturally nuanced right to forgive creates something like a shadow system of justice in Iran, one completely obscured by the monitoring gaze of the international human rights system, which has treated the harsh and public application of sharia law in Iran as a paradigmatic case of gross and state-directed human rights violation.[40] Yet because the culture of forgiveness in Iran is understood by people to express an even more profound Islamic value than retribution, it works as a powerful counterweight to the state criminal justice system and allows Iranians to reshape the contours of law in subtle ways that nevertheless point toward the possibility of institutional reform and even wider social change.

A final example of the dynamic possibilities of pluralism as the basis for a reinvented human rights comes from my own long-term ethnographic research on social and political change and human rights vernacularization in Bolivia. In obvious contrast with postrevolutionary Iran, and even in contrast with Australia, Bolivia was one of the most important sites where human rights activism was fused with international development, beginning in the waning years of the Cold War.

Human rights developmentalism took place in several different ways in Bolivia, but much of the focus was put on linking the economic and social development of the country's marginalized rural areas with the rapidly expanding global discourse of Indigenous rights. Coincidentally, Bolivia's early ratification of the 1989 ILO Convention 169, the "Indigenous and Tribal Peoples Convention," took place in the midst of a national conflict over how to recognize the upcoming five hundredth anniversary of Christopher Columbus's voyage. Like many Indigenous organizations throughout the Americas, Bolivia's highly mobilized Indigenous social movements denounced the narrative of "discovery" and rejected the push to make 1992 a year of celebration.

Inspired by the new unifying language of indigeneity and the new organizing framework of Indigenous rights, communities and social movements in Bolivia's Amazonian lowlands launched a protest march in August 1990 that wound its way through hundreds of kilometers and over difficult terrain, arriving in the political capital of La Paz after more than a month.[41] Along the way, the original protest was joined by hundreds of other Indigenous people from both lowland and highland communities, who formed transethnic and translinguistic alliances in an unprecedented show of collective solidarity.

Although the direct impact of the march was limited, in part because the country was just entering a decade of neoliberal ascendancy, privatization, and land-grabbing, the culture of Indigenous rights mobilization would reemerge with epochal significance through the election of Evo Morales, who was inaugurated in 2006 as the country's first self-identifying Indigenous president. Despite the fact that the Morales government would later be ousted in a right-wing coup d'état in November 2019, after the longest era of political and economic stability in Bolivian history, the period 2006–19 was one in which rights pluralism flourished in important and revealing ways.[42]

A key aspect to what became a longitudinal experiment in the practice of human rights was the fact that it took place within a state-directed program to transform the unitary legal system into a series of "autonomous" Indigenous systems, each with its own set of rules and procedures. A robust orientation based in legal pluralism was given state sanction through the revolutionary 2009 constitution and through a series of new government departments, which were charged with overseeing the liberation of the country from its "republican" and neoliberal shackles and guiding its transformation into a postneoliberal and "plurinational" state.

In addition, the move to rights and legal pluralism as the foundation of the new plurinational state was left intentionally open-ended regarding jurisprudence or new legal codes. Instead, the approach to pluralism was one in which the normative content of distinct Indigenous legal systems—there are theoretically thirty-six in the country[43]—was left untouched by the state, which restricted its policies to the promotion of the value of pluralism itself rather than to any effort to reconcile Indigenous legalities or create an overarching structure of state-level surveillance. As the head of the legal pluralism team based in the new Plurinational Constitutional Tribunal explained to me, there were no plans to draft a "Code of Indigenous Law" in Bolivia, which would require the kind of simplification and normative harmonizing that were anathema to the wide-ranging approach to pluralism being developed throughout the country.[44] Instead, the task was to foster normative diversity by encouraging communities to recover forms of conflict resolution and categories of rights that had long-existed in the shadows of the state.

The results of these radical experiments in state-sponsored rights and legal pluralism in Bolivia were decidedly mixed. On the one hand, the Movement to Socialism (MAS) government confronted something of a structural dilemma: how to use the power of the state to weaken the power of the state, since the vision of a deeply pluralized country based in Indigenous autonomy meant the eventual withdrawal of the state into a minor caretaking function, perhaps focused almost exclusively on foreign relations. This extraordinary intention to relinquish the power of the central government proved to be impossible to sustain, especially in the face of internal opposition by right-wing movements that wanted to overthrow the plurinational regime and to replace it with the kind of hierarchical government that had dominated Bolivian politics for decades.

But on the other hand, even more important was the problem of historical scale. The sheer boldness of the MAS government's experiments in pluralism—and the kinds of social relations and diffused political structures it gestured toward—demanded a scale of transformation that could only be achieved over the *longue durée*. Ideologically, the point of reference was the centuries of colonialism and neocolonialism, something reinforced by the world's only vice ministry of decolonization, which constantly emphasized the enormity of the challenges facing what came to be called the "process of change."

In the end, the highly suggestive possibilities for pluralism in Bolivia were never given the chance to mature over a correspondingly extended period of social and political development. Interestingly, as a reflection of just how potentially transformative pluralism was understood to be by those who violently opposed it, one of the first acts of the revanchist right-wing "interim" government that took power in November 2019 was to refuse to use "plurinational" as the term for the Bolivian state. Instead, the *golpistas* quite ceremoniously reintroduced the "Republic of Bolivia," with all of its nationalist and culturally monolithic implications.

Conclusion: Human Rights as a New Way of Belonging

In making the argument that human rights universalism must be replaced by human rights pluralism as the foundation for a reinvented human rights, it is important to be quite clear about the ways in which cultural difference has been politicized, manipulated, and wielded as a weapon of exclusion and violence. If, as I have argued, the study of the practice of human rights has revealed the dark sides of universalism, something similar can obviously be said about cultural difference.

Indeed, the anthropologist and human rights scholar Richard A. Wilson has reminded us of just how consequential the stakes are when considering the troubled relationship between universal human rights—and the institutions derived from them—and those who would critique their universality based on a variety of opposing ideologies:

> We are currently living in a Weimar-like historical conjuncture in which the number of populist governments has doubled worldwide since the early 2000s. Populist leaders have come to power in, *inter alia*, Brazil, Guatemala, Hungary, India, The Philippines, Poland, Turkey, the United Kingdom, the United States and Venezuela. Populist leaders play the nativist card, blaming international conspiracies and foreigners for their country's difficulties and their own political shortcomings. As part of a "cultural backlash," populist demagogues exalt the local and traditional, rail against international institutions, cosmopolitans, and immigrants, and demand priority for their own country ("America First"), citizens, region, race, or religion, etc.[45]

And we might even push the matter further by reflecting on how the dark sides of "nativism" are far worse than the dark sides of universalism, even if the globalization and imposition of universal human rights and the weaponization of cultural difference at smaller scales stem from the same types of category errors, reflect the same genre of monadic thinking, and express the same inflections of moral and cultural righteousness. Yet in reimagining the future of human rights, it seems to me that this kind of lesser of two evils thinking is only another sign of a prevailing "downsized ambition," a reminder of the "melancholy truth of our failure to invent other ideals and movements" with which to confront the vast spectrum of contemporary crises.[46] Nevertheless, to insist on human rights pluralism is not to suggest that the generative potential of cultural diversity offers neat and tidy guidelines for how to resolve inevitable conflicts over interpretation, future projects, or justifications for collective action.

Indeed, at the time of writing (October 2020), political debate in the United States is bitterly divided over the nomination of Amy Coney Barrett to replace Ruth Bader Ginsburg on the US Supreme Court. Barrett, a conservative Catholic legal scholar, opposes the practice of abortion, since she believes that human life begins at conception. Within the culture of faithful Catholicism, abortion is believed to be a form of unlawful and immoral killing, something to be resisted at all costs. Yet there are many people in the United States—and obviously elsewhere—who don't share this belief, who live their lives within a different "culture of life," who believe that a woman has both a moral and legal right to terminate a pregnancy, at least under the limitations first outlined in the 1973 US

Supreme Court case *Roe v. Wade*. How would an approach rooted in pluralism respond to this seemingly intractable conflict?

Returning to the late-in-life musings on value pluralism by Isaiah Berlin with which this chapter began, both the "pro-life" and "pro-choice" positions at the heart of the conflict over reproductive rights in the United States would represent differing "human values" in Berlin's framing. In other words, thinking reflexively, although I strongly believe in a woman's right to make decisions about her own body, including whether to terminate a pregnancy up to the point at which a fetus becomes a human being (for me, at "viability," or around twenty-eight weeks), I can understand what it would be like to believe that life begins much earlier, at conception, and can imagine what it would mean to organize my moral, social, and political actions in terms of this belief. However, if someone said they belong to a culture that believes that parents have the right to kill their children until they reach the age of eighteen, I would reject such a belief as falling outside the ambiguous, but still finite, "plurality of values" that constitute the deeply heterogenous reservoir of "human values." That is to say, the divergent "pro-life" and "pro-choice" positions would both be accommodated within a framework of human rights pluralism, even though they point to strikingly different outcomes, bases for decision, and even social identities, while the putative culture of child killing would not.

Nevertheless, examples like these don't provide a clear guide to how to resolve the problem suggested by the concept of a "plurality of values"; namely, which values should form the basis of a reinvented human rights, and which values should be deemed to lie beyond the boundaries of "human semblance." Isn't the belief about what are—and are not—part of the plurality of human values itself shaped by particular cultural, political, and intellectual histories? Indeed, from an anthropological perspective, even "human" itself must be seen for what it is: a relatively recent category of belonging that has utterly failed to either account for the diverse realities of attachment or to ground the formation of large-scale translocal alliances in the face of environmental and socioeconomic crisis.[47]

Even so, in the face of inevitable conflicts over the boundaries and limiting cases of human rights pluralism, at least one definitive point can be made: the alternative, the imposition of one narrow system of "human values" over another, the denial and suppression of vast depths of the reservoir in the name of a universal truth, has proven to be a tragic error. As the long-standing conflict over abortion in the United States demonstrates, there are no easy or obvious ways to create social and political alliances between people who hold such fundamentally opposed beliefs about something as elemental as the beginning of human life.

Yet simply to accept the priority of pluralism in this case would completely reorient the terms of the conflict; as Berlin put it, mutual understanding is the precondition for collective action—across cultures, nations, religions, and ethnic groups. It is in this sense that a reinvented human rights represents a different way of belonging, a different logic through which cultural difference becomes a generative resource for creatively responding to problems that are also translocal. Instead of the grand synthesis of universal human rights, human rights pluralism points to a much more diffused framework of alliance and attachment, one that is dynamic, emergent, and ecumenical.

CHAPTER 7

The Subjects of Human Rights

AS WE HAVE SEEN at different points in the book, I was lucky enough to have conducted ethnographic research during the period of the greatest florescence of human rights activism and global power, that is, toward the end of the decade that would soon be described as the Age of Human Rights. These twelve months of fieldwork in a remote region of Bolivia's Potosí Department were arduous, yet life-changing, for reasons both personal and intellectual. Even for someone accustomed to physical hardship and even danger, the experience of studying conflict resolution within forty isolated hamlets in Potosí's Alonso de Ibáñez province—across many months, during different seasons (including the perilous rainy season), and through a number of bouts of illness—presented any number of challenges.

In the middle of the 1999 rainy season, I made the unwise decision to travel alone to the hamlet of Molino T'ikanoma, which was located in a precarious position on the other side of a 4,500 meter pass, about five hours—by foot—from my home base in the provincial capital of Sacaca. I had been focusing my ethnographic research on a fascinating hamlet intellectual who occupied a position in the region's Indigenous socioeconomic system called the *ayllu*. His particular interest was in legal record-keeping, and he was responsible for maintaining the hamlet's *cuaderno de actas*, an oversized notebook in which hamlet authorities kept a record of public actions: the resolution of local conflicts; decisions to collaborate (or not) with international development NGOs; even the fact that a delegation of local leaders had journeyed to La Paz, and returned to the hamlet, after participating in a national march of Indigenous movements.[1]

The narrow path from the high pass to Molino T'ikanoma, which locals called "the Serpent," descended through highly eroded and precipitous terrain that even locals described with some trepidation. (Indeed, as I would come to learn, death from falling was actually common enough to be part of cause-of-death statistics collected by the NGO-funded health clinic in Sacaca. The festival seasons were particularly dangerous, when people traveled at night from hamlet to hamlet, or from Sacaca back to hamlets, after very heavy drinking over multiple days.) Yet instead of continuing down the winding path, which would have taken another hour after passing for about 3 kilometers parallel and above Molino T'ikanoma, for some reason I decided to leave the trail and head directly toward the hamlet. It is true that I was approaching the area in the late afternoon, after having left Sacaca later than I had intended, but the decision to take the spontaneous shortcut proved to be ill-advised and almost fatal.

As I scrambled down the hillside, the gradient became steeper and steeper. I could see the small adobe huts of Molino T'ikanoma below me getting closer, but I could also feel my boots giving way. At a certain point, it became obvious that I had made a terrible mistake: about 10 meters farther down, the ground suddenly gave way to a sheer cliff, dropping away to the rushing T'ikanoma River at least 100 meters below. Just as I turned to try and climb back to safety, both of my boots gave way and I started quickly slipping toward the abyss. As a survival instinct, I began frantically grabbing the soil or anything around me, which consisted of nothing but short, stubby, devilishly spiked cacti. It's difficult to describe the feeling of supporting one's entire weight by clutching a cactus while dozens of spines dig into both hands like a pin cushion, but I was surprisingly calm, focused, and determined to make it through what was by all measures a completely idiotic life-and-death situation.

Little by little, I pulled myself up the hillside, one cactus after another, until I could safely stand up. When I finally reached the trail, after about forty-five minutes, I looked at the palms of my hands and they were completely covered with embedded cactus spines, including the bottoms of all ten fingers. There was very little blood, but there was no way I could even begin to try and remove them. With my life saved, but the research visit to Molino T'ikanoma rendered impossible, I left in a sort of fast trot for Sacaca—holding both hands awkwardly in front of me—so that I had at least a chance of crossing the high pass before the sun went down. Eventually, I stumbled into Sacaca around dusk, with night falling quickly, as it does in the tropics, and went directly to the small clinic, where a young doctor right out of medical school laboriously removed every cactus spine from my hands, one by one, with a pair of tweezers.

Two weeks later, I traveled again to Molino T'ikanoma, this time with my research assistant Javier, a local boy of sixteen. Needless to say, we stayed on the correct trail to the hamlet. Although I had intended to discuss the ways in which authorities in the hamlet had dealt with a recent conflict over a "land invasion"—an ominous-sounding event that actually meant that the children of one family had allowed their llamas to encroach on the potato fields of another family, where they ate seed and generally trampled some of the crops—the hamlet intellectual wanted to talk about human rights.[2] Apparently, in the intervening two weeks between visits, he had attended a human rights "workshop" in the small central plaza of Sacaca in which several NGOs had set up information booths in which the idea of human rights was linked to a number of more basic development initiatives, such as reproductive health and early childhood education.

Although the concept of "rights" didn't hold precise meaning for the hamlet intellectual, either normatively or linguistically, it was, surprisingly, the category of "human" that provoked the greatest curiosity and confusion. Social norms in the hamlet, and indeed throughout the region, could not be described as "rights" in the sense of entitlements that attached to individuals and that could be enforced through local procedures. Rather, people lived their lives in relation to a series of social expectations and obligations regarding conduct, relationships with others, and embeddedness within what has been described as a "unified biological-technological productivity unfolding seamlessly from human-telluric bonds through matrimonial alliance outward to very wide regional alignments and toward cosmological forces."[3] Nevertheless, the presence of a low-level state court, a *juzgado de instrucción*, in the provincial capital meant that people from the hamlets had at least a passing understanding of *derechos*, which they associated exclusively with the laws and procedures of the state court.

It was the "human" in human rights, however, that remained an obscure, even inscrutable, proposition. Although much of the effort behind human rights activism throughout the 1990s had been directed toward the ratification of rights at the national level, or focused on local "capacity-building" intended to teach people that they were rights-bearers with legal and political agency, the fact of humanness was taken for granted, as a kind of a priori global fact that needed very little explanation or justification.

Given that the "human" in human rights derived from the biological category of human beings—a category associated with a long genealogy of classifications, from Aristotle's *History of Animals* to the Scholastic Great Chain of Being to Linnaeus's *Systema Naturae* to the UDHR's "all members of the human family"—and the fact that this putative universal category of being was invested with both moral and social importance, it was treated as the self-evident first principle on which the entire project of human rights depended. Who would have thought it necessary to have to teach people that they were human?

Yet as it turned out, the "human" in human rights proved to be as, or more, problematic in practice than the category of rights. Normativity, in one form or another, turns out to be universal, but humans are not; indeed, quite the contrary. Speaking in a mix of Quechua and Spanish, the intellectual from Molino T'ikanoma put a critical emphasis on something that I had already known: the most important and immediately intelligible category of collective subjectivity for him was *runa*, which in Quechua means something like "the people."[4]

Although runa was reserved as a maximal category, rather than as a way to distinguish different collectivities at more local levels—categories that were defined by hamlet and ayllu—its scope was nevertheless quite limited: it could encompass all Quechua speakers in Bolivia, and perhaps beyond (for example, in Peru), and even Indigenous people from other nations or linguistic groups, but those were the outer boundaries. As an obvious matter, non-Indigenous Bolivians, including urban mestizos, or people with "mixed" origins and identities, were excluded from the maximal category of runa. And it goes without saying that runa couldn't be further, categorically, from that of "humans"—all human beings, everywhere, for all time, members of the species *Homo sapiens*.[5]

For these reasons, it was very difficult for the hamlet intellectual to accept the deeply counterintuitive, counterexperiential, counterfactual idea that all the quotidian realities of local belonging were illusions, masking the truth that we were all members of the same family of "humans." When I explained to him that the most important thing about *derechos humanos* was that it meant we were all the same and that we—meaning everyone in the *world*, a referent with similarly uncertain local purchase—were supposed to treat each other as equals, he gave me a puzzled look.

But we are *not* all the same, he replied matter-of-factly. He didn't mean this in a discriminatory way, even less as a way of saying that runa, "the people," were better than others. He simply meant that his expanding knowledge of the world, which meant his knowledge of Bolivia beyond the boundaries of Alonso de Ibáñez, including the historic departmental capital of Potosí and La Paz, the country's "seat of government,"[6] had taught him that the wider world was much more—not less—diverse than he knew. And his different forays outside the hamlet, ayllu, and mountains and river valleys that normally encompassed his life certainly didn't suggest that he was actually the same as everyone he encountered, just another member of a single global family.[7]

In considering the contours of a reinvented human rights, therefore, the question becomes: should the perplexity of this one local intellectual from rural Bolivia—a narrative of category confusion that could be repeated nearly endlessly, as the anthropology of human rights reveals—be understood as a kind of alienation from his true self, a form of false consciousness that the project of human rights was meant to overcome, however incompletely? Or, rather, should this be taken as evidence for a quite different proposition: the problem lies not with its reception, but with the idea itself, the idea that "freedom, justice and peace in the world" depend on the widespread belief that we form a single collective subject—humanity—and that this collective subject takes precedence over all others, with which it is destined to remain in tension so long as ultimately subsumable categories like "runa" retain their grip on people's everyday lives.

This chapter examines these and related dilemmas in order to clarify and situate the place of the subject(s) within an alternative conception of human rights. In this, I am guided by the analytical framework developed in an innovative volume, which draws a distinction between "who is the subject of human rights," "who is subject to human rights," and "how human rights make subjects."[8] With this framework as a point of departure, the chapter moves beyond the limits created by existing human rights, which necessarily define and give meaning to particular kinds of individual and collective subjects, while excluding others.

If the proposal to reinvent human rights takes aim at the legal and political systems in which rights have traditionally been associated, in seeking to formulate a conception of human rights anchored in social mobilization and translocal solidarity, the same is true of the subjects of this (re-)formulation. In a sense, this is the more difficult task: reimagining the subjects of human rights against a background in which the hegemonic "human" and the many alternatives coexist in unavoidable and unequal tension. What would it mean to relinquish the enduring assumption that our biological identities as human beings should predetermine our social and moral identities, that the unifying fact of our biological sameness should serve as the model for our alliances, our collective projects, our ideologies?

Even more, what would it mean—for a reinvented human rights, but not only—to reconceive our collective subjectivity in such a way that explicitly decenters the human subject, that even, in a spirit of critical reflexivity, regards itself—that is, us, ourselves, our social and political formations—as an existential threat to wider ecologies? This is the ultimate challenge, one that is excruciating to fully contemplate, since it demands forms of thinking and action that are truly difficult to visualize: the reordering of social, political, and economic life at a global level in ways that reflect a fundamental repositioning of human beings; the redistribution and rebalancing of resources on a massive scale; and the presence of a new compact at all levels to live well instead of living better (but only *after* the establishment of new forms of equilibrium).[9]

And yet, despite the formidable odds, despite the sobering acknowledgment that such a sweeping vision will be treated by some as a form of naive futurism, what choice do we really have? If "humanity" has any chance at all of "sav[ing] itself from its low ambitions . . . for the sake of [both] local and global welfare,"[10] my argument is that the category of humanity must first be broken apart and then reassembled along wholly different lines. This is obviously a long-term, collective project, one for which this chapter can only provide signposts. In so doing, I draw in part—as I have done throughout the book—from research on the practice of human rights, which offers suggestive windows into future possibilities, despite the limitations of the international human rights system against which these practices are often responses.

I begin by examining the ways in which the category of "human," the sacrosanct figure at the heart of existing human rights, is given prominence during particular moments in history. Although this historical overture is necessarily limited, it is important to be explicit about how and why the orthodox subject of human rights must be overcome in order to project a different vision for human rights whose ambitions are equal to the manifold crises of the present—and those that are surely coming. Next, I survey the frontiers of contemporary mobilizations for human rights and justice, the outer limits where technology, radical philosophy, and transnational power have created a provocative confluence, one that holds important lessons for the ways in which an *alternatively human*—rather than "posthuman"—subject might return as the agent of translocal alliance-building and movements to resist and replace existing political economies.

The chapter then considers an important body of literature—primarily from the anthropology of human rights—that has revealed the ways in which societies far from the global metropolitan gaze are organized within cultural systems in which rights inhere fundamentally in relationships rather than in people. As will be seen, a relational understanding of rights significantly alters what it means to be entitled to treatment or provision by virtue of something else. From the perspective of rights in relationships, entitlements (and obligations) attach in part to individuals, but not by virtue of anything resembling an immanent quality of humanness or one's status as a free-floating and normatively autonomous person. Instead, rights and obligations flow from and within relational networks, the maintenance and support for which actually define and give meaning to identities—which are, inescapably, social.

Interestingly, recent pleas within legal and social theory for a relational alternative to human rights subjectivity find resonance in some of the earliest critiques of human rights, including Marx's rejection of the abstractions of the "rights of man." As he put it, "human emancipation will only be complete when the real, individual man has absorbed into himself the abstract citizen; when as an individual man, in his everyday life, in his work, and in his relationships, he has become a *species-being*; and when he has recognized and organized his own powers (*forces propres*) as *social* powers."[11]

The chapter concludes by reflecting on what it means for a reinvented human rights to depend on what the anthropologist Ronald Niezen has described as the "rediscovered self": the capacity and willingness to reimagine something as fundamental as (collective) personhood as a precondition for new forms of rights mobilizations.[12] Besides the more practical necessity of privileging conceptions of the subject that are far removed from that which gives rise to the "right of the *circumscribed* individual, withdrawn into himself,"[13] the principle of the rediscovered self also underscores the essential contingency and pluralism of human subjectivity, the ways in which notions of personhood are not permanently fixed—either in culture or in biology—but rather malleable, open to revision or (re-)invention, and capable of grounding new social and political movements for change.

Humanity: An Anthropological History

In considering the genealogy of the human in human rights, and what its history tells us about its ambitions and ultimate limits, it is not necessary to draw a distinction between "human" as a sociolinguistic construct, and something like the thing itself. Put another way: humans, the subjects of this highly consequential construct, don't exist independently of the category; rather, they were created by it. "Human," "humanness," "humanity," and so on, must be understood anthropologically as categories, characteristics, and even moral claims that are related within a particular—even if diverse—lineage in which language, culture, and politics are closely intertwined.

Without making too much of the revelatory power of etymology, the constellation of concepts and words in English that are crystallized by "humanity" were forged through a combination of Anglo-Norman French and earlier antecedents in Latin.[14] To be human, to form part of the collective of humanity, was to display specific characteristics that were believed to distinguish people from animals—and, importantly, to distinguish certain kinds of people from others who might superficially resemble humans, but who were actually different or less than human.

Yet critically, already by the fifth century, these specifically "human" characteristics—such as kindness, refinement, rationality, empathy—had become closely associated with the development of theology around the human nature of Christ, the idea that Christ was both fully human and divine. To be human—and thus part of humanity—from an evolving Christian perspective meant to embody all of the noblest traits celebrated in the New Testament in particular: compassion, forgiveness, tolerance for difference, benevolence. In this sense, the "human" subject encoded from the beginning a complex mix of moral qualities, common affiliation (with varying degrees of exclusion), and an allegiance to a particular worldview, which was originally captured by concepts like "civilization," but which later became more closely connected with Christian doctrine.

Apart from beginning to unpack the historical and cultural roots of humanity—with all its subsequent implications for colonialism, religious proselytism, and racism, among others—the diversion into sociolinguistics also underscores the ways in which the word/concept humanity—or *humanitat* (Catalan), or *humanidad* (Spanish), or *humanité* (French), or *humanidade* (Portuguese), or *umanità* (Italian)—makes both normative and descriptive claims. Normatively, the human subject of humanity, the fallen creature that was nevertheless made in the image of God, is one at least capable of a particular set of feelings and behaviors that must be treated as ideals; although humans, from this perspective, fail to live up to these ideals, they remain as endpoints, as normative objectives that humans, to be humans, must strive to meet. And descriptively, humanity is reserved for those who are born into this collectivity and who endeavor to preserve and guard its boundaries.

In this, humanity is quite different from the much later category of "human beings," which was developed in the early modern period in Europe in order to place humans within wider scientific-taxonomic classifications. Yet the exclusionary moral foundations of humanity were never fully overcome by the development of classification and the rise of "natural" science. One can *perdre son humanité*, even if one can never lose one's status as a member of the biological category "human beings."

In other words, the much older moral sense of humanity—a moral sense, moreover, with a particular legacy that is coextensive with the rise and eventual imposition of European (and then Euro-American) religious, political, and economic ideologies—was always something that demanded specific kinds of actions, specific types of moral behavior, while, by definition, excluding others. As the Sudanese scholar Amal Hassan Fadlalla has put it, within the postwar vision of human rights, humanity is something that must be "performed," according to a carefully curated script, under the watchful gaze of powerful institutions and global publics.[15]

Given this, it becomes easier to understand how the political and discursive process of vernacularizing existing human rights confronted the greatest difficulties and ultimate limitations around the legibility of the subject, rather than around the cross-cultural validity of rights. To return to the local intellectual from the hamlet of Molino T'ikanoma, the problem was that the historical and religious genealogy of the "human" in human rights was one that staked out a set of moral values, within a particular teleology, that clashed with those expressed by the local category runa, a category of collective subjectivity, it must be acknowledged, that was equally contingent, equally the result of a distinct trajectory of historical and cultural development.

And to complicate the dilemma even further, iterations of the "human" in human rights have been part of colonial and neocolonial history in Alonso de Ibáñez province for centuries. Evidence for Catholic missionary work exists throughout the region in the form of dozens of crumbling chapels that date from the mid-seventeenth century. In the provincial capital, Sacaca, the guardians of the historically specific vision of humans-as-Christian subjects are now missionaries from the Spanish Claretian order, which took control of the regional parish in the early 1970s in the wake of Vatican II, the process of institutional reform that gave new impetus to Catholic proselytism within a broader doctrine of liberation theology.

This means that as an Indigenous category of collective personhood, "runa" has evolved over centuries in parallel with, but also in opposition to, that of the Christian "human" promoted by the local Catholic priests. What changed with the coming of human rights discourse to the region in the 1990s was the proposition that this specific conception of personhood gave rise to specific entitlements, and a new capacity to—at least theoretically—make claims on the Bolivian state based on these entitlements.

Illustrations of the ways in which "humanity" has always formed the basis for exclusionary projects of what Gil Gott has described as "imperial humanitarianism"—the supposedly benevolent diffusion of moral truths by powerful actors in which "humanity" forms the dominant side of what Gott calls an "arrested dialectic"—could be further multiplied across any number of cultural and political histories.[16] For example, as was seen in the previous chapter, the landmark initiative to translate the UDHR for the first time into an Aboriginal Australian language—an initiative that was self-consciously meant as a critique of imperial humanitarianism, yet which remained ambiguously intertwined with it—attempted to overcome these category conflicts through the liberal use of textual interpretation.

As with the Quechua spoken throughout Indigenous highland Bolivia, the equivalent to the "human" in human rights doesn't exist within the Aboriginal Pintupi-Luritja language. This creates an immediate and revealing problem: how to translate the UDHR into a specific language if the fundamental word "human" is untranslatable. The project team decided to use the key local concept of *waltja*, which has nothing at all to do with the idea of all human beings in the world, but is rather a "multivalent . . . encapsulating concept" that can refer to possessions, kin members, self, and, again (as with runa), a sense of collective inclusion *through exclusion*.[17] Nevertheless, as Sarah Holcombe explains, the use of "waltja" should not be taken, in the end, as an actual translation of "human"; instead, it must be understood at best as a metaphor that works in both directions to express a sense of "shared identity." Yet it is a metaphor that demands, as she puts it, a "significant leap" in meaning and application.[18]

In laying the groundwork for a reinvented human rights, therefore, we are confronted with yet another significant historical and conceptual difficulty. If it makes any sense at all to preserve "human rights" as the signifier of an alternative logic of translocal collective action, one that demands the formation of alliance-building based on feelings of solidarity that extend beyond existing categories of difference, then the "human" of this formulation must be reappropriated; in a way, it, too, must be reinvented. Instead of the Christian or "civic-bourgeois" "modern subject" expressed by the historical conceit of "humanity," a subject, moreover, that is destined to remain "unfindable,"[19] it is necessary to reimagine the "human" of a (reinvented) human rights more as a metaphor along the lines suggested by *waltja*, a metaphor that conveys a sense of shared identity and of action directed toward common and more emancipatory purposes.

In fleshing out what this metaphor might look like in more detail, the following two sections examine different dimensions of the problem of human rights subjectivity through the practice of existing human rights and justice-seeking. As will be seen, despite the legal, political, and philosophical centrality of the "unfindable" subject of human rights, alternative conceptions of collective personhood have continued to flourish—sometimes in direct opposition to the "human" of human rights, and sometimes simply in its shadows, along the vast outer reaches where the "capillary ends of the contemporary networks of power" register mere traces of their presence.[20]

Frontier Justice

In considering the ways in which an alternatively human subject might return as the agent of translocal alliance-building and mobilizations to resist and replace existing political economies, an important—indeed, necessary—place to look is within growing movements to harness the innovations of new technologies as a strategy of human rights activism. I describe these movements as forms of "frontier justice" for two reasons. First, while inspired by claims for justice or the protection of human rights, these efforts to instrumentalize technology as a new mechanism for social, political, and economic change are developing beyond the boundaries of conventional institutions and ideologies, including courts, nation-states, and rights treaties. In this sense, the emergence of novel approaches to technology-driven and technology-defined justice takes place both at, and beyond, margins—political, social, and even ontological.

And second, the borders at which new technologies are being deployed as a form of alternative human rights activism and collective mobilization are marked by all the characteristics that have long been associated with borders, frontiers, margins. As the Black American author and social activist bell hooks memorably described it, the frontier is a zone of contradictions. At the same time that frontiers and margins are characterized by danger, lawlessness, and cultural ambiguity, they are also—precisely for these same reasons—"site[s] of radical possibility, . . . space[s] of resistance."

As hooks explains, reflecting on her childhood living in a small, segregated town in Kentucky, "I [am] not speaking of a marginality one wishes to lose, to give up, or surrender as part of moving into the center, but rather as a site one stays in, clings to even, because it nourishes one's capacity to resist. It offers the possibility of radical perspectives from which to see and create, to imagine alternatives, new worlds."[21]

In examining the frontiers at which new technologies and new communities are being mobilized in provocative, if uncertain ways, therefore, we likewise are able to imagine how these experiments reveal possibilities for reconceiving human rights subjectivity beyond existing categories: individual and collective, victim and perpetrator, law and politics, state and nonstate, even center and periphery. Indeed, following hooks, we can say that the study of these technological and social frontiers suggests something even more ambitious: the capacity to "cling to" the ambiguities and creative potential of marginal zones as an ongoing project, one in which alliances are forged and solidarity nourished—under the sign of "human rights"—without the need to impose rigid normative systems or, even less, without the need to adopt a single objective, an endpoint toward which the pluralistic practices of a reinvented human rights must eventually converge.

Among these technological and social frontiers of justice-seeking and activism, different types of communities are coalescing, not all of which intervene in ways that offer obvious lessons for the development of new approaches to human rights subjectivity. For example, in her ethnographic research on hackers and the free and open-source software (F/OSS) movement in the United States and Europe, the anthropologist and technology scholar E. Gabriella Coleman has charted the ways in which hacking communities operate in a close dialectical relationship with the global capitalist system that is the frequent target of their breaches.[22]

Although many hackers consider themselves activists working beyond—and against—the boundaries of legal and political regulations, the intention is not to challenge political economic systems or, even less, to work toward solutions to problems such as socioeconomic inequality or global climate change. Instead, as Coleman argues, hackers challenge the legitimacy of copyright and patent law, among others, in order to democratize the economic benefits that are protected as intellectual property and, in so doing, render a quite conventionally liberal understanding of freedom "productive."

Indeed, in a later study of the online activist community known as Anonymous, Coleman suggests that much of hacker activism must be understood as a form of "tricksterism," an ambiguous type of cultural play that is directed toward equally ambiguous ends—or, more commonly, toward no ends at all. As she puts it, the wildly diverse actions of hacker activists "need not be accepted, much less endorsed, to extract positive value. We may see them as edifying us with liberating or terrifying perspectives, symptomatic of underlying problems that deserve scrutiny, functioning as a positive force toward renewal, or as distorting and confusing shadows."[23]

Yet if the practices and ideologies of online communities like Anonymous present (intentionally) equivocal lessons for how innovative technologies facilitate the emergence of the kind of "alternative, new worlds" in which a reinvented human rights might flourish, a much clearer picture emerges when we turn to the more recent rise of digital advocacy organizations, which are typically not anonymous, even though they make use of many of the same tools and technological competencies as "hacktivists." Research that has tracked the development of these online communities has analyzed their implications largely in relation to existing human rights by suggesting ways in which technology might improve the implementation of international human rights law, especially criminal law.[24]

But what concerns me here is something different: the ways in which new technologies are being used as the mechanism through which new collective subjects are confronting powerful actors: states, corporations, and political parties, among others. What we see through these examples is evidence for how people can and do form novel translocal alliances that are inspired by alternative visions for change, in which "justice" and "human rights" function as "summarizing key symbols" rather than as specific legal or political frameworks.[25]

The human rights scholar and anthropologist Ronald Niezen has conducted multisited ethnographic research on the rise and increasing influence of cyberactivist communities, which operate on a global scale to investigate violations and, importantly, to pierce through the webs of state propaganda that rely on deception, misinformation, and the control of flows of information.[26] As Niezen's work demonstrates, the crossroads where new technologies and the "politics of justice claims in practice" meet is a space of both social and ontological creativity in which campaigns for change and justice are being mounted beyond the borders of states, international legal structures, and existing political—especially national—affiliation. More importantly, the creation of these communities takes place through virtual forms of sociality that challenge the conventional bases of collective subjectivity, even as the underlining deceptions and aggressions that trigger virtual mobilization are anchored in long-standing political, cultural, and religious antagonisms.

The digital community at the heart of Niezen's analysis is Bellingcat, an organization that exists in multiple forms: through an investigative journalism website; through online forums and message boards; in reports, case studies, and instructional guides; and through the institutional management of the transnational "collective" from offices in the United Kingdom, under the direction of British journalist Eliot Higgins, who set the Bellingcat community into motion in 2014.[27] Although Bellingcat has intervened in a number of high-profile investigations of violence and state corruption, the organization is most well-known for mobilizing shifting networks of activists, who use open source technologies and search engine algorithms to uncover evidence of violations that is very difficult to manipulate or credibly refute.

For example, amid the clamor of international politics and institutional dissembling, Bellingcat activists, working transnationally through a number of new technologies—such as geolocation, social media networks, and reverse-image searching—quickly established that Iranian Revolutionary Guards were responsible for shooting down a Ukraine International Airlines commercial flight shortly after takeoff from Tehran, killing all 176 people on board.[28]

Although, as Niezen argues, these same technologies are also used by the powerful state and corporate actors who are the targets of Bellingcat's digital activism, the implications for new forms of collective subject-making and alliance-building are clear. In particular, the kinds of frontier justice-seeking by communities like Bellingcat offer the possibility of provocatively different answers to the three questions posed at the beginning of the chapter: who is the subject of human rights?; who is subject to human rights?; and how do human rights make subjects? As Niezen explains:

> Even where it has operated in the absence of tools of encryption, verification, and secure storage, [digital mobilization] has shifted the flow of expertise. Large NGOs like Human Rights Watch and Amnesty International once typically engaged in human rights fact-finding as a process that happens "somewhere else" to people who serve as witnesses through their testimony. . . . When these same witnesses are technologically empowered, however, the pattern of investigation changes. . . . [T]here is now an opportunity for the subjects of human rights violations to actively participate in the investigations that concern them. . . . These advantages are creating conditions for . . . a form of bottom-up claiming of rights, with human rights investigation *transformed into a tool for community mobilization*.[29]

Despite the fact that digital advocacy remains a leading-edge and emergent alternative form of mobilization, it offers any number of key lessons for the broader project to reimagine the subjects of a reinvented human rights. First, online activist communities coalesce through technological platforms that are both transnational and most often mobilized in opposition to states. Far from the fictive pretensions of "humanity," online collectives pursue justice claims based on shared interests, shared competencies, and, as Coleman has argued, an ethics that envisions open source interventions as the expression of a new form of democratic action with global implications.[30]

Second, case studies of frontier justice show that collective subjectivity is closely tied to collective action. Rather than a static, immanent understanding of belonging, digital activist communities conceive of themselves as being constituted through their actions, their interventions, and, most important, through the measurable changes associated with their collective work. Drawing a parallel from a well-known case study from the anthropology of human rights, we can say that digital activists view "rights" and "justice" not as entitlements or normative ideals but as real outcomes of collective action directed toward progressive change.[31]

Third, the rise of transnational digital advocacy communities underscores the ways in which networks represent an alternative, and often subversive, logic of organization, one that embodies both ethical and political values. As Jeffrey S. Juris has shown, a particular form of networking took root during the first decade of the post–Cold War era, toward the end of the Age of Human Rights, specifically as a critique of established forms of state-based rights-claiming and political mobilization.[32] Even then, technology played a key role in constituting antiglobalization movements, despite the fact that what was new then has now become old: email listservs, web pages, and shareware. In this sense, the network should be considered a basic model for imagining how people might organize under the banner of a reinvented human rights.

And finally, these soundings from the study of online activism demonstrate the ways in which collectivities mobilize to confront and undermine the will of dominant actors, not in defense of human rights in the abstract, but as a "positive force toward renewal" based on visions of a world marked by greater equality, transparency, and the redistribution of power beyond—and often against—existing international institutions, corporations, and political ideologies.

Rights in Relationships

If a consideration of the broader implications of digital advocacy mobilization offers part of a solution to the problem of how to reformulate collective subjectivity in ways that are equal to the ambitions of a reinvented human rights, similarly suggestive possibilities are to be found in another area of inquiry: that which explores relationality as an alternative grounding for rights. Here, again, the question is how to imagine human rights in ways that do not revolve around a culturally and historically limiting conception of the atomized "human" subject, one whose problematic genealogy has already been examined. The study of rights in relationships, by contrast, reveals a normative landscape on which entitlements inhere in complex social realties and histories through which individuals conceive their identities and justify their actions.

Yet before surveying this work in more detail, it is worth returning to Marx's critique of the "rights of man," which was principally concerned with the problem of the subject of rights. Although another early critic of human rights, Jeremy Bentham, took issue with the entire philosophical edifice of natural rights, which he famously described as "nonsense on stilts," and "mischievous nonsense" at that, Marx's skepticism flowed from a more specific question: the relationship of the individual to society.[33] For Marx, the conception of the rights-bearing subject at the core of human rights was deeply flawed for two reasons.

First, according to Marx, it was premised on a conception of the individual that was entirely false empirically. The idea that people should be understood as completely distinct and self-contained normative beings flew in the face of everything uncovered by the comparative philosophical and sociological study of societies. Marx narrowed on this point through an analysis of the right to liberty, which was one of the pillars of the French Revolution. As he put it, on this view, "it is a question of the liberty of man regarded as an isolated monad, withdrawn into himself. . . . But liberty as a right of man is not founded upon the relations between man and man, but rather upon the separation of man from man. It is the right of such separation. The right of the *circumscribed* individual, withdrawn into himself."[34] Although a monadic understanding of the subject might have had currency within the culturally and historically bounded world of European Enlightenment philosophy, it had no relation at all—according to Marx—to the reality of social relations within any societies (including those within Europe) of which he was aware.[35]

And second, as a social and political project, that is, as a framework for revolutionary change, Marx viewed human rights to be fatally flawed, because it inverted the order of priority between individuals and societies that would be necessary for transformative collective action. The "allegorical" subject of the "rights of man" was nothing other than a philosophical phantasm, yet another specter that was haunting Europe, except for different reasons and with—as we know in retrospect—much broader and historically more lasting implications. According to Marx, society did not exist to serve the interests of "egotistical man"; instead, emancipation would only be possible through a "*restoration* of the human world and of human relationships" organized around, and toward, a common purpose.[36]

This wider historical context, therefore, changes the way we view empirical data on the workings of social systems in which rights, as such, are derived from complex social networks through which individuals collaborate in common moral and economic projects. If Marx's critique has enduring validity—as I am suggesting—it means that the subject of human rights at the center of the post-war international legal and political order must be treated as something like the continuation of a long-standing figment of the European philosophical imagination, a figment that nevertheless became hugely consequential, not the least as the basis for a society in which autonomous individuals could "freely" enter into contracts within a market economy, as Henry Sumner Maine had imagined.[37]

Although many examples could be given for how nonmonadic rights systems work in practice, some of the clearest and most remarkable come from research on normativity throughout Melanesia, which has been held out as a striking counterpoint to the deformations of Western individualism since at least the early twentieth century writings of the anthropologist Bronislaw Malinowski and the sociologist Marcel Mauss.[38] Joel Robbins, who has conducted ethnographic research in Papua New Guinea (PNG) since the early 1990s, has studied the ways in which local systems that privilege "rights in relationships" have come into conflict with human rights norms and national law. As he explains, relational rights systems are based on three principles. First, people in Melanesia value social and kinship relationships above all others, and maintaining these relationships occupies the highest priority in daily life. As Robbins puts it, "relationships . . . play a role equivalent to that played by the individual in Western societies."[39]

Second, Melanesians understand rights to inhere in complex relational webs into which they are born; in this sense, they believe in natural rights, but in relationships rather than in individuals. As Robbins puts it, "persons are microcosms of relationships," and "much of the social process of people's lives consists in realizing these various already existing relationships by attending to them, and by making new relationships that at once allow people . . . to establish a wider social world in which to move."[40]

And third, relational rights are not static, they are not inert norms that exist as timeless abstractions. Instead, rights in relationships are made and remade through the performance of sociality, especially reciprocal exchange, which structures even the most quotidian of activities, such as preparing and eating food.

As Robbins explains, people nourish rights in relationships by exchanging food even though these exchanges are not necessary for daily sustenance. As he puts it, "people refer to eating food one has produced oneself, rather than giving it away and eating food given to oneself by others, as 'eating for nothing.' This kind of eating, they say, is bad because it does no relational work."[41]

Yet when the culture of rights in relationships confronted human rights activism and the power of national courts in PNG, the contrast between the two normative worlds was put into stark relief. Robbins examines what came to be known as the "Compo Girl" case, in which an eighteen-year-old woman was offered as part of a claim for compensation for the death of an older man, whose clan demanded from the woman's clan (which was held responsible) money, pigs, and a marriageable woman. The young woman objected to being part of the "head payment" and told her story to one of the national newspapers in PNG. On the basis of this news article, a human rights NGO in the capital filed a case in the high court on her behalf, which sought to enjoin the compensation settlement as a violation of her human rights.

During the hearings in the high court, Justice Salamo Injia heard testimony from a range of witnesses and studied affidavits on the question from different perspectives, including one submitted by a professor of anthropology at the University of Papua New Guinea, who was also a member of one of the two clans involved in the underlying dispute.[42] Dr. John Muke described in detail the system of relationality in the PNG highlands and the ways in which interclan marriages functioned as the fundamental mechanism for creating and maintaining wider relational networks.

As he explained, the killing of someone embedded in these networks causes harm—and potentially catastrophic harm—to the networks themselves. The victim of a killing is first and foremost the relational web of which the deceased is a "microcosm." The giving of a woman in marriage, therefore, was understood locally as a form of restorative justice. By contrast, to follow national law and punish the killer by putting him in prison would only cause further harm to the relational system. Despite being responsible for the death, he was still obligated to continue to respect rights in relationships through reciprocal exchange, ritual prestations, and by participating in future marriage alliances as a member of his clan.

Although he was sympathetic to the arguments for the legitimacy of the compensation payment and was someone who came from the highlands himself,[43] Justice Injia ruled in favor of the human rights NGOs, finding that the system of rights in relationships could not take precedence over the "dictates of our modern national laws."[44] In effect, the court ruled that relational systems of justice at the center of highland life throughout PNG came into tension per se with the human rights norms adopted into national law, since the subjects of both systems were fundamentally, irreconcilably, opposed to each other. In the face of such a conflict, according to Justice Injia, international human rights must prevail.

In reflecting on what the outcome of the "Compo Girl" case has to say more generally about the possibilities for reconfiguring human rights and conceptions of justice around alternative accounts of the subject, Robbins argues that relationality—as opposed to the individualism of existing human rights—has a much better claim to translocal validity, since relationality everywhere "become[s] translated into expectations about acts and behavior."[45]

Although the specific facts of the Compo Girl case generated controversy on a number of levels,[46] it is an important heuristic with which to think through the ways in which orthodox human rights norms "occlude[d]"[47] the central place of relationality as a distinct subject *of* and *for* rights as well as the ways in which subjects are *made* through relational networks.[48]

Conclusion: Human Rights and the Rediscovered Self

In an earlier study of the rise of Indigenous rights discourse and mobilizations for cultural justice, Ronald Niezen makes a broader, and more fundamental, argument about the ways in which rights movements have demanded transformations in subjectivity as much as in law and politics.[49] As he puts it, rights frameworks—especially those that take shape as a form of revelation, as a breakthrough solution to existing social and political problems—depend on a process of "rediscovery" in which people are asked to reimagine themselves as different kinds of subjects within different kinds of social worlds.

Indeed, the invention of existing human rights, to invoke Lynn Hunt's formulation, was even more the invention of a new and powerfully agentic subjectivity within Euro-American history, a specific kind of subjectivity that went on to form the basis for European and American colonialism, the eventual conquests of global capitalism, and, over the course of time, modern human rights activism. To make this point at a much more granular level: as we have seen, I was witness to the importance of the "rediscovered self" within human rights development work in Bolivia during the late 1990s.

The first and most important task for the numerous human rights NGOs was to sensitize the region's Indigenous agro-pastoralists to the importance of thinking of themselves in a completely different way: as bearers of individual rights that defined them and that created clear lines of normative separation where they didn't traditionally exist—between husbands and wives, between children and parents, and between different hamlets within the same ayllu. Yet at the same time, this conception of the rediscovered self demanded lines of normative separation that left people isolated and confused, because the human rights subject was conceived as an abstract universal, without social or moral grounding, without any resonance at all with people's lived experiences.

The practical implications of promoting human rights as a revelatory framework, despite the fact that the conception of the monadic human rights subject bore no relation to local lifeworlds, was that people kept human rights activism at a distance by refusing to remake their social and moral lives in its image. Instead, as the years passed, *derechos humanos* was reduced to something much less transformative: just another set of rules that were associated with the provincial capital and its little-used state court, rules that might be invoked in principle during disputes, but rarely were. In effect, the more profound claims around subjectivity were largely ignored, reducing human rights to just another foreign import, one that took its place within the region's wider legal and political universe, but in a way that dramatically limited its long-term measurable impact.

In light of this, and given what has been unpacked and examined throughout the chapter, how *should* the subjects of human rights be conceived? First, in thinking about a reinvented human rights beyond existing ontological and normative categories, it should be clear that subjectivity must be regarded as dynamic rather than fixed. From this perspective, human rights subjectivity becomes something quite different: a shifting and open-ended category that is marked by greater or lesser degrees of adherence rather than permanent ascription. In this way, although the three-part analytical framework Danielle Celermajer and Alexandre Lefebvre proposed retains its usefulness, only the third part provides specific guidance. In other words, if human rights subjectivity is emphatically detached from its historical and philosophical origins, it becomes much less possible to answer, definitively and without exception, either who is the subject of human rights or who is subject to human rights. Instead, most of the concern will be with the third problem: how human rights make subjects.

Second, an enduring conception of human rights subjectivity should not be one that does violence to *actual* subjectivity, which describes a diverse landscape of ways and means of belonging. As we have seen, the normatively specific conception of the "human" in existing human rights emerged through a philosophical, social, and economic history in which the monadic account of the person served specific purposes. The claimed universality for this specific conception of the person was merely the ideological justification meant to make these purposes all the more inevitable. Nevertheless, I am convinced that the monadic human of human rights must be relegated to a place of mere historical interest, if not necessarily abandoned altogether, if human rights subjectivity is to be reanimated for the future.

In "thinking and feeling beyond" the intentionally abstracted "human" of existing human rights,[50] I am compelled by the translocal prevalence of relationality as well as by the spirited arguments for it as an alternative basis for human rights subjectivity. Without wanting to prefigure the possibilities, even less to suggest replacing one fixed vision (individualist) with another (relationalist), it is important to recognize that the kinds of "rights in relationships" systems that have been widely documented point to the need to *begin* with collective subjects and then imagine how individuals might work together to ensure that these collective subjects of human rights flourish.[51]

And finally, to return to the framing suggested by Holcombe, based on lessons learned from the landmark project to translate the UDHR into an Aboriginal Australian language for the first time, I would argue that the category of human rights subjectivity must, in the end, be understood metaphorically rather than literally. Instead of conceiving the subjects—whether individual, relational, or otherwise—of a reinvented human rights as bounded entities, ready for codification, the entire concept of human rights subjectivity should be understood as a metaphor for new and more efficacious forms of collective action and belonging, forms—to reinforce this essential point yet again—that demand the creation of alliances beyond existing categories of difference.

Although this proposition might appear implausible, one only needs to turn to Holcombe's account to be reminded of why and how a model like this already exists. In the remote stretches of the Western Desert Lands, the Pintupi-Luritja people organize themselves through the "multivalent . . . [yet] encapsulating concept" of *waltja*,[52] which serves as a profoundly resonant metaphor for shared identity, collective purpose, and a willingness to struggle for a more interdependent and durable future.

CHAPTER 8

Human Rights in a G20 World

OVER THE COURSE OF TWO DAYS in November 2008, in a strange and cavernous building in Washington, DC, the path of global power was fixed in seismic ways that nevertheless remained largely hidden from critical scrutiny or even general awareness. Whether the momentousness of this turning point was meant to be obscured, its far-reaching significance camouflaged by the deadening languages of financial regulation and institutional collaboration, is another question. What is not in doubt, however, is what this moment represented: the point in time when global economic and political power were definitively fused, when the promotion of "international financial stability" was accepted as the truly visionary logic for a global capitalist political economy that had taken undisputed center stage, a position of dominance that downgraded alternatives like the United Nations could only look on with worried envy.

The incongruous meeting place for this epochal event, which took place over two short days during which we—collectively, globally—were pushed across the Rubicon without even realizing it, was a massive red-brick structure built in the 1880s to house thousands of office clerks, whose only job was to process pension requests from veterans, nurses, and widows of Union soldiers killed during the US Civil War. Although meant as an office building, it was constructed in that burst of exuberant historicism that is so prevalent across the history of American architecture: with actual interior office space minimized or even concealed, the building was modeled after several Italian Renaissance palaces. Even though the legions of clerks presumably found ways to manage their work during the decades in which the building served as the national pension bureau, it was known more for its vast "Great Hall" interior, where several of the tallest Corinthian columns in the world tower over an immense covered courtyard.[1]

It was in the middle of this dizzying expanse, around a large table placed on a raised, purpose-built platform, that members of an elite political economic club called the "Group of Twenty," or the G20, met to decide how to work collaboratively to promote "financial markets and the world economy." Summoned to Washington, DC, by George W. Bush, in the waning days of a controversial two-term presidency, the leaders of nineteen countries plus representatives of the European Union gathered along with national central bankers and the heads of the World Bank and International Monetary Fund. Although the summit brought together leaders from less than 10 percent of the world's nation-states, the G20 accounts for 90 percent of the global GDP (and about 85 percent of the world's fossil fuel emissions).

Politically, the G20 includes all five permanent members of the UN Security Council (China, France, Russia, the United Kingdom, and the United States); both the most populous (Indonesia) and influential (Saudi Arabia) Islamic states; the most powerful Latin American states (Argentina, Brazil, and Mexico); and an assortment of other global and regional powers (Japan, Turkey, South Korea, India, Australia). Of the fifty-four countries on the African continent, only one, South Africa, is a "core member" of the G20. The G20 also grants several "extraordinary" guest invitees permission to enter the club, including the only "permanent" guest country invitee, Spain, whose desperate campaign to be invited to the historic 2008 meeting became a "Spanish national obsession that transcend[ed] party politics," a frenzied last-minute process that led the Spanish prime minster at the time—ironically, the socialist José Luis Rodríguez Zapatero—to be willing to endure "almost any diplomatic humiliation."[2]

Ideologically, the G20 encompasses a vast spectrum of approaches and histories: representative democracy, parliamentary democracy, constitutional monarchy, authoritarian democracy, Islamic absolute monarchy, and one-party Marxist-Leninist socialism. Along any number of other criteria—cultural diversity, linguistic diversity, religious diversity, landmass, national biodiversity, colonial histories—the G20 reflects a sweeping global range, a panorama whose scope was perfectly symbolized by the capacious surroundings of its fateful 2008 summit.

Yet around the G20's table, in the midst of this global multiplicity, a powerfully opposing current is at work. It is, in fact, the dominant current that justifies the G20 and explains its world-historical significance. Although 2008 marked a key juncture in both political economic history and in the organizational history of the G20 itself, it is important to note that the G20 was launched almost a decade earlier, in 1999. Even though the first years of the post–Cold War ushered in the Age of Human Rights, they also served as a powerful reminder of just how much capitalism—globally, regionally, and nationally—was subject to periodic crises and pervasive, systemic, socioeconomic insecurity.

With the free-fall of the traditional left marked by the rise of "new" left parties in strongholds like the United Kingdom and the United States, an ideological transformation that was described at the time as a "third way,"[3] resistance to capitalism was replaced by centrist approaches that sought to displace the struggle for justice from economics to social identity. This transition, which would prove so debilitating to the cause of progressive politics over the succeeding decades, had the more immediate effect of yielding to the power of global capitalism, now unhindered by any broadly legitimate countervailing economic system.

At the same time, the "people's republic" of China, now almost a decade into its breathtaking transformation from a command economy into an authoritarian capitalist state, entered a period of explosive growth as a "socialist" market economy. With the Cold War coming to a close, the writing was on the wall: China, under the leadership of Deng Xiaoping (who had set China on the road to capitalism in 1979) and then Jiang Zemin, could not afford to be left behind as history "ended"[4] and the future became a permanent struggle for economic supremacy *between* capitalist superpowers.

Yet this period of post–Cold War global market fervor and increasing integration provoked a series of regional jolts to the wider capitalist system, tremors that were worrying enough for the leading capitalist states to take steps to reinforce global economic structures and alliances, most importantly through the launch of the G20, after a number of debt and financial crises in so-called emerging markets. Nevertheless, even as capitalist economic growth continued—albeit unevenly—in the years after 1999, the far-reaching importance of the G20 remained latent as the attacks of September 11, 2001, and the resulting mobilizations around national security and global surveillance, sidelined the cause of "international financial stability."

The global financial crisis of 2007–8 completely changed the calculation: despite ongoing wars of religion, politics, and ethnicity, the unifying imperative to protect the global capitalist system at all costs was embraced by the leading powers with renewed urgency. With loses of more than $2 trillion from the global economy looming as a reminder of just how dangerous capitalism can be when its different contradictions become too much for the system's safety valves to handle, the G20 was relaunched in November 2008 with a dramatically expanded mandate: first, to reaffirm the existing consensus that capitalism would be the only global political economy, despite the many regional and national variations; and second, to deepen collaboration between national and international financial institutions and central banks to ensure that the protection of the global capitalist system would become the unquestioned baseline, the overriding principle that would transcend, and serve as an ultimate check on, national politics and international relations.

The urgency and significance of the "new" G20 were marked in different ways over the next decade, beginning with the fact that the global 10 percent club met twice a year for the first two years, then settled on yearly summits beginning in 2011. Regardless of what took place during high-level meetings of the increasingly marginalized "international community" in Geneva and New York City, it was the yearly gatherings of the G20 that crystallized the aims and intentions of global power. And even if the global capitalist economy took years to recover the wealth lost during the 2007–8 financial crisis, with recovery uneven within different national economies, economic growth and the unequal creation of wealth returned as the central pillars of a world that was being remade under the careful watch of the twenty members of what is euphemistically described as an "international forum."

China's gambit, in particular, to finally abandon any lingering attachments to its association with Marxist anticapitalism paid off in spectacular ways. As Evan Osnos documents in compelling detail, the years after China's declaration of allegiance to global capitalism at the 2008 G20 meeting in Washington, DC, were a veritable Gilded Age: when more wealth was produced in the shortest amount of time in global economic history (exceeding all the wealth created during the entire Industrial Revolution); when more billionaires were made in the shortest amount of time; and, inevitably, when levels of economic and social inequality in China exploded, as economic ambition replaced social welfare as the foremost public value.[5]

And finally, despite the sudden shock to national economies caused by the historically unprecedented lockdowns during the global COVID-19 pandemic, the global capitalist economy grew in the years after 2008 exactly in the way the G20 wanted: without major system-wide crises and without any serious signs of political resistance, even as the costs of ever-expanding economic growth became more and more "brutal," as the "expulsions" of contemporary capitalism became more and more the inevitable consequence of the system's complex rapaciousness.[6]

By 2021, the G20 club sat collectively at the controls of a global capitalist economy whose relentless inexorability had become almost as important as its socioeconomic and environmental ramifications. With two of the five remaining communist countries fully aligned with the political economic certainty of capitalism (China, Vietnam), the almost absurd global marginality of the other three (Cuba, Laos, North Korea) merely reinforces the wider point: despite the catastrophic implications, it has become "easier to imagine the end of the world than the end of capitalism."[7]

These, then, are the contours of what has become a G20 world. It is also the reason I reserved the most formidable chapter for the book's conclusion: in considering the prospects for a reinvented human rights, it is vitally important to be as clear-eyed as possible about the wider political economic and global context within—and against—which such a project must necessarily take shape. Although "real utopian" thinking demands that we push against the boundaries of both the imaginable and the possible, as Erik Olin Wright argued,[8] it is also equally important to not lose touch with what Isaiah Berlin called the "sense of reality."[9]

It is in this spirit that this concluding chapter examines in more detail the nuances of our G20 world, the ways in which what might be described as a "postinternationalist" fusion of global economic and political power is reflected in social, institutional, and technological formations—among others—that create significant challenges for human rights, even as they reveal points of weakness that remind us of just how much capitalism remains riddled by "inner contradictions,"[10] despite its obvious resilience.

In the next section, the chapter takes up the phenomenon of "passive colonialism," the ways in which the international human rights system has been increasingly co-opted by key players at the center of the G20 as a means of legitimating political economic interests *through* human rights. As will be seen, passive colonialism in this sense has usually been misinterpreted as a kind of deception or disingenuousness, the false engagement with international human rights norms and institutions in order to promote national interests by other means. Instead, I argue that manipulation of the UN Human Rights Council, for example, expresses something else: the way in which the contemporary postinternational world order was anticipated by the international system itself, with human rights providing the normative language through which the system's eventual impotence could be explained and justified.

The chapter then turns to one of the most revealing developments over the last twenty years: the movement to overcome the barriers of state sovereignty by making major transnational corporations directly responsible for the protection of human rights. This movement reached its apogee in 2011, when the United Nations adopted a set of guiding principles on business and human rights, otherwise known as the "Ruggie Principles." These were named after the diplomat and scholar John Ruggie, the indefatigable architect of the campaign to find some way, however unlikely, of holding private transnational corporations to account for human rights abuses.

By examining several areas in which the quixotic "corporate social responsibility" movement is believed to have had its greatest impact, however, the true scope of the challenge for a reinvented human rights comes into unsettling focus. If states—and not only those in the G20—must necessarily remain in structural opposition to the cause of a reinvented human rights, the same is true—except much more so—for the corporate actors whose interests are of paramount concern for states.

The chapter then moves beyond the more obvious ways in which the fusion of global economic and political power is refracted through existing human rights to consider emergent challenges, especially those in which new technologies are changing the face of contemporary capitalism and the status of humans themselves—as consumers, as workers, but even more, as a category of embodied capital. As will be seen, new technologies are rapidly changing the ways in which the postinternational world order is taking shape. What this suggests, among other things, is that a reinvented human rights will confront the power of a global political economy that exerts pressure as much through people's embodied selves—actions, gestures, habits, and even genetic profiles—as through social and economic policies that depend on the expulsions of our G20 world.

The book concludes by reflecting on what it would really mean to push against, and ideally beyond, the current political economic conjuncture as the most critical task for both the present and future. If capitalism fundamentally depends on multiple, systemic, and enduring forms of dispossession, then the task of a reinvented human rights must be understood as one of *repossession*, of recovery, and of renewal.

Human Rights and the Passive Colonialism of Global Power

It is a mistake to overread the postwar history of human rights as one in which the international human rights system either remained largely irrelevant within global politics or developed in stark antagonism to global networks of economic and political power. Both narratives contain elements of truth, but they also obscure crucial subtleties in the ways in which existing human rights norms and institutions have been appropriated strategically over the decades. It would be more accurate to say that the international human rights system has always been critically important, but not in the ways the proponents of the system imagined. And instead of an antagonistic relationship, the international human rights system has—in different ways, for different actors, during different historical periods—become a useful instrument, a means of protecting the prerogatives of global power rather than confronting or undermining them.

Even more, the instrumentalization of the international human rights system can be understood as a form of "passive colonialism," a means of consolidating and projecting political economic control through modes of engagement with formal human rights bodies. In this sense, passive colonialism is much more than merely a form of colonialism that dare not speak its name; it is, in a way, more brazen and more degrading. Given that human rights norms and institutions were the only basket into which all the postwar international eggs were placed, the sole legal and moral framework on which "freedom, justice and peace in the world" depended, it is especially vexing to recognize the many ways in which this framework has become a preferred means to justify or legitimate the opposite of freedom, justice, and peace. Indeed, in a nod to classic forms of colonialism, the passive colonialism through which international human rights become instrumentalized is often marked by the reinterpretation of key concepts, including "human rights" itself, a culturalist version of passive colonialism for which China, in particular, has become the leading example.[11]

Yet even if the passive colonialism of global power through human rights continues to be the leitmotif of the contemporary international human rights system, this should not be seen as an unintended consequence of wider geopolitical struggles, or a structural failure of the system, something that couldn't have been anticipated from the beginning. Instead, early developments showed how the wider international system was rendered vulnerable to instrumentalization even before the UDHR was adopted in 1948; in this sense, the human rights project proved to be useful as a mechanism of passive colonialism long before the global capitalist convergence of the post–Cold War.

As we have seen at different points throughout this book, the history of the UNESCO human rights survey, which took place during 1947 and 1948, has provided a critical lens through which to observe fundamental institutional, political, and ideological dynamics that would come to characterize the broader international human rights system, even though the UNESCO survey took place in the shadows of the UN CHR and the high-level debates over what became the UDHR.

One dynamic that is of particular significance is the way in which leading powers—all of which would become central players in the G20 a half a century later—used their disproportionate financial importance to the main international institutions in order to steer developments behind the scenes, far from the visibility of plenary sessions and beyond what could be captured through the permanent records of meeting minutes.

The United States proved to be especially adept at using the leverage of financial support for the United Nations, and its specialized agency UNESCO, to exert pressure over the course that the human rights project—legally and politically—would take. More often than not, this back-channel pressure included the threat to withdraw funding or political support for institutional leaders. For example, when representatives of the United States government finally learned of the surprising ambitions of UNESCO to uncover the cross-cultural principles on which a human rights declaration should be based, they took immediate steps to undermine the upstart agency.

In May 1947, at a critical moment for both the UNESCO human rights survey and the work of the UN CHR, the US State Department made contact with UNESCO to insist that work on its meddlesome human rights survey be scaled way back. The US State Department announced that it would closely monitor UNESCO to ensure that its human rights survey did not clash with the ongoing work of the UN CHR, which the United States was also carefully monitoring and steering.[12]

In order to underscore just how much the United States intended to dictate the terms of human rights diplomacy by excluding the potentially far-reaching work of UNESCO, it gave the job of suppressing the human rights survey to Arthur Compton. Compton, writing at the behest of the US State Department, was a Nobel Prize–winning physicist who played a leading role in the development of the atomic bombs that had expressed US power in more brutal ways at the end of the recent world war. Compton's letter to Julian Huxley, the controversial director-general of UNESCO who had dared challenge the authority of the United States within the human rights project, leaves no doubt that UNESCO had crossed a boundary and would soon face the consequences.

And indeed, that is precisely what happened. Six months after putting UNESCO on notice that its plans to change the carefully managed course of the UDHR drafting process would not be tolerated, the UN CHR, under the direction of Eleanor Roosevelt, issued an extraordinary censure of UNESCO during a December 1947 closed session. Describing the UNESCO human rights survey as a "dangerous precedent," the UN CHR decided to quash the survey's findings by preventing them from being sent to UN member states, and, most important, by refusing to consider them at all during deliberations over the text of the UDHR.[13]

With the United States having set the original precedent through which passive colonialism would come to shape the international human rights system across the decades,[14] this model would later be refined even further by China, which came to view human rights as a superb weapon in an intra-G20 struggle with the United States, a fight for supremacy *within* the global 10 percent club. Among other things, the clash between China and the United States, despite their common commitment to global capitalism, shows how quickly the struggle for global power can become a zero-sum game, with lines of inequality and conflict stretching even into the highest circles of political economic alliance.

China's passive colonial relationship with the international human rights system reflects years of careful planning and strategic maneuvering. Although China had been viewed as a perennial pariah by human rights organizations such as Human Rights Watch and Amnesty International, a notoriety first linked to its government's brutal suppression of a nascent prodemocracy movement in Tiananmen Square in 1989, its leaders realized just how useful human rights institutions could be for the country's long-term political economic plans. What is so notable is the extent to which China's increasing involvement in human rights diplomacy paralleled almost exactly the country's meteoric rise as a global capitalist juggernaut. By the time China's GDP had come to dwarf that of Japan, putting the Chinese economy on track to surpass the United States by 2030 at the latest, it had become the most influential "maker and constrainer" within the international human rights system.

As Rana Siu Inboden has shown, in a remarkable longitudinal study of China's passive colonialism through human rights, China developed a multidimensional approach that allowed it to shape the functioning of key institutions like the Human Rights Council on the one hand, and, on the other, to condition economic assistance and the development of trading partnerships on support for its moves at the international level.[15] As her research reveals, China took a leading role in the negotiations that led to the creation of the Human Rights Council in 2006.

Moreover, China has developed an elaborate set of strategies ever since to ensure that the council refuses to seriously examine the manifold human rights abuses within China, while working to keep the council itself mired in internal conflict and bureaucratic wrangling, which another study has characterized as "repetitious statements, bloc voting, and vote-bartering," tactics that are precisely calculated to "undermine[ ] the legitimacy of some, if not many, Council discussions and actions."[16]

As Inboden's study demonstrates, China has managed to bolster its image within the international human rights community by supporting institutions and processes to a much greater extent than the United States, in particular, while at the same time taking steps to make certain that these same institutions and processes facilitate, rather than hinder, its broader political economic objectives. Since 2013, China's wider global strategy has been dominated by the Belt and Road Initiative, through which hundreds of billions of dollars in infrastructure assistance are being given to countries throughout Asia, Africa, and Latin America as part of a multidecade project to replace the United States as the world's only true superpower. From this long-term perspective, the global capitalist system will still be the only political economy, and the United States and its various capital and labor markets will still be essential for China's own economic growth and stability. The difference is that in this future version of our G20 world, China will sit at the head of the table and set the global agenda.

If the existing international human rights system has become a mechanism through which members of the global 10 percent club engage in different forms of passive colonialism at the service of national economic and political interests, and the wider capitalist economy on which these national interests ultimately depend, then the lessons for a reinvented human rights are not difficult to draw. Without necessarily declaring the vast apparatus of international human rights treaty negotiation and monitoring defunct, it must be, at the least, seen for what it is, and, more important, what it is not.

In the very best of circumstances, tenuous linkages *are* formed between the institutional centers of the international human rights system and the distant places in which actual struggles take place, linkages that can provide inspiration for those on the frontlines of social, economic, and political conflict.[17] Yet these are linkages that connect the bureaucratic and political machinations of the Human Rights Council, for example, with the diffuse practice of human rights very much despite, not because of, the wider system of which the council is both the symbol and organizational anchor.

More commonly, the international human rights system provides no framework whatsoever for organizing resistance to a global political economy whose exclusions and dependence on accumulation by dispossession are the driving forces behind many of the world's systemic crises. In the same way in which a reinvented human rights must be developed apart from the control of individual states, the same is true of the existing international human rights system, which a powerful subset of states "make and constrain"[18] as an instrumental of both national and global control.

Human Rights, Risk Management, Capital Bondage

The problem of how to extend the reach of legal enforcement and account-ability to nonstate actors has become one of the most enduring dilemmas of the existing international human rights system. Nevertheless, among the range of "nonstate actors"—a category that derives from both the Westphalianism of the system and arid legal analysis for which such distinctions are jurispruden-tially relevant—some are much more significant than others. In states like China and Saudi Arabia, major corporations are either directly owned or controlled by the government.[19] But in most instances, corporate ownership is discon-nected enough from the state that companies have no formal obligations under international human rights law, although private companies—depending on jurisdiction—might have rights as "legal" persons.

For many reformers working within the international human rights system, the exclusion of transnational corporations from the framework of legal obliga-tion and enforcement was increasingly viewed as an obvious defect particularly as the post–Cold War unleashed the twin genies of capitalist expansion and human rights policy making. Although obscure and rarely used instruments like the US Alien Tort Statute had provided at least a theoretical mechanism through which corporations could be held to account for human rights violations (in this case, under national law),[20] and even though regional bodies like the European Court of Human Rights had allowed "indirect approaches" to corporate liability,[21] corporations were largely shielded from either the threat of direct human rights prosecutions or the more general scrutiny of naming-and-shaming.

This was all the more worrying for human rights activists because of the increasing economic power of transnational corporations, whose portfolios became more diversified and financialized, and because of the ways in which corporations were influencing national policy making, especially around re-source extraction. At the same time, although major multinational corpora-tions exerted tremendous social and economic pressure in the countries in which they exploited raw materials, provided work, or sold products, their entire institutional orientation—or "business model"—had absolutely noth-ing to do with the protection of human rights, except if such a concern could be monetized consistent with the overriding—usually statutory—objective to increase corporate value.

Indeed, as human rights scholars came to realize, multinational corpora-tions were not fundamentally "bad" actors, even those in resource industries who were responsible for vast environmental degradation, violence against local populations who deigned to struggle against corporate encroachments, and the corruption of relatively weak national political systems. Rather, like sharks, mul-tinational capitalist corporations were just extremely efficient at doing what they were designed to do: maximize profits, increase value to shareholders, capture surplus value, and mitigate risk, all while working to ensure that wider political and economic conditions remained as favorable as possible to the corporation's interests.[22]

As a response, during the late 1990s and into the early 2000s, an unlikely and ultimately doomed global movement took shape that was committed to holding transnational corporations accountable for human rights abuses beyond the narrow boundaries of state sovereignty. This movement traced its origins to the early 1970s and the outrage sparked by the involvement of US-based corpora-tions in the 1973 coup d'état in Chile, which overthrew the democratically elected government of Salvador Allende.[23] Although the resulting activism led the United Nations to adopt a "Code of Conduct on Transnational Corporations" in 1974, the negotiations over the code took place with almost no participation from any of the major socialist countries, whose perspective at the time on multinational corporations was dismissive. From the vantage point of the Soviet bloc and of Maoist China, transnational corporations were seen as "poisonous flowers on the dung-heap of a dying capitalism."[24]

Despite the initial impetus, the 1974 Code of Conduct played almost no role in regulating corporate behavior over the next decade, and it died a slow but inevitable death within the international system, with the United States, in particular, working through its embassies around the world to ensure the final "termination of the Code."[25] As Karl Sauvant argues, the failure of this first effort to hold multinational corporations liable for a range of economic, political, and environmental abuses can be explained quite simply: the convergence of state and multinational corporate power became too useful for both sides, as foreign policy and global corporate strategy were increasingly intertwined under the rubric of "foreign direct investment."

Nevertheless, although this intertwining had only tightened in the years since, culminating in the G20 synthesis of 2008, the international community returned to the problem, this time under the supervision of the Human Rights Council. In fact, also in 2008, a UN-appointed special representative, John Ruggie, completed a much-anticipated report on business and human rights. This report then became the basis for the UN Guiding Principles on Business and Human Rights, which the council endorsed in 2011. Neither a General Assembly–adopted declaration (like the UDHR), nor, obviously, a human rights treaty, the so-called Ruggie Principles are based on three general pillars, the second of which is the "corporate responsibility to respect human rights."

Perhaps nothing quite captures the unique combination of self-interestedness and folly in the international human rights system as the idea that multinational corporations should be trusted to restructure their operations so as to protect human rights around the world, all because of an earnest commitment to the value of corporate social responsibility (CSR) and a willingness to perform human rights "due diligence." Given that the entire CSR movement—in relation to human rights and beyond—relies on the market forces of capitalism to give weight to what amounts to a set of completely voluntary suggestions, it is not surprising that this pretty please approach has utterly failed to alter the nature of corporate behavior in the ways CSR idealists imagined.

This is not to say that corporations around the world have remained aloof to the CSR mandate; indeed, quite the contrary. The problem is that the impact has been largely the opposite of what many business and human rights activists longed for during the halcyon days of the 1990s, when anticorporate and anti-globalization movements reluctantly turned—disastrously, as we now know—to human rights discourse as the new language of resistance. Likely blinded by the pervasive optimism and sense of historical certainly that was so characteristic of the Age of Human Rights, the CSR movement in fact offered to multinational corporations a powerful new tool for risk management, yet another mechanism through which global capital could shape its public image and draw attention away from the ruinous long-term ecological and socioeconomic consequences of its mode of production.

As many studies have documented in predictable yet still dispiriting detail, multinational corporations in a variety of industries have eagerly embraced the new mantra of human rights due diligence, the international *suggestion* to act, if not exactly "in a spirit of brotherhood," then in ways that demonstrate a sense of good corporate citizenship. Indeed, as Christian Scheper has shown, an entire subsector of global capitalism has emerged that is dedicated to perfecting, and monetizing, the art of "knowing and showing."[26] Multinational corporations "know" human rights standards by referencing them in corporate documents and through public outreach; they "show" their commitment to these standards by making an often tenuous or vague link between them and business decisions. As Scheper's research reveals, the prevalence of CSR as a corporate strategy reflects its sheer impotence as a form of human rights activism at the same time it reaffirms the capacity of capitalism more generally to absorb social critique and transform it into a factor of production.[27]

This capacity has also been documented across the proliferating range of so-called voluntary regimes in which entire industries have banded together to establish CSR guidelines and self-monitoring procedures. In this way, the financializing power of voluntary compliance with human rights standards becomes a broader and more deeply embedded aspect of global capitalism, especially within the resource extraction sector, which depends on a toxic combination of access to (usually nonrenewable) resources, the acquiescence of local political officials, and favorable legal conditions.

In an innovative study of these voluntary regimes, Christelle Genoud conducted empirical research on the ways in which they worked to obscure ongoing business and productive practices that perpetuated resource conflicts and environmental damage. As she argues, these negative impacts are made worse *because of* the presence of CSR as a new corporate value.[28] If corporations can now claim to be socially responsible institutions that regulate their business activities in order to protect human rights, then resource conflicts or environmental degradation that seem to be closely associated with corporate operations must be, at worst, unintended consequences for which multinational corporations bear much less responsibility. This now-pervasive ability to smother critical scrutiny in the languages of human rights and CSR has been a boon not only to multinational corporations, as Genoud's comparative research reveals; it has also proven useful for investors, who view CSR as a powerful new mechanism for mitigating risk to their investments, especially when the underlying company is engaged in land-grabbing.

Genoud studied three voluntary regimes: the Round Table on Sustainable Palm Oil (RSPO); the Voluntary Guidelines on the Responsible Governance of Tenure of Land, Fisheries and Forests (VGGT), which was developed by the UN Food and Agriculture Organization (FAO) in close collaboration with dozens of industry representatives; and the Principles for Responsible Agricultural

Investment that Respect Rights, Livelihoods and Resources (PRAI), another "voluntary and non-binding" FAO initiative developed under the close watch of major multinational corporations and financial institutions. In all three voluntary regimes, Genoud traces an elaborate network of corporate and investor manipulation through which the respective human rights guidelines are used to divert attention away from the ongoing impact of extractive and productive activities, and, even more disturbingly, the actual lines of ownership and control.

For example, within the notoriously destructive palm oil industry, Genoud examines the role of the US commodity trader Cargill, which uses a specialized investment arm called Black River Asset Management to make investments in palm oil properties as part of a global hedging strategy.[29] Yet while Cargill is listed as a "palm oil processor and trader" for purposes of the RSPO's voluntary regime, the role of Black River Asset Management, which is the real source of funding—and therefore of power over palm oil producers in places like Indonesia, Malaysia, and Colombia—is completely omitted. Given the fox-in-the-henhouse nature of the RSPO guidelines—and all the other voluntary guidelines—one must conclude that these sorts of elisions and diversions were the reason the guidelines were developed in the first place, despite the well-meaning human rights rhetoric of institutions like the HRC or the FAO.

If the ill-fated business and human rights movement not surprisingly reveals, yet again, the ways in which economic and political power are increasingly mutually constitutive in our G20 world, what does this mean for a reinvented human rights? If the state-corporate assemblages that form the foundation of capitalism are at the center of our most significant crises, then it would be the height of naivety to imagine that corporations could be reliable allies in the struggle against the economic, environmental, and social problems that are an inevitable consequence of capitalism as a mode of production. Although, as Marina Welker has argued, multinational corporations should not be understood as monolithic entities, organizational "instantiations of *Homo economicus* who know just what they want and how to get it," this approach merely shows that corporations are indeed complex organizations.[30]

What it does not do, however, is change our understanding of the broader political economic context in which corporations—working in collaboration with states, working effectively *as* states, or working beyond the boundaries of state control—dictate the ways and means of contemporary life for reasons that have nothing to do with human flourishing or ecological sustainability. It is critically important, again, not to view the global hegemony of multinational corporations through a simplistic moral lens; if corporations are not "instantiations of *Homo economicus*," neither are they instantiations of socioeconomic malevolence. Indeed, as the engines of global capitalism, a mode of production that has produced inconceivable amounts of wealth in stunningly short periods, corporations are a social invention that merit a certain amount of respect.

Yet as David Harvey has argued, this is a kind of respect that can only come through understanding the true scope of the problem, which he illustrates by following what he calls the "paths of capital circulation."[31] As he shows, these paths come to encompass vast political, economic, labor, and financial spheres in ways that make them both interdependent and inescapable, a condition that he describes as "capital bondage."

These are the concrete interconnections that are interpreted, more ideologically, as capitalist inevitability, the proposition that there is no way out from the political economic singularity of our G20 world. But this is precisely what the proposal for a reinvented human rights calls for: to break the shackles of inevitability, to resist allegiance to existing human rights in the name of naive pragmatism, and to ground a vision of the future in which profit maximization is relegated as the dominant value so that a more radically "ambitious and successful moral program"[32] can be given shape and form.

Surveillance Capitalism and the Biometric Human

Finally, if the fusion of economic and political power creates the most imposing set of obstacles that a reinvented human rights must nevertheless navigate, it is important to recognize that some of the expressions of this power permeate swaths of social and technological life that have very little to do with legal or political norms. On the one hand, these social and technological domains are defined by the materialities of various digital and information infrastructures. And on the other hand, the socio-technological expressions of contemporary political economy are increasingly embodied, that is, filtered through and encoded on human bodies. Given the ways in which the social and technological dimensions of political economic control constitute a paradigmatic example of *biopouvoir*, the limits of existing human rights are brought into even sharper relief. In the face of new technologies that translate political economic imperatives into questions of computing speed, the creation of metadata, and artificial intelligence, among others, what use is a set of legal and political norms that still have the strong odor of the eighteenth century about them?

Even more, the multidimensional proliferation of new technologies is modifying the nature of capitalism. This is not to say that these profound shifts are taking place in similar ways across the entire global political economic landscape. In the same way that it is a mistake to use the category of post-Fordism to analyze forms of capitalist production more generally, since industries in many parts of the world remain dependent on mass production by unskilled workers, so too with the impact on capitalism of the increasing dominance of industries based on the financialization of data, the capacity to predict behavior, and the exploding marketization of "undefended human experience."[33] The economics and social consequences of palm oil production in Indonesia, or cement production in India, or even the manufacture of automobiles (from which the concept of Fordism derives), continue to be defined by classic forces of supply and demand, the cultivation of consumer markets, and, above all, the never-ending quest to maximize surplus value.

However, parallel to the ongoing global reproduction of capitalism based on some combination of both Fordist and post-Fordist principles, something quite different is also taking place. As Shoshana Zuboff has argued, a new form of capitalism is emerging that seeks to transform the logic of existing markets, reorder the relationship of consumers to producers, and, most worryingly, limit the possibilities for collective action against the abuses of what she describes as "surveillance capitalism."[34] Zuboff describes the ambitions of surveillance capitalism in the following way:

> Instead of claiming work (or land, or wealth) for the market dynamic as industrial capitalism once did, surveillance capitalism audaciously lays claim to private experience for translation into fungible commodities that are rapidly swept up into the exhilarating life of the market. Invented at Google and elaborated at Facebook in the online milieu of targeted advertising, surveillance capitalism embodies a new logic of accumulation. Like an invasive species with no natural predators, its financial prowess quickly overwhelmed the networked sphere, grossly disfiguring the earlier dream of digital technology as an empowering and emancipatory force.[35]

Beyond the ways in which surveillance capitalism is reshaping political economic and social relations within core G20 economies based on data practices that are themselves global, this "exhilarating" shift has also been remarkably profitable. As Zuboff explains, Google and Facebook rapidly reached the heights of market capitalization after only several years, even though they employed relatively few workers in relation to the scale of their corporate value. By contrast, "General Motors took four decades to reach its highest market capitalization of $225.15 billion in 1965, when it employed 735,000 women and men. Most startling is that GM employed more people during the Great Depression than either Google or Facebook employs at their heights of market capitalization."[36]

According to Zuboff, these discontinuities in the comparative history of capitalism reflect the fact that surveillance capitalism is flourishing because of what she calls the "absence of consumer reciprocities [and] the absence of employment reciprocities," a rupture in capitalist space-time in which a "small, highly educated workforce leverages the power of a massive capital-intensive knowledge-production infrastructure."[37] Even more, this "knowledge-production infrastructure" has become embedded in the very fabric of everyday life, both within and beyond the wealthiest G20 countries. As she puts it, "Google's Home and Amazon's Alexa are frontier examples. Disguised as engines of 'personalization,' digital assistants operate as complex supply chains for continuous automatic extraction of behavioral surplus from human experience, its predictive value ultimately realized in markets for future behavior."

From the perspective of surveillance capitalism, the consumers whose behavior feeds the explosive market capitalizations that characterize the Digital Age are also the system's main producers, thereby further twisting this mutated form of capitalism into something whose long-term consequences are difficult to predict, which is ironic given that predictability forms the basis for these new digital supply chains.

Even so, what worries Zuboff about the more subtle transformations of surveillance capitalism is also what creates an immediate dilemma for a reinvented human rights: the fact that the possibilities for social action are being diminished as individual lives become data points in a vast process of "experiential dispossession,"[38] in which people are being refashioned—and, perhaps more troubling, refashioning themselves—into "users" who are ever more dependent on virtual lives constructed within what are actually *anti*-social networks.

If "industrial civilization flourished at the expense of nature and threatens to cost us the earth," the rise of surveillance capitalism and its digital dislocations threaten the human capabilities necessary to resist such an ecological crisis, "especially the hard-won capacities associated with self-determination and moral autonomy."[39] Without characterizing the forms that resistance to the transformations of surveillance capitalism must take, Zuboff argues that such resistance will necessarily "define a key battleground on which the next generation of collective action will be contested at the new frontier of power."[40]

If surveillance capitalism indeed marks a new frontier of power within our G20 world, a frontier at which the mobilizations inspired by a reinvented human rights must in part be concentrated, another site of contestation will be the human body itself, which has become its own "key battleground" in the struggle over data, identity, and autonomy. Biometrics are a range of technologies and statistical approaches that generate information about people that is of a highly unusual type, particularly in the way that biometrics are supposed to elicit data that cannot be modified, except under equally unusual circumstances (like eye or throat surgery that is undertaken explicitly to defeat biometric identification). As one scholar who studies the intersections between biometrics and human rights explains, they are data about

> unique and individual physical characteristics that differ from one human being to the next and that remain unaltered for life (e.g., DNA samples, fingerprint images, pictures of the iris or the retina and voice-recording). Biometric data are very reliable means of authentication because they allow one to prove a very strong connection between an individual and his alleged identity through the verification of an individual's unique physical . . . data.[41]

Even more, what makes biometric data so valuable in the information marketplace is the fact that they are very difficult to manipulate. This is important because verified identification has become a commodified process, one that drives many other aspects of economic, social, and political life. As Paul De Hert puts it, "in comparison with other means of authentication, such as badges or passwords, biometric data reduce the chance of abuse because they cannot be transferred to third parties."[42]

The increasing importance of biometrics creates any number of problems for existing human rights protections, according to De Hert. These are primarily associated with "covert data capture, lack of transparency and [the absence of] consent."[43] More troubling still is the way in which "second generation" biometric technologies are being developed that create greater distances between the technologies themselves and the individuals whose identities are being captured. Sophisticated sensor technologies are being installed in public and private spaces around the world that can identity people and track and trace them surreptitiously without losing any precision in the authentication process. In relation to the fusion of economic and political power in our G20 world, it is critical to recognize that these advanced biometrics are being used both to better predict consumer behavior and to monitor social and political action as a tool of governance.

However, although scholars like De Hert focus on the legal and regulatory responses to the proliferation of biometric authentication, my concern here is somewhat different. As I have argued at different places (especially in chapters 6 and 7), a reinvented human rights must be based on a conception of the human that breaks free from a particular genealogy, one in which the human subject was invested with a set of specific—and therefore exclusionary—moral, religious, and civic values.

But in imagining what it would mean to reconceive of the "human" in a *reinvented* human rights as a signifier of an alternative logic of translocal action, or as a metaphor that conveys a new sense of shared identity, it is important to remember that this future formulation will clash not only with the image of the "unfindable" civic-bourgeois subject at the heart of the postwar human rights project.[44]

As debates over the implications of biometric technologies reveal, yet another conception of the human is central to monitoring, authentication, and surveillance economies, a conception that might be considered the "biometric human." From this perspective, the body plays a key role in generating information for which there are rapidly expanding markets and for providing the data points on which the underlying biometric technologies learn, adapt, and become more sophisticated. The hyper-embodied nature of biometrics was something that preoccupied the Dutch ethicist and philosopher of science Irma van der Ploeg from the early years, when biometrics were being adapted into an essential instrument for economic and political control, especially in relation to immigration.[45]

Ploeg draws a distinction between the much more accepted and well-established ways in which the body is "knowable" within biomedicine and the much more ambiguous ways in which the body is "readable" within biometrics. As she puts it, biometrics "transforms the body's surfaces and characteristics into digital codes and ciphers to be 'read' by a machine. . . . Thus transformed into readable 'text,' the meaning and significance of the biometric body [are] contingent upon 'context,' and the relations established with other 'texts.'"[46]

Moreover, the biometric human is not one that can be easily "read" by other humans—whether conceived biometrically or not. As Ploeg argues, the biometric body is only "readable by the appropriate equipment rather than by human beings, but in a world increasingly populated and policed by sensing, knowing, and remembering . . . computers, it matters not that much that biometric inscriptions on the body are invisible to the human eye."[47] More provocative still is the question of whether or not the prevalence of biometrics in our daily lives is rendering people more sensitive and even willing to being read in these ways, that is, to ensuring that we make our "machine-readable bodies" available for analysis and processing in a widening range of social and institutional settings.[48]

Given the fact that the long-term implications of the biometric revolution are difficult to assess, especially when certain applications—such as contact tracing during the global COVID-19 pandemic—don't immediately conjure nightmarish scenarios of bodily control drawn straight from science fiction, it is equally difficult to locate these transformations in relation to a reinvented human rights. Yet there is no question that our G20 world is increasingly characterized by networks of surveillance capitalism that depend on citizen-consumers who themselves—through their bodies—constitute a new form of capital, a form, moreover, that can be deployed for a variety of security, political, and even ideological purposes in ways that will make emancipatory collective action that much more difficult to organize and sustain.

Conclusion: Mobilizing for Repossession through Human Rights

As the Age of Human Rights was overturned by a period of violent transition marked by the imperatives of national and global security on the one hand, and, on the other, by the ongoing consolidation of neoliberal and developmental capitalism (the latter under the sign of the "Washington Consensus"), the economic geographer David Harvey took stock of the emerging realignments that would soon culminate in the historic fusion of global economic and political power.[49]

Writing five years before the 2008 turning point, in which the pretensions of the postwar international order were finally made redundant through the unabashed re-creation of the G20, Harvey narrowed on the most significant aspect of the intensifying political economic world order: its reliance on dispossession. As he argues, dispossession is the driving engine and most corroding long-term consequence of capitalism, well beyond questions of commodity exchange or the exploitation of labor. On the contrary, dispossession has become the most pervasive feature of a world marked by historical economic growth and the unequal creation and distribution of wealth at unimaginable scales. Harvey locates the permutations and forms of dispossession in most areas of economic, political, and social life. As he explains:

> The escalating depletion of the global environmental commons . . . and proliferating habitat degradations that preclude anything but capital-intensive modes of agricultural production have likewise resulted from the wholesale commodification

of nature in all its forms. The commodification of cultural forms, histories, and intellectual creativity likewise entails wholesale dispossessions. . . . The corporatization and privatization of hitherto public assets (such as universities) . . . indicate a new wave of "enclosing the commons." As in the past, the state is frequently used to force such processes through even against popular will. The rolling back of regulatory frameworks designed to protect labor and the environment from degradation [is also a form of dispossession]. The reversion of common property rights won through years of hard class struggle (the right to a state pension, to welfare, to national health care) to the private domain has been one of the most egregious of all policies of dispossession.[50]

Moreover, as we have seen, in the years after the "new imperialism" of the G20 became the dominant political economic logic of our time, the imperatives of dispossession were extended beyond what Harvey could have imagined even as late as 2003. The rise of surveillance capitalism and the rapid diffusion of biometric technologies have brought the workings of dispossession into the most intimate spaces of individual identity, self-control, and even consciousness. As Zuboff has emphasized, what makes dispossession of these most personal of capacities so dangerous is that it makes the possibility of classic forms of resistance—what Harvey calls "hard class struggle"—that much more difficult to realize.

From this perspective, dispossession must be understood as something like the vast negative space that is the inevitable counterpart to the positive space of capitalist accumulation. Viewing our G20 world—in all of its forms—as one based on the production of dispossession, rather than wealth, clarifies the stakes and underscores just how daunting it will be to envision a counter-response that is equal to the task. Indeed, even Harvey seemed ready to raise the white flag, to capitulate to the inevitability of a world in which capitalist accumulation and widespread dispossession constituted the dialectical bedrock of a postinternational global order. As he puts it, we must

> rise above nostalgia for that which has been lost and likewise be prepared to recognize the positive gains to be had from . . . discriminat[ing] between progressive and regressive aspects of accumulation by dispossession and seek to guide the former toward a more generalized political goal that has more universal valency than the many local movements, which often refuse to abandon their own particularity.[51]

Yet leaving aside an appreciation for just how bleak the future must have looked for Harvey to have settled on the "progressive" aspects of dispossession as the foundation for a *variation on*—not alternative to—capitalist hegemony, my argument is that our collective and varied counter-responses to the dispossessions of the G20 synthesis must go much further. In giving shape and form to the objectives toward which a reinvented human rights must be directed, objectives that might very well be seen to have "universal valency," the more transformative place to begin is with the opposite of dispossession, that is, with *repossession*. In other words, if the political economic logic of our G20 world—one whose consequences are at the root of most of our contemporary crises, from climate change to systemic socioeconomic inequality—is a logic of dispossession, then our responses to this condition must seek to recover what has been lost and to undermine the forces of dispossession going forward.

This, then, is the ultimate meaning of a reinvented human rights, its widest vantage point. It is an argument for meeting the bold fusion of economic and political power in our G20 world on its own terms, with an equally bold reformulation of a much older framework. As a movement of *repossession*, the collective mobilizations inspired by a reinvented human rights must demand the return of all that has been, and is being, dispossessed, taken away, denied: the "environmental commons"; "cultural forms, histories, and intellectual creativity"; public goods of all kinds; labor power; social wealth; our identities; and our bodies.

Acknowledgments

This book is the culmination of many factors, including the support of students, colleagues, and institutions; the opportunity over a number of years to present different ideas that coalesced into the proposal to reinvent human rights to a wide and diverse range of audiences; and the space to reflect on the future of human rights over the intellectual *longue durée*, amid other research projects, professional and teaching obligations, and, as always, an ever-present commitment to my family.

To begin, I must acknowledge the generous support I receive from different entities at the University of Lausanne, including the Faculty of Social and Political Sciences, the Institute of Social Sciences, and the Laboratory of Cultural and Social Anthropology (LACS), for which I served as director for much of the time spent conducting research and writing. The University of Lausanne has been my institutional home since 2014, and it has been a privilege to work in such a congenial and *solidaire* academic environment, one, moreover, that has been deeply connected to the public life and history of the region since 1537.

I was fortunate to have two excellent research assistants over the years, whose bibliographic detective work and editorial suggestions proved crucial to the final foundation: Alice Welland and Hanna Josefine Berg.

Many of the concepts in the book were first mooted during lectures and discussions in my regular graduate seminar at the University of Lausanne titled "Human Rights and Social Change: Anthropological Perspectives." I thank the dozens of former students in the seminar for their insight and participation and acknowledge the important role played by my colleague Dr. Mina Rauschenbach, a social psychologist and expert on transitional justice and collective memory, with whom I cotaught the seminar between 2016 and 2020.

During the period (2015–18) in which I was finalizing research for what became *Letters to the Contrary: A Curated History of the UNESCO Human Rights Survey*, whose findings figure prominently at different places in the current book and in my thinking more generally about the past and future of human rights, I was lucky to have been invited to be a member of an innovative network of human rights historians, funded by the Leverhulme Trust. I express my deepest gratitude to these colleagues for bringing an anthropologist into the historical fold, where I was able to see the importance of regarding human rights through what I would later describe as a "period eye." I participated in meetings of the Leverhulme network at the University of Warwick, Sciences Po Paris, the Paris Institute for Advanced Studies, Harvard Law School, and, finally, the University of Lausanne. Particular thanks and appreciation are owed to Christian Christiansen, Nicolas Delalande, Philip Kaisary, Steven Jensen, Sam Moyn, Paul-André Rosental, Stephen Sawyer, Claudia Stein, and Charles Walton.

I am enormously grateful to have been invited to give presentations on various parts of the proposal to reinvent human rights in a number of different academic and nonacademic settings over the years, most notably the following: New York University School of Law (November 2019); National University of Singapore (Centre for Legal Theory, College of Law, October 2019); Yale-NUS College, Singapore (Department of Sociology and Anthropology, October 2019); Australian National University (Centre for Law, Arts and the Humanities, College of Law, August 2019); University of Geneva (Centre for Children's Rights Studies, May 2019); Graduate Institute of International and Development Studies (Department of Anthropology and Sociology and the Global Health Center, February 2019); UNESCO Headquarters (Section for Intercultural Dialogue, Division of Social and Human Sciences, September 2018); Royal Irish Academy (June 2017); Utrecht University (Netherlands Institute of Human Rights and the Montaigne Centre for Judicial Administration and Conflict Resolution, April 2017); The Hebrew University of Jerusalem (Minerva Center for Human Rights, Faculty of Law, January 2017); University of Michigan Law School (October 2016); and the Venice Academy of Human Rights (European Inter-University Centre for Human Rights and Democratization, July 2016).

Special mention must be made of two events in particular, during which the book project was presented and discussed in a nearly complete form. The first was a talk cosponsored by the Australian Human Rights Institute, the University of New South Wales, and the University of Sydney, in August 2019. It is a pleasure to recognize the generosity of the hosting collective in Sydney:

Danielle Celermajer, Ben Golder, Alexandre Lefebvre, Claudia Tazreiter, and Jessica Whyte. The second event took place at the end of February 2020, with the specter of the global COVID-19 pandemic looming just in the distance. I warmly thank Steven Jensen, Stéphanie Lagoutte, and Hans-Otto Sano for welcoming me to the Danish Institute for Human Rights in Copenhagen for a critical workshop on the book's themes.

The editorial and production teams at Stanford University Press were, as always, a joy to work with during the different phases of publication. I want to acknowledge the singular importance of Michelle Lipinski, who believed in the project from the beginning and then followed it supportively right up to the moment in which she decided to move to another university press. From then on, editorial responsibility was taken over by Kate Wahl, who provided incomparable feedback while also serving as editor-in-chief and publishing director of the press. Among other things, Kate convinced me of the wisdom in making some final structural changes, which greatly improved the manuscript.

Saving the most important for last, I acknowledge the love and support I receive from my family: my son Isaiah and my daughter Dara, my raisons d'être; and my wife Romana, who inspires me every day with her poetry, her capacity for what she describes as "simple hearing," and her strength. *Te iubesc, minunea mea, viața mea.*

The book is formally dedicated to the memory of Sally Engle Merry, who passed away in September 2020. Sally was a highly influential anthropologist whose research and writing underscored the importance of putting the cross-cultural practice of human rights at the center of theory and policy making. She was also a key mentor to me and close friend for over twenty years, a scholar whose generosity of spirit touched many people around the world. Hers was an academic career in full—widely lauded, moving steadily and creatively forward for over four decades, and filled to the brim with what Einstein (adapting Spinoza) described as "intellectual love."

Notes

Chapter 1

1. Ai Weiwei, "Human Dignity Is in Danger," *The Guardian* (January 1, 2019), www.theguardian.com/commentisfree/2019/jan/01/human-dignity-danger-ai-weiwei. Subsequent quotes in this section are taken from this article.

2. Kofi Annan, "The Age of Human Rights," *Project Syndicate*, 2000, www.project syndicate.org/commentary/the-age-of-human-rights?barrier=true. Although Annan doesn't say so explicitly, his invocation of the Age of Human Rights finds echoes in the well-known study by Louis Henkin, published ten years earlier, that examined, in particular, US foreign policy within what he described as an "Age of Rights." Louis Henkin, *The Age of Rights* (New York: Columbia University Press, 1990).

3. Saskia Sassen, *Expulsions: Brutality and Complexity in the Global Economy* (Cambridge, MA: Belknap Press of Harvard University Press, 2014).

4. See, e.g., Rhoda E. Howard-Hassmann, *In Defense of Universal Human Rights* (Cambridge: Polity, 2018).

5. A signal example of this much more common form of quietism in human rights scholarship is the proposal by Hurst Hannum to "rescue" existing international human rights by returning to a less complicated approach through which human rights are reduced to a particular category of binding legal obligations. Hurst Hannum, *Rescuing Human Rights: A Radically Moderate Approach* (Cambridge: Cambridge University Press, 2019).

6. Erik Olin Wright, *Envisioning Real Utopias* (London: Verso, 2010).

7. Lynn Hunt, *Inventing Human Rights: A History* (New York: W. W. Norton, 2007).

8. For a fascinating alternative history of the invention of the "human" in human rights that can be read as a companion to *Inventing Human Rights*, see Surekha Davies's study of "maps and monsters" during the European Renaissance. Her research suggests that the "man" who would appear several centuries later in the "rights of man" was largely invented by Renaissance cartographers as a means of coming to terms with the ontological dislocations of early colonialism. Surekha Davies, *Renaissance Ethnography and the Invention of the Human: New Worlds, Maps and Monsters* (Cambridge: Cambridge University Press, 2016).

9. Jack Donnelly, "Human Rights as Natural Rights," *Human Rights Quarterly* 4, no. 3 (1982): 391–405, 391 (emphasis in original).

10. In this regard, it is worth noting the reaction of Morris L. Ernst, the American civil rights lawyer and one of the founders of the American Civil Liberties Union (ACLU), to the proposal to draft a declaration of human rights as the basis for the postwar settlement. In an April 1947 letter to Richard McKeon of the University of Chicago, who was also working at the time for UNESCO, Ernst writes that, "it seems to me that we are finished with the era of passing general resolutions in regard to liberty and freedom. I am not opposed to the creation of new, neatly worded symbols for man to use as goals. But the continued yapping . . . for the free flow of thought seems to me at this time to be doing little more than creating cynicism." Quoted in Mark Goodale, ed., *Letters to the Contrary: A Curated History of the UNESCO Human Rights Survey* (Stanford, CA: Stanford University Press, 2018), 298–99.

11. There are many examples that could be given for this strand of what might be called human rights disenchantment, but an exemplary case is that of Stephen Hopgood, the British scholar who conducted a long-term sociological study of Amnesty International. Stephen Hopgood, *Keepers of the Flame: Understanding Amnesty International* (Ithaca, NY: Cornell University Press, 2006). Despite obviously sharing many of the same goals as Amnesty International—he begins his study with a "shocking" account of torture in Chile that he describes as the "very essence of human misery"—Hopgood later turned decisively against the international human rights system, which he accused of promoting a form of moral imperialism under the guise of global human rights activism. Stephen Hopgood, *The Endtimes of Human Rights* (Ithaca, NY: Cornell University Press, 2013). *The Endtimes of Human Rights* understandably provoked a strong reaction, not the least from major global human rights actors like Amnesty. Nevertheless, after reflecting on the different responses to his apocalyptic vision, Hopgood reaffirmed his position that since human rights were "on the road to nowhere," the time had come to definitively abandon what he viewed as an obsolete "global brand." See Hopgood, "Human Rights on the Road to Nowhere," in *Human Rights Futures*, ed. J. Snyder, L. Vinjamuri, and S. Hopgood (Cambridge: Cambridge University Press, 2017), 283–310.

12. See, e.g., the robust intervention by the prominent human rights scholar and political scientist Kathryn Sikkink, who dismisses much contemporary criticism of human rights as a kind of social contagion that is disconnected from the realities of human rights implementation and enforcement around the world. Kathryn Sikkink, *Evidence for Hope: Making Human Rights Work in the 21st Century* (Princeton, NJ: Princeton University Press, 2017). For Sikkink, what is most important is to continue the struggle for international human rights without becoming complacent or giving in to despair, guided always by "patience and the knowledge that human rights and democracy are won by means of long, drawn-out effort" (245).

13. For other efforts to forge a middle path between disenchantment and defiance, albeit grounded in approaches quite different from the one taken here, see Alison Brysk, *The Future of Human Rights* (Cambridge: Polity, 2018); and Alicia Ely Yamin, *When*

Misfortune Becomes Injustice: Evolving Human Rights Struggles for Health and Social Equality (Stanford, CA: Stanford University Press, 2020).

14. The practice of human rights is an ethnographic category developed by anthropologists to organize the proliferation of cross-cultural research on the legal, political, and discursive realities of human rights. See Mark Goodale and Sally Engle Merry, eds., *The Practice of Human Rights: Tracking Law between the Global and the Local* (Cambridge: Cambridge University Press, 2007). "Practice dependency," by contrast, is a way that philosophers of human rights draw a distinction between *theories* that take account—even if largely in the abstract—of historical, cultural, social, or institutional contexts and those that don't, which are described as "practice-independent" theories. For work in political philosophy that is particularly congruent with the orientation to the practice of human rights developed throughout this book, see the writings of Charles Beitz, for example, *The Idea of Human Rights* (Oxford: Oxford University Press, 2009).

15. Howard Zinn, *A People's History of the United States* (New York: Harper and Row, 1980).

16. Margaret Keck and Kathryn Sikkink, *Activists beyond Borders: Advocacy Networks in International Politics* (Ithaca, NY: Cornell University Press, 1998).

17. The political version of this critique was most prominently represented by the so-called Asian Values Debate, in which leaders from different East and Southeast Asian countries took turns denouncing criticism of their human rights records by a range of state and nongovernmental actors from the "West." See, e.g., Bilahari Kausikan, "Asia's Different Standard," *Foreign Affairs* (June 1993): 24–41; Kausikan, "An East Asian Approach to Human Rights," *Buffalo Journal of International Law* 2, no. 2 (1995): 263–83. The academic version was associated primarily with postcolonial scholars. See, e.g., Makau Mutua, "Savages, Victims, and Saviors: The Metaphor of Human Rights," *Harvard International Law Journal* 42, no. 1 (2001): 201–45; and Antony Anghie, *Imperialism, Sovereignty and the Making of International Law* (Cambridge: Cambridge University Press, 2005).

18. Important works in this pro-universalist campaign include Paul Lauren Gordon, *The Evolution of International Human Rights: Visions Seen* (Philadelphia: University of Pennsylvania Press, 1998); Johannes Morsink, *The Universal Declaration of Human Rights: Origins, Drafting, Intent* (Philadelphia: University of Pennsylvania Press, 1999); and especially Mary Ann Glendon, *A World Made New: Eleanor Roosevelt and the Universal Declaration of Human Rights* (New York: Random House, 2001).

19. UNESCO, *Human Rights: Comments and Interpretations* (London: Allan Wingate, 1949).

20. For the full documentary history of the UNESCO human rights survey, which includes extensive interpretation and editorial annotations, see Goodale, *Letters to the Contrary.*

21. See Steven L. B. Jensen, *The Making of International Human Rights: The 1960s, Decolonization, and the Reconstruction of Global Values* (Cambridge: Cambridge University Press, 2016); see also Roland Burke, *Decolonization and the Evolution of International Human Rights* (Philadelphia: University of Pennsylvania Press, 2010).

22. Robert Hayden, "Constitutional Nationalism in the Formerly Yugoslav Republics," *Slavic Review* 51, no. 4 (1992): 654–73; Sarah E. Holcombe, *Remote Freedoms: Politics, Personhood, and Human Rights in Aboriginal Central Australia* (Stanford, CA: Stanford University Press, 2018).

23. A well-known example of such an organic reformulation took place during and after the Zapatista uprising against the Mexican state in the mid-1990s. As documented by Shannon Speed, Indigenous communities in Chiapas reimagined human rights as a logic of collective social action in which "human rights" only existed "in their exercise" and only when they proved useful in "improving the path of resistance." As Speed explains, these organic reformulations "challeng[ed] not only . . . the state, but also [the] liberal and neoliberal conceptualizations of rights and their relationship to the law." Shannon Speed, *Rights in Rebellion: Indigenous Struggle and Human Rights in Chiapas* (Stanford, CA: Stanford University Press, 2008), 156–57.

24. Mark Goodale, "The Power of Right(s): Tracking Empires of Law and New Modes of Social Resistance in Bolivia (and Elsewhere)," in Goodale and Merry, *Practice of Human Rights*, 130–62.

25. Samuel Moyn, *Not Enough: Human Rights in an Unequal World* (Cambridge, MA: Belknap Press of Harvard University Press, 2018).

26. Moyn, *Not Enough*, 220. Jessica Whyte has made a powerful case that the relationship between human rights and neoliberalism is much more closely correlated, that human rights are the source for what she calls the "morals of the market." Jessica Whyte, *The Morals of the Market: Human Rights and the Rise of Neoliberalism* (London: Verso, 2019).

27. Sassen, *Expulsions*.

28. For a remarkable study of the relationship between human rights and data technologies, see Ronald Niezen, *#Human Rights: The Technologies and Politics of Justice Claims in Practice* (Stanford, CA: Stanford University Press, 2020).

29. Moyn, *Not Enough*, 220.

30. See, e.g., Eric Hobsbawm, *The Age of Capital: 1848–1875* (1975; London: Abacus, 2004).

31. Quoted in Hobsbawm, *Age of Capital*, 103.

32. Charter of the United Nations, Article 1, "Purposes and Principles."

33. It is an intriguing historical coincidence that the United States became the world's leading economic power, measured by gross domestic product, in the year 1871 (passing Great Britain), a status it has maintained ever since.

34. Nancy Fraser, "From Redistribution to Recognition? Dilemmas of Justice in a 'Post-Socialist' Age," *New Left Review* 212 (July/August 1995): 68–93.

35. Although there is a debate about the origin of the slogan "We are the 99%," various sources attribute it to Graeber and a small group of anarchists in New York who established what they called the "New York City General Assembly." Jeff Sharlet, "Inside Occupy Wall Street," *Rolling Stone*, November 24, 2011, www.rollingstone.com/politics/politics-news/inside-occupy-wall-street-236993/.

36. Axel Honneth, *The Struggle for Recognition: The Moral Grammar of Social Conflicts* (Cambridge, MA: MIT Press, 1996).

37. Pheng Cheah and Bruce Robbins, *Cosmopolitics: Thinking and Feeling beyond the Nation* (Minneapolis: University of Minnesota Press, 1998).

38. This is a line from Dr. King's "I Have a Dream" speech of August 29, 1963, delivered on the steps of the Lincoln Memorial in Washington, DC, during an iconic event in the US civil rights movement that was significantly called the "March on Washington *for Jobs* and Freedom" (emphasis mine).

Chapter 2

1. Julian Huxley, *UNESCO: Its Purposes and Its Philosophy* (London: Preparatory Commission of the United Nations Educational, Scientific, and Cultural Organization, 1946), 61, 41.

2. This introductory section draws from Mark Goodale, ed., *Letters to the Contrary: A Curated History of the UNESCO Human Rights Survey* (Stanford, CA: Stanford University Press, 2018).

3. Quoted in Goodale, *Letters to the Contrary*, 286.

4. Quoted in Goodale, *Letters to the Contrary*, 109.

5. Quoted in Goodale, *Letters to the Contrary*, 110.

6. Quoted in Goodale, *Letters to the Contrary*, 112. Lewis explains that "'natural rights,' while they have the appearance of being general and absolute, are really particular (defending or asserting concrete needs) and strictly relative to the occasion. They are not general rights appertaining to man as such, under all conditions and for all time." Quoted in Goodale, *Letters to the Contrary*, 113. By contrast, see the widely cited definition given by Jack Donnelly (in the late twentieth century, no less), in which human rights are conceived as "*natural rights*: namely, rights (entitlements) held simply by virtue of being a person (human being). Such rights are natural in the sense that their source is human nature." Jack Donnelly, "Human Rights as Natural Rights," *Human Rights Quarterly* 4, no. 3 (1982): 391–405, 391 (emphasis in original).

7. Quoted in Goodale, *Letters to the Contrary*, 113.

8. Quoted in Goodale, *Letters to the Contrary*, 113.

9. Quoted in Goodale, *Letters to the Contrary*, 115.

10. Note that the Virginia Declaration of Rights, which preceded and influenced both the 1776 US Declaration of Independence and the 1789 US Bill of Rights, establishes the right of "acquiring and possessing property" as one of the three foundational natural and inherent human rights (the other two being "the enjoyment of life and liberty" and the pursuit of "happiness and safety").

11. Quoted in Goodale, *Letters to the Contrary*, 115.

12. Presaging the crisis over anti-Semitism in the British Labour Party in the aftermath of Jeremy Corbyn's catastrophic defeat in the 2019 national elections in the United Kingdom, Levy was expelled from the British Community Party in 1958 after criticizing the persecution of Jewish intellectuals in the Soviet Union in his 1957 book *Jews and the National Question*.

13. Quoted in Goodale, *Letters to the Contrary*, 168–69.

14. Quoted in Goodale, *Letters to the Contrary*, 176.

15. Dobb was a professor of economics at Cambridge University and one of the leading Marxist economists of the twentieth century. His tenure at Cambridge was both famous (or, depending on the position, infamous) and shrouded in a certain amount of intrigue. Dobb founded the Communist Party Historians Group with E. P. Thompson and Christopher Hill (author of the 1972 *The World Turned Upside Down*, a Marxist reinterpretation of the English Civil War) and taught a long line of students who would go on to influential careers, including Amartya Sen, Eric Hobsbawm, and Kim Philby, who would later become a Soviet double agent within British intelligence.

16. Quoted in Goodale, *Letters to the Contrary*, 177.

17. Quoted in Goodale, *Letters to the Contrary*, 177.

18. Quoted in Goodale, *Letters to the Contrary*, 177.

19. Indeed, Friedmann had just published his Marxism-inflected study of the relationship between labor, automation, and industrial management, which launched the French "sociology of work" and also reinforced the anticapitalist preoccupations of French sociology more generally. Georges Friedmann, *Problèmes humains du machinisme industriel* (Paris: Gallimard, 1946).

20. Quoted in Goodale, *Letters to the Contrary*, 126.

21. See Tim Andrew Obermiller, "Will the Real Richard McKeon Please Stand Up?," *University of Chicago Magazine* (December 1994), http://magazine.uchicago.edu/9412/Feat4.html.

22. UNESCO Archives, AG 8 Secretariat Records, Central Registry Collection, file Human Rights—Enquiry, document UNESCO/Phil/9/1947.

23. Goodale, *Letters to the Contrary*, 84–85. The "tyranny of the masses" is the phrase used by Charles Malik, the strongly anticommunist Lebanese philosopher and member of the UN CHR, who opposed the consideration of Marxist and socialist ideas during the UDHR drafting process.

24. UNESCO Archives, AG 8 Secretariat Records, Central Registry Collection, file Human Rights—Enquiry, Letter from Carr to Huxley, September 29, 1947.

25. Francis Fukuyama, *The End of History and the Last Man* (New York: Free Press, 1992).

26. Samuel Moyn, *Not Enough: Human Rights in an Unequal World* (Cambridge, MA: Belknap Press of Harvard University Press, 2018), xii.

27. Moyn, *Not Enough*, 218.

28. Moyn, *Not Enough*, 218.

29. Thomas Piketty, *Capital in the Twenty-First Century* (Cambridge, MA: Belknap Press of Harvard University Press, 2014), 9.

30. Piketty, *Capital in the Twenty-First Century*, 9.

31. Piketty, *Capital in the Twenty-First Century*, 10.

32. In his quasi-ethnographic reflection on his two years spent as a young apprentice at a paper mill in Manchester, *The Condition of the Working Class in England in 1844*, Friedrich Engels memorably captured the extent of this political economic toxicity: "Everywhere heaps of *débris*, refuse, and offal; standing pools for gutters, and a stench which alone would make it impossible for a human being in any degree

civilised to live in such a district. . . . Everything which here arouses horror and indignation is of recent origin, belongs to the *industrial epoch* . . . the industrial epoch alone enables the owners of these [tenements] to rent them for high prices to human beings, to plunder the poverty of the workers, to undermine the health of thousands, in order that they *alone*, the owners, may grow rich." Quoted in Robert C. Tucker, ed., *The Marx-Engels Reader*, 2nd ed. (New York: W. W. Norton, 1978), 582, 584 (emphases in original).

33. As Guy Standing, a leading historian of the ILO (and himself a former ILO economist) explains, the organization was founded as a "means of locking in the international division of labor . . . to the advantage of the affluent capitalist countries." Guy Standing, "The ILO: An Agency for Globalization?," *Development and Change* 39, no. 3 (2008): 355–84, 357. Another ILO historian, Donald Richards, is even blunter. As he puts it, the ILO exists in order to ensure the stability of what he describes as the "global capitalist state." Donald Richards, *Intellectual Property Rights and Global Capitalism: The Political Economy of the TRIPS Agreement* (Armonk, NY: M. E. Sharpe, 2004), 105.

34. Piketty, *Capital in the Twenty-First Century*, 10.

35. "The Dictatorship of the Proletariat," in *The Lenin Anthology*, ed. Robert C. Tucker (New York: W. W. Norton, 1975), 489–91.

36. On the rhetorical categories of the Cambodian genocide, see Alexander Laban Hinton, *Man or Monster? The Trial of a Khmer Rouge Torturer* (Durham, NC: Duke University Press, 2016).

37. Piketty, *Capital in the Twenty-First Century*, 571–72.

38. Piketty, *Capital in the Twenty-First Century*, 571.

39. Piketty, *Capital in the Twenty-First Century*, 571.

40. Piketty, *Capital in the Twenty-First Century*, 572–73.

41. David Graeber, "Savage Capitalism Is Back—and It Will Not Tame Itself," *The Guardian*, May 30, 2014, www.theguardian.com/commentisfree/2014/may/30/savage-capitalism-back-radical-challenge. Likely as a response to criticism such as this, Piketty followed up *Capital in the Twenty-First Century* with a sequel in which he develops the alternatives to what he now calls "hypercapitalism" in much more detail. These more ambitious proposals include the promotion of a form of democratic socialism he calls "participatory" socialism, support for social property regimes, and the development of international systems and laws to require the sharing of knowledge, especially technological knowledge. Thomas Piketty, *Capital and Ideology* (Cambridge, MA: Belknap Press of Harvard University Press, 2020).

42. Christopher Ingraham, "Wealth Concentration Returning to 'Levels Last Seen during the Roaring Twenties,' according to New Research," *Washington Post*, February, 2019, www.washingtonpost.com/us-policy/2019/02/08.

43. See Piketty, *Capital and Ideology*.

44. A classic statement of this moral justification for capitalism is Friedrich Hayek, *The Road to Serfdom* (Chicago: University of Chicago Press, 1944).

45. Jessica Whyte, *The Morals of the Market: Human Rights and the Rise of Neoliberalism* (London: Verso, 2019).

46. Karl Marx, "On the Jewish Question," in *The Marx-Engels Reader*, 2nd ed., ed. Robert C. Tucker (New York: W. W. Norton, 1978).

47. Marx, "On the Jewish Question," 42 (emphasis in original).

48. Marx, "On the Jewish Question," 43, 46 (emphasis in original).

49. For a granular history of the drafting of the UDHR, including the struggles by countries and blocs of countries to ensure the inclusion of economic and social rights, see Johannes Morsink, *The Universal Declaration of Human Rights: Origins, Drafting, Intent* (Philadelphia: University of Pennsylvania Press, 1999).

50. Christopher N. J. Roberts, *The Contentious History of the International Bill of Human Rights* (Cambridge: Cambridge University Press, 2015).

51. Roberts, *Contentious History of the International Bill of Human Rights*, 210.

52. Roberts, *Contentious History of the International Bill of Human Rights*, 196.

53. Roberts, *Contentious History of the International Bill of Human Rights*, 196.

54. Roberts, *Contentious History of the International Bill of Human Rights*, 209–10.

55. Roberts, *Contentious History of the International Bill of Human Rights*, 210.

56. Roberts, *Contentious History of the International Bill of Human Rights*, 223.

57. See, e.g., Steven L. B. Jensen, *The Making of International Human Rights: The 1960s, Decolonization, and the Reconstruction of Global Values* (Cambridge: Cambridge University Press, 2016). I return to the question of the relationship between decolonization and human rights (existing and future) in chapter 5.

58. The full extent of the tragedy of economic and social rights was powerfully expressed in the final report issued to the UN Human Rights Council in July 2020 by the outgoing UN Special Rapporteur on Extreme Poverty and Human Rights, Philip Alston. Alston, an international lawyer and law professor whose five years in office were marked by a singular, even heroic, effort to advance the cause of economic and social rights around the world, concluded that the human rights system was failing, that "extreme poverty" was being ignored by "governments, economists, and human rights advocates," who could only focus on "a standard of miserable subsistence." Echoing Piketty's reminder that economic systems are not inevitable or inherent in the nature of things, Alston puts it quite clearly: "Poverty is a political choice." Philip Alston, "The Parlous State of Poverty Eradication," report presented to the Human Rights Council, June 1, 2020, https://chrgj.org/wp-content/uploads/2020/07/Alston-Poverty-Report-FINAL.pdf.

59. Evan Osnos, *Age of Ambition: Chasing Fortune, Faith, and Truth in the New China* (New York: Farrar, Straus, and Giroux, 2014). Osnos, who was the China correspondent for the *New Yorker* from 2008 to 2013, won the 2014 National Book Award in nonfiction for *Age of Ambition*.

60. Moyn, *Not Enough*.

61. Thomas Piketty, Li Yang, and Gabriel Zucman, "Capital Accumulation, Private Property, and Rising Inequality in China," *American Economic Review* 109, no. 7 (2019): 2469–96.

62. Jiandong Chen, Dai Dai, Ming Pu, Wenxuan Hou, and Qiaobin Feng, "The Trend of the Gini Coefficient in China," *Brooks World Poverty Institute Working Paper*, No. 109, 2012, https://ssrn.com/abstract=2161034.

63. This moral vision not only characterized the rise and expansion of capitalism from the beginning. It also worked its way into societies in which the relationship between capitalism and bondage was more direct. In his magisterial history of the Australian transportation system, Robert Hughes writes about the ways in which the discovery of gold hastened the end of the colony's convict economy, a process driven by "the unrelenting, go-getting, land-grabbing, cash-and-gold obsessed materialism of free Australian colonists." As he puts it, "nowhere in the world was the Victorian equation between wealth and virtue rammed home more brutally than in mid-nineteenth-century Australia." Robert Hughes, *The Fatal Shore: The Epic of Australia's Founding* (London: William Collins, 1986), 588.

Chapter 3

1. Before 2008, some of the United Nations human rights treaty bodies were based at the UN headquarters in New York City.

2. Sally Engle Merry, *Human Rights and Gender Violence: Translating International Law into Local Justice* (Chicago: University of Chicago Press, 2006).

3. Merry, *Human Rights and Gender Violence*, 113.

4. See the discussion of compensation payments within in the relational systems of Melanesia in chapter 7. For a comparative analysis of different approaches to conflict resolution, see Mark Goodale, *Anthropology and Law: A Critical Introduction* (New York: New York University Press, 2017).

5. Merry, *Human Rights and Gender Violence*, 114–15.

6. Merry, *Human Rights and Gender Violence*, 116.

7. Merry, *Human Rights and Gender Violence*, 239n9.

8. Merry, *Human Rights and Gender Violence*, 239n9.

9. Merry, *Human Rights and Gender Violence*, 132.

10. Annelise Riles, "Infinity within the Brackets," *American Ethnologist* 25, no. 3 (1998): 378–98.

11. For a sweeping global history of the relationship between nation-states and human rights, see Eric D. Weitz, *A World Divided: The Global Struggle for Human Rights in the Age of Nation-States* (Princeton, NJ: Princeton University Press, 2019).

12. On the importance of "seeing like a state" as a basic value of institutional legitimacy, see James C. Scott, *Seeing Like a State: How Certain Schemes to Improve the Human Conditions Have Failed* (New Haven, CT: Yale University Press, 1998).

13. Makau Mutua, "Savages, Victims, Saviors: The Metaphor of Human Rights," *Harvard International Law Journal* 42, no. 1 (2001): 201–47.

14. Christopher N. J. Roberts, *The Contentious History of the International Bill of Human Rights* (Cambridge: Cambridge University Press, 2015), 72.

15. J. L. Brierly, *The Law of Nations* (1928; Oxford: Oxford University Press, 1963), 12.

16. Brierly, *Law of Nations*, 6–7.

17. Eric Hobsbawm, *The Age of Empire: 1875–1914* (London: Abacus, 1987), 142.

18. The global malleability of sovereignty as an unquestioned fact of political embodiment and national separateness extends even to so-called failed states or to what Agathe Mora has described as "black hole" states. Agathe Mora, "Black Hole State: Human Rights

and the Work of Suspension in Post-War Kosovo," *Social Anthropology* 28, no. 1 (2020): 83–95.

19. Roberts, *Contentious History of the International Bill of Rights*, 89.

20. Roberts, *Contentious History of the International Bill of Rights*, 89–90.

21. See the discussion in chapter 5.

22. I make this point despite the fact that some wistful US-based human rights scholars and activists like to look back on the ill-fated Carter administration (1977–81) as a kind of glorious, if fleeting, period in which the United States promoted human rights around the world.

23. The original quote is "bureaucracy and social harmony are inversely proportional to each other," taken from Trotsky's 1937 *The Revolution Betrayed: What Is the Soviet Union and Where Is It Going?*, published three years before the exiled Trotsky was murdered in Mexico City on the orders of Stalin.

24. See, e.g., Ilana Gershon, "Neoliberal Agency," *Current Anthropology* 52, no. 4 (2011): 537–55; Eugene Dili Liow, "The Neoliberal-Developmental State: Singapore as Case Study," *Critical Sociology* 38, no. 2 (2015): 241–64; Linda Lobao, Mia Gray, Kevin Cox, and Michael Kitson, "The Shrinking State? Understanding the Assault on the Public Sector," *Cambridge Journal of Regions, Economy, and Society* 11, no. 3 (2018): 389–408; and Rajesh Venugopal, "Neoliberalism as Concept," *Economy and Society* 44, no. 2 (2015): 165–87.

25. For more on the CEDAW centers in Bolivia and the history of the center in Sacaca, see Mark Goodale, *Dilemmas of Modernity: Bolivian Encounters with Law and Liberalism* (Stanford, CA: Stanford University Press, 2008).

26. Julie Mertus, *Human Rights Matters: Local Politics and National Human Rights Institutions* (Stanford, CA: Stanford University Press, 2009).

27. Mertus, *Human Rights Matters*, 3.

28. Mertus, *Human Rights Matters*, 3.

29. Mertus, *Human Rights Matters*, 138.

30. Mertus, *Human Rights Matters*, 138.

31. Mertus, *Human Rights Matters*, 23.

32. Mertus, *Human Rights Matters*, 23.

33. Mertus, *Human Rights Matters*, 22, quoting from an interview with Hans-Otto Sano.

34. Mertus, *Human Rights Matters*, 22.

35. Mertus, *Human Rights Matters*, 28.

36. As of 2021, the DIHR conducted research and NHRI advocacy in the following countries or territories: Burkina Faso, China, Ethiopia, Ghana, Greenland (an autonomous territory of Denmark), Jordan, Kenya, Kyrgyzstan, Mali, Morocco, Myanmar, Niger, Palestinian Territories, Tunisia, Ukraine, and Zambia. www.humanrights.dk/where-we-work.

37. Beyond its chart-topping placement in the proliferating array of more conventional social and economic indexes, Denmark was also famously ranked as the "happiest" country in the world in the highly competitive global happiness stakes, a position from which it was later bumped by its Nordic neighbor Finland, which proved—among other

things—that quantitative indicators have no way of measuring the experience of living through a winter in Helsinki.

38. Stephen D. Krasner, *Sovereignty: Organized Hypocrisy* (Princeton, NJ: Princeton University Press, 1999).

39. "Disregard and contempt for human rights" are the twin evils evoked by the UDHR as the root causes of the world's most "barbarous acts."

40. Martti Koskenniemi, "What Use for Sovereignty Today?," *Asian Journal of International Law* 1, no. 1 (2011): 61–70.

41. Koskenniemi, "What Use for Sovereignty Today?, 63.

42. Koskenniemi, "What Use for Sovereignty Today?, 70.

43. Koskenniemi, "What Use for Sovereignty Today?, 69.

44. Koskenniemi, "What Use for Sovereignty Today?, 70.

45. Koskenniemi, "What Use for Sovereignty Today?, 70.

46. Koskenniemi, "What Use for Sovereignty Today?, 70.

47. Jacques–Guillaume Thouret, "Report on the Basis of Political Eligibility," quoted in Lynn Hunt, ed., *The French Revolution and Human Rights: A Brief Documentary History* (New York: Bedford/St. Martins, 1996), 82.

Chapter 4

1. See Mark Goodale, *Dilemmas of Modernity: Bolivian Encounters with Law and Liberalism* (Stanford, CA: Stanford University Press, 2008).

2. During my research, I offered to catalog and organize this rural legal archive in exchange for research access. As I have discussed elsewhere, in many rural areas, a legal archive is often the only place where written local history is collected. Given that these legal histories coexist with oral and artifactual forms of history, the question of how legal documents organize information in particular ways becomes critical. Mark Goodale, "Legal Ethnohistory in Rural Bolivia: Documentary Culture and Social History in the *norte de Potosí*," *Ethnohistory* 49, no. 3 (2002): 583–609.

3. In fact, through archival research, I discovered that there had been 202 homicide cases filed in the small court between 1883 and 1999.

4. See, e.g., Abdullahi Ahmed An-Na'im, "The Spirit of Laws Is Not Universal: Alternatives to the Enforcement Paradigm for Human Rights," *Tilburg Law Review* 21, no. 2 (2016): 255–74.

5. Kieran McEvoy, "Beyond Legalism: Towards a Thicker Understanding of Transitional Justice," *Journal of Law and Society* 34, no. 4 (2007): 411–40.

6. For an insightful overview to key developments within the field of transitional justice, see Brianne McGonigle Leyh, "The Socialization of Transitional Justice: Expanding Justice Theories within the Field," *Human Rights and International Legal Discourse* 11, no. 1 (2017): 83–95.

7. See, e.g., Kathryn Sikkink, *Evidence for Hope: Making Human Rights Work in the 21st Century* (Princeton, NJ: Princeton University Press, 2017); Christopher J. Fariss, "Yes, Human Rights Practices Are Improving Over Time," *American Political Science Review*

113, no. 3 (2019): 868–81; Dustin Sharp, "Pragmatism and Multidimensionality in Human Rights Advocacy," *Human Rights Quarterly* 40, no. 3 (2018): 499–520.

8. E. P. Thompson, *Whigs and Hunters: The Origin of the Black Act* (London: Penguin, 1977).

9. E. P. Thompson, *The Making of the English Working Class* (London: Victor Gollancz, 1963).

10. Thompson, *Whigs and Hunters*, 22.

11. Marx analyzes this political economic chain reaction in chapter 27, volume 1, of *Das Kapital*, in which he describes how "free peasant proprietors" in England were forced to become wage-laborers when the "rapid rise of the Flemish wool manufacturers, and the corresponding rise in the price of wool in England" led authorities to use either legal means or direct violence to transform "arable land into sheep-walks." Quoted in Robert C. Tucker, ed., *The Marx-Engels Reader*, 2nd ed. (New York: W. W. Norton, 1978), 434.

12. Thompson, *Whigs and Hunters*, 21. Note also how the expansion of the penal transportation system to Australia later in the eighteenth century—when the social ravages of enclosure were well established in English cities like London—was used primarily to exile people who had committed even minor property crimes, like the theft of small amounts of food from stores. The "lives and liberties . . . of the propertied" were "preserved" by shipping almost 200,000 men, women, and children to the brutal police state in the antipodes (until the system ended in 1868), where they endured years of physical and psychological abuse and also formed the basis for the economic development of the colony, which relied for decades on the slave-like conditions of convict labor. See Robert Hughes, *The Fatal Shore: The Epic of Australia's Founding* (London: William Collins, 1986).

13. Samuel Moyn, *Not Enough: Human Rights in an Unequal World* (Cambridge, MA: Belknap Press of Harvard University Press, 2018), xii. See the discussion of the moral dimensions of capitalism in chapter 2.

14. Thompson, *Whigs and Hunters*, 81.

15. This irreversible transformation has recently become the concern of an underground movement in England that is attempting to claw back some of the ancient commons by asserting what it calls a "right to roam." As George Monbiot puts it, this movement is a form of resistance against the fact that "almost all of us, in England and many other nations, are born on the wrong side of the law. The disproportionate weight that the law gives to property rights makes nearly everyone a second-class citizen before they draw their first breath, fenced out of the good life we could lead." George Monbiot, "English Landowners Have Stolen Our Rights. It Is Time to Reclaim Them," *The Guardian*, August 19, 2020, www.theguardian.com/commentisfree/2020/aug/19/pandemic-right-to-roam-england.

16. Thompson, *Whigs and Hunters*, 264–65.

17. Richard Thompson Ford, *Rights Gone Wrong: How Law Corrupts the Struggle for Equality* (New York: Farrar, Straus and Giroux, 2011).

18. Ran Hirschl, *Towards Juristocracy: The Origins and Consequences of the New Constitutionalism* (Cambridge, MA: Harvard University Press, 2004).

19. Heinz Klug, *Constituting Democracy: Law, Globalism, and South Africa's Political Reconstruction* (Cambridge: Cambridge University Press, 2000).

20. Robert Hayden, "Constitutional Nationalism in the Formerly Yugoslav Republics," *Slavic Review* 51, no. 4 (1992): 654–73, 670. For an innovative study that analyzes the problematic relationship between human rights, law, and nationalism through the framework of "human rights memorialization," see Lea David, *The Past Can't Heal Us: The Dangers of Mandating Memory in the Name of Human Rights* (Cambridge: Cambridge University Press, 2020).

21. Mark Goodale, *Anthropology and Law: A Critical Introduction* (New York: New York University Press, 2017), especially chapter 8 on "Ethnonationalism and Conflict Transformation."

22. An-Na'im, "Spirit of Laws Is Not Universal," 255–74.

23. See, e.g., Javier A. Couso, Alexandra Huneeus, and Rachel Sieder, eds., *Cultures of Legality: Judicialization and Political Activism in Latin America* (Cambridge: Cambridge University Press, 2010); Martin Shapiro and Alex Stone Sweet, *On Law, Politics, and Judicialization* (Oxford: Oxford University Press, 2002); and Rachel Sieder, Line Schjolden, and Alan Angell, eds., *The Judicialization of Politics in Latin America* (New York: Palgrave Macmillan, 2005).

24. See Jürgen Habermas's theory of communicative action, in which he examines what he describes as the "colonization of the lifeworld" by modern bureaucratic systems. Jürgen Habermas, *Lifeworld and System: A Critique of Functionalist Reason* (Boston: Beacon Press, 1987).

25. Sally Engle Merry, *Getting Justice, Getting Even: Legal Consciousness among Working-Class Americans* (Chicago: University of Chicago Press, 1990).

26. See, e.g., Rachel Sieder, "Legal Cultures in the (Un)Rule of Law: Indigenous Rights and Juridification in Guatemala," in *Cultures of Legality: Judicialization and Political Activism in Latin America*, ed. Javier A. Couso, Alexandra Huneeus, and Rachel Sieder (Cambridge: Cambridge University Press, 2010), 161–81; see also Mark Goodale, "Dark Matter: Toward a Political Economy of Indigenous Rights and Aspirational Politics," *Critique of Anthropology* 36, no. 4 (2010): 439–57.

27. James Ferguson, *The Anti-Politics Machine: "Development," Depoliticization, and Bureaucratic Power in Lesotho* (Cambridge: Cambridge University Press, 1990).

28. See, e.g., Saturnino Borras and Jennifer Franco, "Contemporary Discourses and Contestations around Pro-Poor Land Policies and Land Governance," *Journal of Agrarian Change* 10, no. 1 (2010): 1–32; Karen Engle, *The Elusive Promise of Indigenous Development: Rights, Culture, Strategy* (Durham, NC: Duke University Press, 2010); Goodale, "Dark Matter"; and Stuart Kirsch, "Juridification of Indigenous Politics," in *Law against the State: Ethnographic Forays into Law's Transformations*, ed. Julia Eckert, Brian Donahoe, Christian Strümpell, and Zerrin Özlem Biner (Cambridge: Cambridge University Press, 2012), 23–43.

29. Borras and Franco, "Contemporary Discourses and Contestations around Pro-Poor Land Policies and Land Governance."

30. Nancy Fraser, "From Redistribution to Recognition? Dilemmas of Justice in a 'Post-Socialist' Age," *New Left Review* 212 (July/August 1995): 68–93.

31. James Boyd White, *Heracles' Bow: Essays on the Rhetoric and Poetics of the Law* (Madison: University of Wisconsin Press, 1985).

32. H. L. A. Hart, *The Concept of Law* (Oxford: Oxford University Press, 1961).

33. Bronislaw Malinowski, *Crime and Custom in Savage Society* (1926; Totowa, NJ: Littlefield, Adams, 1976), 55.

34. Although the Nuremberg and Tokyo trials took place immediately after the end of World War II and before the UDHR drafting process had even begun, the concept of mass human rights violations had been discussed at least since Raphaël Lemkin invoked the Armenian "Genocide" (the term hadn't been coined yet) at a 1933 League of Nations conference in Madrid. As is well known, Lemkin worked tirelessly to have the crime of genocide recognized in international law, including throughout World War II, where dozens of his relatives perished in the Holocaust. Lemkin's advocacy influenced the legal basis for the postwar trials, which adopted "crimes against humanity" as one of the counts, and resulted in the Genocide Convention, which was adopted by the UN General Assembly on December 9, 1948, the day before the UDHR was adopted. See Douglas Irvin-Erickson, *Raphaël Lemkin and the Concept of Genocide* (Philadelphia: University of Pennsylvania Press, 2017).

35. The troubled status of the ICC can perhaps be inferred in part by the fact that a majority of the permanent members of the UN Security Council are nonparties to the Rome Statute.

36. See, e.g., Geoff Dancy and Kathryn Sikkink, "Ratification and Human Rights Prosecutions: Toward a Transnational Theory of Treaty Compliance," *NYU Journal of International Law and Politics* 44, no. 3 (2012): 754–77; and Hunjoon Kim and Kathryn Sikkink, "Explaining the Deterrence Effect of Human Rights Prosecutions for Transitional Countries," *International Studies Quarterly* 54, no. 4 (2010): 939–63.

37. Sikkink, *Evidence for Hope*, 208–9.

38. Kathryn Sikkink, *The Justice Cascade: How Human Rights Prosecutions Are Changing World Politics* (New York: W. W. Norton, 2011); Sikkink, *Evidence for Hope*, 209.

39. But see Sally Engle Merry, *The Seductions of Quantification: Measuring Human Rights, Gender Violence, and Sex Trafficking* (Chicago: University of Chicago Press, 2016); Sally Engle Merry, Kevin E. Davis, and Benedict Kingsbury, eds., *The Quiet Power of Indicators: Measuring Governance, Corruption, and the Rule of Law* (Cambridge: Cambridge University Press, 2015); and Richard Rottenburg, Sally Engle Merry, Sung-Joon Park, and Johanna Mugler, eds., *The World of Indicators: The Making of Governmental Knowledge through Quantification* (Cambridge: Cambridge University Press, 2016).

40. Alexander Laban Hinton, *The Justice Facade: Trials of Transition in Cambodia* (New York: Oxford University Press, 2018).

41. See also Alexander Laban Hinton, ed., *Genocide: An Anthropological Reader* (Oxford: Blackwell, 2002); Alexander Laban Hinton, ed., *Annihilating Difference: The Anthropology of Genocide* (Berkeley: University of California Press, 2002); Alexander Laban Hinton, *Why Did They Kill? Cambodia in the Shadow of Genocide* (Berkeley: University

of California Press, 2004); Alexander Laban Hinton, ed., *Transitional Justice: Global Mechanisms and Local Realities after Genocide and Mass Violence* (New Brunswick, NJ: Rutgers University Press, 2010); Alexander Laban Hinton, Thomas La Pointe, and Douglas Irvin-Erickson, eds., *Hidden Genocides: Power, Knowledge, Memory* (New Brunswick, NJ: Rutgers University Press, 2013); Alexander Laban Hinton, "The Paradox of Perpetration: A View from the Cambodian Genocide," in *Human Rights at the Crossroads*, ed. Mark Goodale (Oxford: Oxford University Press, 2014), 153–62; and Alexander Laban Hinton, *Man or Monster? The Trial of a Khmer Rouge Torturer* (Durham, NC: Duke University Press, 2016).

42. Hinton, *Justice Facade*, 250. For another powerful critique of the disjunctures between the global transitional justice imaginary and local cultural and religious complexities, also based on research in Cambodia, see Carol A. Kidron, "The 'Perfect Failure' of Communal Genocide Commemoration in Cambodia: Production Friction or 'Bone Business'?" *Current Anthropology* 61, no. 3 (2020): 304–34.

43. Hinton, *Justice Facade*, 251.

44. Kenneth Roth, "Africa Attacks the International Criminal Court," *New York Review of Books* 61, no. 2 (February 6, 2014), www.nybooks.com/articles/2014/02/06/africa-attacks-international-criminal-court/.

45. Kamari Maxine Clarke, *Affective Justice: The International Criminal Court and the Pan-Africanist Pushback* (Durham, NC: Duke University Press, 2019).

46. Kamari Maxine Clarke, *Fictions of Justice: The International Criminal Court and the Challenge of Legal Pluralism in Sub-Saharan Africa* (Cambridge: Cambridge University Press, 2009).

47. For a provocative study of the ways in which international women's rights advocacy has refracted many of these same colonial and neocolonial tropes in the effort to bring heightened—or even exclusive—attention to the problem of sexual violence in conflict, see Karen Engle, *The Grip of Sexual Violence in Conflict: Feminist Interventions in International Law* (Stanford, CA: Stanford University Press, 2020).

48. Makau Mutua, "Savages, Victims, Saviors: The Metaphor of Human Rights," *Harvard International Law Journal* 42, no. 1 (2001): 201–47.

49. Antony Anghie, "Francisco de Vitoria and the Colonial Origins of International Law," *Social and Legal Studies* 5, no. 3 (1996): 321–36; Antony Anghie, *Imperialism, Sovereignty, and the Making of International Law* (Cambridge: Cambridge University Press, 2005); and Antony Anghie, "The Evolution of International Law: Colonial and Postcolonial Realties," *Third World Quarterly* 27, no. 5 (2006): 739–53.

50. Julie Fraser and Brianne McGonigle Leyh, eds., *Intersections of Law and Culture at the International Criminal Court* (Cheltenham, UK: Edward Elgar, 2020).

51. Edward Sapir, "Culture, Genuine and Spurious," *American Journal of Sociology* 29, no. 4 (1924): 401–29; see also Mark Goodale, "Afterword: Culture, Genuine and Juridical," in *Intersections of Law and Culture at the International Criminal Court*, ed. Julie Fraser and Brianne McGonigle Leyh (Cheltenham, UK: Edward Elgar, 2020), 397–405.

52. Marie-Claire Foblets and Alison Dundes Renteln, eds., *Multicultural Jurisprudence: Comparative Perspectives on the Cultural Defense* (Oxford: Hart Publishing, 2009).

53. Thania Paffenholz, "Unpacking the Local Turn in Peacebuilding: A Critical Assessment towards an Agenda for Future Research," *Third World Quarterly* 36, no. 5 (2015): 857–74.

54. Fiona C. Ross, "An Acknowledged Failure: Women, Voice, Violence, and the South African Truth and Reconciliation Commission," in *Localizing Transitional Justice: Interventions and Priorities after Mass Violence*, ed. Rosalind Shaw and Lars Waldorf (Stanford, CA: Stanford University Press, 2010), 69–91.

55. Mariane Ferme, *The Underneath of Things: Violence, History, and the Everyday in Sierra Leone* (Berkeley: University of California Press, 2001).

56. Tania Li, "Indigeneity, Capitalism, and the Management of Dispossession," *Current Anthropology* 53, no. 3 (2010): 385–414, 386.

57. For measured, yet critical, empirical accounts of hybrid tribunals, see Phil Clark, *The Gacaca Courts, Post-Genocide Justice and Reconciliation in Rwanda: Justice without Lawyers* (Cambridge: Cambridge University Press, 2010); and Tim Kelsall, *Culture under Cross-Examination: International Justice and the Special Court for Sierra Leone* (Cambridge: Cambridge University Press, 2009).

58. Michael Hardt and Antonio Negri, *Empire* (Cambridge, MA: Harvard University Press, 2000), 313.

59. Hinton, *Justice Facade*, 247.

60. See, e.g., Ugo Mattei and Laura Nader, *Plunder: When the Rule of Law is Illegal* (Malden, MA: Blackwell, 2008).

61. David Kennedy, *The Dark Sides of Virtue: Reassessing International Humanitarianism* (Princeton, NJ: Princeton University Press, 2005).

62. Thompson, *Whigs and Hunters*, 265.

Chapter 5

1. Javier Malagón Barceló, "The Role of the *Letrado* in the Colonization of America," *The Americas* 18, no. 1 (1961): 1–17, 4.

2. See Gordon S. Wood, *The Radicalism of the American Revolution* (New York: Vintage Books, 1993). Wood's study is particularly valuable in bringing nuance to the question of the contradictory relationship between slavery and the human rights revolution of 1776. As he explains, colonial American society was based on a vast hierarchy of unfreedom, with the "half million Afro-Americans reduced to the utterly debased position of lifetime hereditary servitude" and thus the most "conspicuously unfree." However, tens of thousands of white indentured servants made up between one-half and two-thirds of all immigrants to the colonies, bonded servants who "shared some of the chattel nature of black slaves." As Wood puts it, "newly arriving Britons were astonished to see how ruthlessly Americans treated their white servants," which explains why "slavery could be regarded . . . as merely the most base and degraded status in a society of several degrees of unfreedom." In claiming that "all men are created equal," therefore, we see how this revolutionary assertion of human rights was never meant to undo a society based on multiple degrees of unfreedom but rather to eliminate unfreedom only as it applied

to white, male, colonial subjects, who would use their hard-won freedom to build what Wood calls a "middle-class order" (51–56).

3. Christopher N. J. Roberts , *The Contentious History of the International Bill of Rights* (Cambridge: Cambridge University Press, 2015). See especially chapter 4, "Saving Empire."

4. Roberts, *Contentious History of the International Bill of Rights*, 136–37.

5. Roberts, *Contentious History of the International Bill of Rights*, 137.

6. Quoted in Mark Goodale, ed., *Letters to the Contrary: A Curated History of the UNESCO Human Rights Survey* (Stanford, CA: Stanford University Press, 2018), 240 (emphasis in original).

7. Quoted in Goodale, *Letters to the Contrary*, 240, 239.

8. Quoted in Goodale, *Letters to the Contrary*, 240.

9. Quoted in Goodale, *Letters to the Contrary*, 240–41.

10. The other anthropologist was A. P. Elkin, an Australian Anglican clergyman and professor at the University of Sydney. Elkin, whose response to the UNESCO survey was titled "The Rights of Primitive Peoples," was a controversial figure within the Australian academy, since he played an important role as a governmental advisor on the country's Aboriginal peoples and believed, at the same time, that they should eventually be assimilated to Australia's majority society.

11. The AAA published the "Statement on Human Rights" in the association's flagship journal, *American Anthropologist*, in December 1947, a full year before the adoption of the UDHR.

12. Quoted in Goodale, *Letters to the Contrary*, 314–15.

13. On the various controversies surrounding the 1947 "Statement on Human Rights," particularly as this quasi-official anthropological position was received by anthropologists decades later, see Mark Goodale, *Surrendering to Utopia: An Anthropology of Human Rights* (Stanford, CA: Stanford University Press, 2009). The 1947 "Statement" was eventually repudiated in 1999 by the AAA's "Declaration on Anthropology and Human Rights," which endorsed the UDHR and implored anthropologists to use their research as a form of human rights activism. The 1999 "Declaration" was itself superseded by the more multilayered 2020 "Statement on Anthropology and Human Rights," for which I was one of the "drafters." See www.americananthro.org/ParticipateAndAdvocate/AdvocacyDetail.aspx?ItemNumber=25769.

14. Goodale, *Letters to the Contrary*, 315.

15. Herskovits goes on to issue what is perhaps the clearest critique of human rights from the perspective of cultural relativism ever made: "Ideas of right and wrong, good and evil, are found in all societies, though they differ in their expression among different peoples. What is held to be a human right in one society may be regarded as anti-social by another people, or by the same people in a different period of their history. The saint of one epoch would at a later time be confined as a man not fitted to cope with reality. Even the nature of the physical world, the colors we see, the sounds we hear, are conditioned by the language we speak, which is part of the culture into which we are born." Quoted in Goodale, *Letters to the Contrary*, 317.

16. Jacques Havet, "Distinguished World Thinkers Study Bases of Human Rights," *UNESCO Courier* 1, no. 7 (1948): 8.

17. See Mark Goodale, *A Revolution in Fragments: Traversing Scales of Justice, Ideology, and Practice in Bolivia* (Durham, NC: Duke University Press, 2019); see also Penelope Anthias, *Limits to Decolonization: Indigeneity, Territory, and Hydrocarbon Politics in the Bolivian Chaco* (Ithaca, NY: Cornell University Press, 2019).

18. Max Horkheimer and Theodor W. Adorno, *Dialectic of Enlightenment: Philosophical Fragments* (1944; Stanford, CA: Stanford University Press, 2002), xv.

19. For a penetrating history of this experience, and the ways in which it grounded the eventual "strange triumph" of human rights, see Mark Mazower, "The Strange Triumph of Human Rights, 1933–1950," *Historical Journal* 47, no. 2 (2004): 379–98.

20. Roberts, *Contentious History of the International Bill of Rights*, 57. The Potsdam Conference took place in August 1945, two months after Germany's unconditional surrender, between leaders of the United States, Great Britain, and the Soviet Union. Among other peculiarities of the Potsdam Conference, this was the first major international event at which the newly installed US president, Harry S. Truman, represented the United States, Roosevelt having died in April 1945. In addition, the British prime minister, Winston Churchill, was unceremoniously replaced in the middle of the conference by the newly elected prime minister Clement Attlee, who had just taken power after a historic pro-Labour victory (and who would soon oversee the creation of the National Health Service and the partition of India).

21. Roberts, *Contentious History of the International Bill of Rights*, 58.

22. See, e.g., Roland Burke, *Decolonization and the Evolution of International Human Rights* (Philadelphia: University of Pennsylvania Press, 2010); Steven L. B. Jensen, *The Making of International Human Rights: The 1960s, Decolonization, and the Reconstruction of Global Values* (Cambridge: Cambridge University Press, 2016); and A. Dirk Moses, Marco Duranti, and Roland Burke, eds., *Decolonization, Self-Determination, and the Rise of Global Human Rights Politics* (Cambridge: Cambridge University Press, 2020). See also A. W. Brian Simpson, *Human Rights and the End of Empire: Britain and the Genesis of the European Convention* (Oxford: Oxford University Press, 2001).

23. See this chapter's next section for a critical discussion of the use of the binary Global North/Global South.

24. Mary Ann Heiss, "Privileging the Cold War over Decolonization: The US Emphasis on Political Rights," in *Decolonization, Self-Determination, and the Rise of Global Human Rights Politics*, ed. A. Dirk Moses, Marco Duranti, and Roland Burke (Cambridge: Cambridge University Press, 2020), 132–50.

25. See Roland Burke, *Decolonization and the Evolution of International Human Rights* (Philadelphia: University of Pennsylvania Press, 2010).

26. See Jensen, *Making of International Human Rights*. Marco Duranti has described the human rights mobilizations of anticolonial leaders around the right of self-determination during these years as an effort to also decolonize the United Nations itself. Marco Duranti, "Decolonizing the United Nations: Anti-Colonialism and Human Rights in the French Empire," in *Decolonization, Self-Determination, and the Rise of Global Human Rights*

Politics, ed. A. Dirk Moses, Marco Duranti, and Roland Burke (Cambridge: Cambridge University Press, 2020), 54–78.

27. The right of self-determination, as an emergent human right that reflects the lived realities of colonial violence and anticolonial resistance, must be distinguished from the principle of sovereignty, the abstract doctrine that grounded the rise of modern states, especially after the 1648 Peace of Westphalia (see the discussion in chapter 3). Despite the fact that the concept of "sovereignty" was certainly invoked on occasion as a stand-in for self-determination, the anticolonial struggles for freedom were also struggles against an international politico-legal order in which the principle of sovereignty protected colonial prerogatives.

28. On the use of "rekindling" as an apt metaphor to describe this second sense of subversion through human rights, see chapter 3 in Jensen, *Making of International Human Rights*.

29. Bonny Ibhawoh, "Seeking the Political Kingdom: Universal Human Rights and the Anti-colonial Movement in Africa," in Moses, Duranti, and Burke, *Decolonization, Self-Determination, and the Rise of Global Human Rights Politics*, 35–53, 35.

30. Ibhawoh, "Seeking the Political Kingdom," 45.

31. The colonial and neocolonial histories of South Africa are complicated by the fact that earlier anticolonial resistance took place during the nineteenth and early twentieth centuries by both native peoples (particularly the Zula and Xhosa peoples) and the Boers, a population of Dutch settlers who had arrived in southern Africa with the Dutch East India Company beginning in the middle of the seventeenth century. However, after South Africa was granted independence in 1931, the dominant National Party instituted the internal colonial policy of apartheid (formalized in 1948), which subjugated and exploited the country's Black majority, so that the end of apartheid in 1994 could be seen as the end of a second, much more insidious, period of (neo-)colonial history in South Africa. For a study of apartheid South Africa's efforts to navigate early postwar debates over human rights, which "posed a mortal threat to the apartheid project," see Roland Burke, "'A World Made Safe for Diversity': Apartheid and the Language of Human Rights, Progress, and Pluralism," in Moses, Duranti, and Burke, *Decolonization, Self-Determination, and the Rise of Global Human Rights Politics*, 316–39.

32. The transcript of Mandela's "I Am Prepared to Die" speech can be found through many sources, for example, at the UN website dedicated to Nelson Mandela International Day, which falls on July 18 each year. www.un.org/en/events/mandeladay/court_statement_1964.shtml.

33. Meredith Terretta, "'We Had Been Fooled into Thinking That the UN Watches Over the Entire World': Human Rights, UN Trust Territories, and Africa's Decolonization," *Human Rights Quarterly* 34, no. 2 (2012): 329–60.

34. Terretta, "We Had Been Fooled into Thinking That the UN Watches Over the Entire World," 333.

35. Terretta, "We Had Been Fooled into Thinking That the UN Watches Over the Entire World," 331. It should be noted that Terretta is critical of many of the revisionist histories of human rights and decolonization, including some of the sources already cited.

She argues that these works focus too heavily on debates within the United Nations and on high-level anticolonial politicians, a perspective that imparts a "top-down quality that obfuscates the agency of [grassroots] anti-colonial activists who *did* invoke human rights as a way of delegitimizing colonial rule." Terretta, "We Had Been Fooled into Thinking That the UN Watches Over the Entire World," 331 (emphasis in original).

36. Terretta underscores the importance of a number of these anticolonial lawyers, including "Ralph Millner, British Barrister-at-Law and member of the International Association of Democratic Lawyers, Dudley J. Thompson, Jamaican Pan-Africanist who began practicing law in Kenya and Tanganyika in the 1950s, and Robert Delson, Esq., of Delson, Levin & Gordon, General Counsel for the Brotherhood of Sleeping Car Porters and legal counsel to the Republic of Indonesia." Terretta, "We Had Been Fooled into Thinking That the UN Watches Over the Entire World," 336.

37. Terretta, "We Had Been Fooled into Thinking That the UN Watches Over the Entire World," 335–36.

38. Terretta, "We Had Been Fooled into Thinking That the UN Watches Over the Entire World," 333.

39. Terretta, "We Had Been Fooled into Thinking That the UN Watches Over the Entire World," 352–53, quoting from Aimé Césaire, *Discourse on Colonialism* (1955; New York: Monthly Review Press, 2000), 15. Césaire played a formative role in the education of Frantz Fanon, who he taught in high school in Martinique during the early 1940s.

40. Harold Laski, 1947, "Towards a Universal Declaration of Human Rights," quoted in Goodale, *Letters to the Contrary*, 126.

41. Humayun Kabir, 1947, "The Rights of Man and the Islamic Tradition," quoted in Goodale, *Letters to the Contrary*, 220–21. Kabir's response was sent in April 1947, just three months before the partition of colonial India into independent India and Pakistan.

42. S. V. Puntambekar, "Human Freedoms," quoted in Goodale, *Letters to the Contrary*, 237. Puntambekar, who was at the time a professor of history and political science at the Hindu University in Benares, opposed the creation of a secular state for India after independence from the British Empire. As he put it, "there are no politics without religion. Politics bereft of religion are a death trap because they kill the soul." S. V. Puntambekar, "Human Freedoms," quoted in Goodale, *Letters to the Contrary*, 236.

43. F. S. C. Northrop, "Toward a Bill of Rights," quoted in Goodale, *Letters to the Contrary*, 249.

44. Mark Goodale, "The Myth of Universality: The UNESCO 'Philosophers' Committee' and the Making of Human Rights," *Law and Social Inquiry* 43, no. 3 (2018): 596–617.

45. In Goodale, *Letters to the Contrary*, 250. I return to questions of pluralism and universality in relation to the future of human rights in chapter 6 of this volume.

46. Johannes Morsink, *The Universal Declaration of Human Rights: Origins, Drafting, Intent* (Philadelphia: University of Pennsylvania Press, 1999), 29; see also John P. Humphrey, *Human Rights and the United Nations: A Great Adventure* (New York: Transnational Publishers, 1984).

47. See, e.g., José-Manuel Barreto, *Human Rights from a Third World Perspective: Critique, History and International Law* (Cambridge: Cambridge Scholars Publishing,

2013); José-Manuel Barreto, "Epistemologies of the South and Human Rights: Santos and the Quest for Global and Cognitive Justice," *Indiana Journal of Global Legal Studies* 21, no. 2 (2014): 395–422; Silvia Rivera Cusicanqui, "The Notion of 'Rights' and the Paradoxes of Postcolonial Modernity: Indigenous Peoples and Women in Bolivia," *Qui Parle* 18, no. 2 (2010): 29–54; Nikita Dhawan, *Decolonizing Enlightenment: Transnational Justice, Human Rights, and Democracy in a Postcolonial World* (Berlin: Verlag Barbara Budrich, 2014); Boaventura de Sousa Santos, ed., *Another Knowledge Is Possible: Beyond Northern Epistemologies* (London: Verso, 2008); Julia Suárez-Krabbe, "Race, Social Struggles, and 'Human' Rights: Contributions from the Global South," *Journal of Critical Development Studies* 6 (2015): 78–102; and Lynn Welchman, Elena Zambelli, and Ruba Salih, "Rethinking Justice beyond Human Rights: Anti-colonialism and Intersectionality in the Politics of the Palestinian Youth Movement," *Mediterranean Politics*, 2015, doi.org/10.1080/1362 9395.2020.1749811.

48. Indeed, during the time of the UNESCO human rights survey, the binary "East-West" appeared frequently as an explanatory device for both the respondents and the committee of experts who evaluated survey responses and prepared a report for the UN CHR. For example, F. S. C. Northrop had just published his most influential work, *The Meeting of East and West: An Inquiry Concerning World Understanding*, the year before the UNESCO survey.

49. Étienne Balibar, "L'introuvable humanité du sujet moderne: L'universalité 'civique-bourgeoise' et la question des differences anthropologiques," *L'Homme* 3–4, no. 203–4 (2012): 19–50.

50. Boaventura de Sousa Santos, *The End of the Cognitive Empire: The Coming of Age of Epistemologies of the South* (Durham, NC: Duke University Press, 2018).

51. See Balibar, "L'introuvable humanité du sujet moderne."

52. Eleanor Roosevelt, "The Promise of Human Rights," *Foreign Affairs* 26, no. 3 (1948): 470–77.

53. I thank an anonymous reviewer for pointing out the irony in the fact that Roosevelt made this argument about the transformative and inclusive potential of human rights in the pages of *Foreign Affairs*, a leading outlet for international relations that began its institutional life as the *Journal of Race Relations*, a journal associated with eugenics, race science, and imperialism. See Robert Vitalis, *White World Order, Black Power Politics: The Birth of American International Relations* (Ithaca, NY: Cornell University Press, 2015).

54. See Jane Cowan, Marie-Bénédicte Dembour, and Richard A. Wilson, eds., *Culture and Rights: Anthropological Perspectives* (Cambridge: Cambridge University Press, 2001); and Mark Goodale and Sally Engle Merry, eds., *The Practice of Human Rights: Tracking Law between the Global and the Local* (Cambridge: Cambridge University Press, 2007).

55. Mark Goodale, *Dilemmas of Modernity: Bolivian Encounters with Law and Liberalism* (Stanford, CA: Stanford University Press, 2008). The basis for this creative extension of human rights is a common complaint among young peasant women in the region that they are forced to carry a heavier burden when walking from place to place, the only way to travel throughout the province's mountainous terrain. The local rules about how to distribute loads are heavily gendered. For example, men always carry agricultural tools,

such as the *chaqui tajlla*, or foot plow, and women carry nearly everything else, including small children, who are bundled on women's backs in a *q'epi*, or folded blanket. The problem comes when couples are traveling for reasons other than agricultural work. It is quite common in these cases to see men walking with nothing on their backs and women heavily laden.

56. Published in English as Paulo Freire, *Pedagogy of the Oppressed* (New York: Continuum, 1970).

57. Boaventura de Sousa Santos, "Para além do Pensamento Abissal: Das linhas globais a uma ecologia de saberes," *Revista Crítica de Ciências Sociais* 78 (2007): 3–46.

Chapter 6

1. Isaiah Berlin, "My Intellectual Path," *New York Review of Books* 45, no. 8 (1998): 53–60, reprinted in Isaiah Berlin, *The Power of Ideas*, ed. Henry Hardy (Princeton, NJ: Princeton University Press, 2000).

2. Berlin, *Power of Ideas*, 15–16.

3. Berlin, *Power of Ideas*, 16. Berlin adapts the chilling phrase "engineers of human souls" from a speech that Stalin gave at the house of Maxim Gorky in October 1932 to a group of Soviet writers, in which he defined the role of artists with the Soviet state.

4. Berlin, *Power of Ideas*, 14.

5. Berlin, *Power of Ideas*, 11–12.

6. Berlin, *Power of Ideas*, 12. In this, Berlin follows Hannah Arendt's perspective that the Nazis were not "pathological or insane" but rather people who "comit[ted] the most unspeakable crimes" while nevertheless retaining their "human semblance." For a study that explores similar questions of humanity and inhumanity in relation to the Cambodian genocide, see Alexander Laban Hinton, *Man or Monster? The Trial of a Khmer Rouge Torturer* (Durham, NC: Duke University Press, 2016).

7. I take up the concept of "humanity" and the historical construction of the "human" in human rights through a more critical lens in chapter 7 of this volume.

8. Berlin, *Power of Ideas*, 12.

9. See, e.g., Sally Engle Merry, *Human Rights and Gender Violence: Translating International Law into Local Justice* (Chicago: University of Chicago Press, 2006).

10. Tine Destrooper, "Introduction: On Travel, Translation, and Transformation," in *Human Rights Transformation in Practice*, ed. Tine Destrooper and Sally Engle Merry (Philadelphia: University of Pennsylvania Press, 2018), 1–26.

11. See, e.g., Annette Förster, "The Concept of Human Rights: Dissolving the Universality-Plurality Puzzle," *Human Rights & International Legal Discourse* 10, no. 2 (2016): 185–99.

12. For a provocative study of the political implications of "pluriversality," see Arturo Escobar, *Pluriversal Politics: The Real and the Possible* (Durham, NC: Duke University Press, 2020).

13. Jack Donnelly, "Human Rights as Natural Rights," *Human Rights Quarterly* 4, no. 3 (1982): 391–405, 391.

14. For a more recent effort to develop a sociological approach to the problem of

human rights universality, see Alison Dundes Renteln, *International Human Rights: Universalism versus Relativism* (1990; Newbury Park, CA: Sage Publications, 2013). Renteln proposes an open-ended research model that is oriented toward the sociological search for cross-cultural universals, a model that she describes more generally as a "cross-cultural approach to validating international human rights." One cross-cultural universal that receives particular attention from Renteln is the principle of "retribution tied to proportionality," the fact that all cultures apparently modulate levels of punishment based on the perceived seriousness of the underlying infraction.

15. See chapter 5 for a discussion of the relationship between human rights universality and colonialism during the UNESCO survey. From a methodological perspective, the final results of the UNESCO human rights survey speak to the ultimate limits of the sociological approach to universality. Despite the very difficult technical and political circumstances, the UNESCO survey managed to elicit opinions on the question from an impressive range of respondents. But the final tally, the database on which the formal UNESCO report could confidently reaffirm the universality of human rights, reveals a ludicrously unrepresentative and numerically limited sample: at most sixty responses received; nearly 45 percent of replies from American or British respondents; and another 40 percent spread among respondents from several countries in Western Europe, Australia, Canada, and apartheid South Africa. Put another way, 85 percent of the sixty replies to the survey came from respondents from only about nine countries, all arguably "Western"; in addition, only one woman sent a reply, the English Quaker prison reformer Margery Fry. Even more, as we have seen in earlier chapters, a small majority of the "Western" respondents actually rejected—on different grounds—the universality of human rights.

16. Eleanor Roosevelt, "The Promise of Human Rights," *Foreign Affairs* 26, no. 3 (1948): 470–77. For more on the pedagogical dimensions of human rights, see the concluding section of chapter 5.

17. See Jane Cowan, Marie-Bénédicte Dembour, and Richard A. Wilson, introduction to *Culture and Rights: Anthropological Perspectives*, ed. Jane Cowan, Marie-Bénédicte Dembour, and Richard A. Wilson (Cambridge: Cambridge University Press, 2001), 11–13. This early work in the anthropology of human rights was based on a conference held at the University of Sussex in 1997, in which mostly anthropologists reflected on lessons learned in conducting ethnographic research on the practice of human rights in the early years of the post–Cold War. By 1997, the authors had found the idea that a global culture of human rights was emerging "increasingly persuasive" (12).

18. The international legal scholar Elena Baylis has examined the ways in which this inside/outside approach to human rights universality can take more disingenuous, self-interested forms, particularly among the small cadre of elite lawyers who become "post-conflict justice junkies," as Baylis puts it, "tribunal-hopping" their way through human rights and justice promotion to careers as high-profile law professors, diplomats, and international development consultants. Elena Baylis, "Tribunal-Hopping with the Post-Conflict Justice Junkies," *Oregon Review of International Law* 10 (2008): 361–90.

19. Cowan, Dembour, and Wilson, introduction, 3.

20. While conducting research in rural Bolivia during the late-1990s, I observed the ways in which human rights NGOs were particularly active in linking the reduction and sorting process to specific aid projects, which had the result of creating conflicts even between villages with populations of only several hundred people. Complicating matters was the fact that human rights NGOs competed, in a sense, with North American evangelical churches in the region, which were aggressively trying to convert people to the "true" religion. Of course, long before human rights development or Protestant proselytizing, the Catholic Church had been active in the region, bringing what was one of the first globalized universalisms to the Aymara and Quechua speakers of the highlands. See Mark Goodale, *Dilemmas of Modernity: Bolivian Encounters with Law and Liberalism* (Stanford, CA: Stanford University Press, 2008).

21. David Kennedy, *The Dark Sides of Virtue: Reassessing International Humanitarianism* (Princeton, NJ: Princeton University Press, 2005).

22. The practical nuances of this paradox have been documented across a wide range of anthropological studies, which collectively show how international human rights is promoted as a discourse of inclusion that can also deny, negate, and silence. See, e.g., Lori Allen, *The Rise and Fall of Human Rights: Cynicism and Politics in Occupied Palestine* (Stanford, CA: Stanford University Press, 2013); Kamari Maxine Clarke, *Fictions of Justice: The International Criminal Court and the Challenge of Legal Pluralism in Sub-Saharan Africa* (Cambridge: Cambridge University Press, 2009); Harri Englund, *Prisoners of Freedom: Human Rights and the African Poor* (Berkeley: University of California Press, 2006); and Rita Kesselring, *Bodies of Truth: Law, Memory, and Emancipation in Post-Apartheid South Africa* (Stanford, CA: Stanford University Press, 2017).

23. Charles R. Hale, "Does Multiculturalism Menace? Governance, Cultural Rights, and the Politics of Identity in Guatemala," *Journal of Latin American Studies* 34, no. 3 (2002): 485–524.

24. For a more sustained analysis of the neoliberal management of soft and hard markers of justice through national Indigenous rights legislation, see Mark Goodale, "Dark Matter: Toward a Political Economy of Indigenous Rights and Aspirational Politics," *Critique of Anthropology* 36, no. 4 (2016): 439–57.

25. Hale has argued more recently that the thirty-year "era of neoliberal multiculturalism" is coming to an end, given that many states have found that even symbolic accommodations of cultural diversity are no longer politically expedient. Instead, states have returned to more violent strategies for responding to internal demands for cultural recognition, especially when such demands so much as gesture toward redistribution or challenge extractivist national planning. Charles R. Hale, "Using and Refusing the Law: Indigenous Struggles and Legal Strategies after Neoliberal Multiculturalism," *American Anthropologist* 122, no. 3 (2020): 618–31.

26. See the UNESCO Universal Declaration on Cultural Diversity and supporting materials at www.unesco.org/new/fileadmin/MULTIMEDIA/HQ/CLT/pdf/5_Cultural_Diversity_EN.pdf.

27. A. L. Kroeber and Clyde Kluckhohn, *Culture: A Critical Review of Concepts and*

Definitions. Papers of the Peabody Museum of American Archaeology and Ethnology 47 (Cambridge, MA: Harvard University and the Museum, 1952), 181.

28. For a more recent study of the tensions between international human rights law and culture, see Julie Fraser and Brianne McGonigle Leyh, eds., *Intersections of Law and Culture at the International Criminal Court* (Cheltenham, UK: Edward Elgar, 2020). See also Eve Darian-Smith, *Laws and Societies in Global Contexts: Contemporary Approaches* (Cambridge: Cambridge University Press, 2013).

29. On the vernacularization of human rights, see Sally Engle Merry, "Transnational Human Rights and Local Activism: Mapping the Middle," *American Anthropologist* 108, no. 1 (2006): 38–51; Sally Engle Merry, *Human Rights and Gender Violence: Translating International Law into Local Justice* (Chicago: University of Chicago Press, 2006); and Mark Goodale, "Our Vernacular Futures," in *Human Rights Transformation in Practice*, ed. Tine Destrooper and Sally Engle Merry (Philadelphia: University of Pennsylvania Press, 2018), 251–62.

30. Sarah E. Holcombe, *Remote Freedoms: Politics, Personhood, and Human Rights in Aboriginal Central Australia* (Stanford, CA: Stanford University Press, 2018).

31. The full text of the UDHR translated into Luritja can be found at the website of the UN Office of the High Commissioner for Human Rights: www.ohchr.org/en/udhr/pages/Language.aspx?LangID=piu.

32. Holcombe, *Remote Freedoms*, 45–46.

33. Holcombe, *Remote Freedoms*, 46.

34. Holcombe, *Remote Freedoms*, 46. See also Fred Myers, *Pintupi Country, Pintupi Self: Sentiment, Place, and Politics among Western Desert Aborigines* (Washington, DC: Smithsonian Institution Press, 1986).

35. Holcombe, *Remote Freedoms*, 50.

36. See Arzoo Osanloo, *The Politics of Women's Rights in Iran* (Princeton, NJ: Princeton University Press, 2009); and Arzoo Osanloo, *Forgiveness Work: Mercy, Law, and Victims' Rights in Iran* (Princeton, NJ: Princeton University Press, 2020).

37. In this regard, see the Cairo Declaration of Human Rights in Islam (CDHRI), adopted by the Organization of Islamic Cooperation in 1990 just as the Cold War was about to give way to the Age of Human Rights. Iranian officials and religious scholars played a key role during the 1980s, the first decade after the Islamic revolution in Iran, in pushing for the adoption of an Islamic alternative to the UDHR.

38. Osanloo, *Politics of Women's Rights in Iran*.

39. Osanloo, *Forgiveness Work*.

40. Iran has also been the target for decades of high-level naming-and-shaming by major human rights NGOs like Amnesty International. For example, a 2020 report on Iran published by Amnesty was titled "Trampling Humanity." www.amnesty.org/en/documents/mde13/2891/2020/en/.

41. The 1990 "March for Territory and Dignity" in Bolivia has been the subject of numerous analyses from a variety of disciplines and perspectives. However, perhaps the most compelling is the eyewitness chronicle by the historian and educator Arnaldo Lijerón Casanovas, who participated in the march and soon after interpreted it in a work that

combines firsthand observation with a kind of lyrical reportage. Arnaldo Lijerón Casanovas, *De la resistencia pacifica a la interpelacion historica: Crónica preliminar de la Marcha Indígena por el Territorio y la Dignidad* (Trinidad, Bolivia: Centro de Investigación y Documentación para el Desarrollo del Beni, 1991).

42. See Mark Goodale, *A Revolution in Fragments: Traversing Scales of Justice, Ideology, and Practice in Bolivia* (Durham, NC: Duke University Press, 2019). See also Eija M. Ranta, *Vivir Bien as an Alternative to Neoliberal Globalization: Can Indigenous Terminologies Decolonize the State?* (Abingdon, UK: Routledge, 2018); Almut Schilling-Vacaflor, "Bolivia's New Constitution: Towards Participatory Democracy and Political Pluralism?" *European Review of Latin American and Caribbean Studies* 90 (2011): 3–22; and Nicole Fabricant, "Good Living for Whom? Bolivia's Climate Justice Movement and the Limitations of Indigenous Cosmovisions," *Latin American and Caribbean Ethnic Studies* 8, no. 2 (2013): 159–78.

43. The thirty-six Indigenous "peoples and nations" of Bolivia are recognized in Art. 5 of the 2009 constitution.

44. Goodale, *Revolution in Fragments*.

45. Richard A. Wilson, "Affective Justice Symposium: Commentary on Kamari Clarke's *Affective Justice*," *OpinioJuris* (May 28, 2020), opiniojuris.org/2020/05/28/.

46. Samuel Moyn, *Not Enough: Human Rights in an Unequal World* (Cambridge, MA: Belknap Press of Harvard University Press, 2018), 6, xii.

47. See chapter 7.

Chapter 7

1. Mark Goodale, *Dilemmas of Modernity: Bolivian Encounters with Law and Liberalism* (Stanford, CA: Stanford University Press, 2008). For a more extended description of the ayllu in rural Bolivia, see the introductory section of chapter 4 in this book.

2. My use of "intellectual" is part of a wider analysis of legal and political leaders in rural Bolivia that represents an extension of the Gramscian distinction between "traditional" and "organic" intellectuals. See Goodale, *Dilemmas of Modernity*; see also Steven Feierman, *Peasant Intellectuals: Anthropology and History in Tanzania* (Madison: University of Wisconsin Press, 1990).

3. Frank Salomon, "Review of *To Make the Earth Bear Fruit: Ethnographic Essays on Fertility, Work, and Gender in Highland Bolivia* (Olivia Harris)," *Journal of Latin American Studies* 33, no. 3 (2001): 654–56, 654.

4. The phrase for the Quechua language in the Bolivian dialect is *runa simi*, literally "language of the people."

5. Nevertheless, various dictionaries, after correctly translating "runa" as "the people" in this more exclusive sense, will add "human" as a second possible translation. No doubt this reflects an attempt to expand the category of runa to make it synonymous with the equally culturally and historically particular category of "human."

6. Bolivia divides its government between a political capital—often referred to as the "seat of government"—in La Paz, where the executive and legislative branches are located, and the legal capital, which is located in the city of Sucre.

7. For a similar account of categorical incommensurability within the literature on the practice of human rights, an account based on research in northern Thailand, see David M. Engel, "Vertical and Horizontal Perspectives on Rights Consciousness," *Indiana Journal of Global Legal Studies* 19, no. 2 (2012): 423–55.

8. Danielle Celermajer and Alexandre Lefebvre, eds., *The Subject of Human Rights* (Stanford, CA: Stanford University Press, 2020).

9. Here, I make reference to—and amplify—the goal of movements, most notably in South America, to replace the social ideology of "living better" that underpins global capitalism with a pan-Indigenous ideology of "living well," which requires the equitable distribution of resources, economic restraint, and the protection of ecological diversity and health, even at the cost to growth and economic development. See Eduardo Gudynas, "Buen vivir: Sobre secuestros, domesticaciones, rescates y alternativas," in *Bifurcación del buen vivir y el sumak kawsay*, ed. Atawallpa Oviedo Freire (Quito: Ediciones Yachay, 2014), 23–45; Eija M. Ranta, *Vivir Bien as an Alternative to Neoliberal Globalization: Can Indigenous Terminologies Decolonize the State?* (Abingdon, UK: Routledge, 2018); Boaventura de Sousa Santos, "Hablamos del Socialismo del Buen Vivir," *América Latina en Movimiento* 452 (2010): 4–7; and Óscar Vega Camacho, *Errancias: Aperturas para vivir bien* (La Paz: CLASCO and Muela del Diablo, 2011).

10. Samuel Moyn, *Not Enough: Human Rights in an Unequal World* (Cambridge, MA: Belknap Press of Harvard University Press, 2018), 220.

11. Karl Marx, 1844, "On the Jewish Question," in *The Marx-Engels Reader*, 2nd ed., ed. Robert C. Tucker (New York: W. W. Norton, 1978), 46 (emphases in original). I retain the gendered use of "man" in this quote to underscore how Marx, in developing a critique of capitalism that he believed would lead to social liberation, nevertheless remained shaped by other biases and prejudices.

12. Ronald Niezen, *The Rediscovered Self: Indigenous Identity and Cultural Justice* (Montreal: McGill-Queen's University Press, 2009).

13. Marx, "On the Jewish Question," 42.

14. See the "humanity" entry in the Oxford English Dictionary, which can be found online at www.oed.com/view/Entry/89280?redirectedFrom=humanity#eid. Importantly, the analysis here would not differ greatly if the source language were Catalan, Spanish, Portuguese, or Italian, in which the meanings of "humanity" share a similar Latinate origin and historical and cultural development.

15. Amal Hassan Fadlalla, *Branding Humanity: Competing Narratives of Rights, Violence, and Global Citizenship* (Stanford, CA: Stanford University Press, 2019).

16. Gil Gott, "Imperial Humanitarianism: History of an Arrested Dialectic," in *Moral Imperialism: A Critical Anthology*, ed. Berta Esperanza Hernández-Truyol (New York: New York University Press, 2002), 19–38.

17. See Sarah E. Holcombe, *Remote Freedoms: Politics, Personhood, and Human Rights in Aboriginal Central Australia* (Stanford, CA: Stanford University Press, 2018), 48.

18. Holcombe, *Remote Freedoms*, 48.

19. Étienne Balibar, "L'introuvable humanité du sujet moderne: L'universalité 'civique-bourgeoise' et la question des différences anthropologiques," *L'Homme* 203-4 (2012): 19–50.

Even here, between English and French, the problem of cultural and conceptual incommensurability reveals itself. Although "unfindable" exists in English usage, it is extremely rare and, I suspect, a direct adaptation of the French *introuvable*. According to the OED, "unfindable" was used first in English in 1791 by the utilitarian philosopher and social reformer Jeremy Bentham, who was certainly fluent in at least written French, since he carried on a well-known correspondence with leading figures of the French Revolution. www.oed.com/view/Entry/213343?redirectedFrom=unfindable#eid. Although *introuvable* is usually translated in English as "not found," this is not what this word means in French. The essence of *introuvable* is something—for Balibar, "humanity"—that can never be found, no matter how hard or long one looks.

20. Michael Hardt and Antonio Negri, *Empire* (Cambridge, MA: Harvard University Press, 2000), 313.

21. bell hooks, "Marginality as a Site of Resistance," in *Out There: Marginalization and Contemporary Cultures*, ed. Russell Ferguson, Martha Gever, Trinh T. Minh-ha, and Cornel West (Cambridge, MA: MIT Press, 1990), 341.

22. See E. Gabriella Coleman, *Coding Freedom: The Ethics and Aesthetics of Hacking* (Princeton, NJ: Princeton University Press, 2012).

23. E. Gabriella Coleman, *Hacker, Hoaxer, Whistleblower, Spy: The Many Faces of Anonymous* (London: Verso, 2014), 34–35.

24. See, e.g., Molly Land and Jay Aronson, eds., *New Technologies for Human Rights Law and Practice* (Cambridge: Cambridge University Press, 2018).

25. As Sherry Ortner explained, in a classic study, "summarizing key symbols" are those that express important political and cultural values through summarization, by evoking meanings in ways that foster collective identity while remaining ambiguous and resistant to finely-grained parsing. Sherry Ortner, "On Key Symbols," *American Anthropologist* 75, no. 5 (1973): 1338–46.

26. Ronald Niezen, *#Human Rights: The Technologies and Politics of Justice Claims in Practice* (Stanford, CA: Stanford University Press, 2020).

27. The name "Bellingcat" is presented by the community as "bell¿ngcat," with the inverted question mark representing a bell hanging around a cat's neck. "Belling the cat" was taken from a fable about a mouse who suggested to other mice that they should hang a bell around the housecat's neck so they could hear it coming. The other mice agreed it was an excellent idea, but the problem was: which mouse would agree to bell the cat?

28. Philip Bump, "How Open-Source Investigators Quickly Identified Iran's Likely Role in the Crash of Flight 752," *Washington Post*, January 10, www.washingtonpost.com/politics/2020/01/10/.

29. Niezen, *#Human Rights*, 90–91 (emphasis mine).

30. See Coleman, *Coding Freedom*.

31. The reference here is to Shannon Speed's study of Indigenous Zapatista communities in their struggles against the repressive Mexican state, who formulated a novel theory of human rights in which rights were seen to exist only "in their exercise," rather than as natural entitlements of individuals or groups. Shannon Speed, *Rights in Rebellion:*

Indigenous Struggle and Human Rights in Chiapas (Stanford, CA: Stanford University Press, 2008).

32. Jeffrey S. Juris, *Networking Futures: The Movements against Corporate Globalization* (Durham, NC: Duke University Press, 2008).

33. Bentham's phrase appears in an essay that was written during the French Revolution itself, but only published in 1816—and not in English, but in a French translation (in Geneva, Switzerland), with the title (chosen by the translator, not Bentham) of *Sophismes anarchiques*. The English version, titled "Anarchical Fallacies: Being an Examination of the Declaration of Rights Issued during the French Revolution," wasn't published in English until 1834, two years after Bentham's death. On the curious publication history of Bentham's blistering critique of human rights, see Hugo Adam Bedau, "'Anarchical Fallacies': Bentham's Attack on Human Rights," *Human Rights Quarterly* 22, no. 1 (2000): 261–79.

34. Marx, "On the Jewish Question," 42 (emphasis in original).

35. For a more extended critique of how monadism (originally derived from the philosophy of Leibniz) remained a conceptual Trojan Horse at the heart of the modern human rights project, see Mark Goodale, "The Misbegotten Monad: Anthropology, Human Rights, Belonging," in Celermajer and Lefebvre, *The Subject of Human Rights*, 48–63.

36. Marx, "On the Jewish Question," 46 (emphasis in original).

37. In 1861, when the Industrial Revolution had already unleashed the power of capitalist production, Maine—who was an English jurist and colonial official—published his influential *Ancient Law*, a quasi-anthropological work that purported to show how the rise of contracts as the basis for modern society represented the final stage in an inevitable, and universal, process of cultural evolution.

38. See Bronislaw Malinowski, *Argonauts of the Western Pacific* (London: Routledge and Kegan Paul, 1922); and Marcel Mauss, "Essai sur le don: Forme et raison de l'échange dans les sociétés archaïques," *L'Année Sociologique*, nouvelle série, 1ère année, 30–186.

39. Joel Robbins, "Recognition, Reciprocity, Justice: Melanesian Reflections on the Rights of Relationships," in *Mirrors of Justice: Law and Power in the Post-Cold War Era*, ed. Kamari Maxine Clarke and Mark Goodale (New York: Cambridge University Press, 2010), 171–90, 175.

40. Robbins, "Recognition, Reciprocity, Justice," 175.

41. Robbins, "Recognition, Reciprocity, Justice," 176.

42. Robbins, "Recognition, Reciprocity, Justice," 184.

43. Justice Salamo Injia later became the Chief Justice of PNG's National Court, serving between 2008 and 2018. He was also the victim of an intended assassination attempt linked to another killing and claim for compensation. According to news reports, Justice Injia was attacked because his clan was accused of not paying compensation for the death of a man who was believed to have been killed through sorcery. Helen Davidson, "Papua New Guinea Chief Justice Attacked as Sorcery-Related Violence Escalates," *The Guardian*, January 10, 2018, www.theguardian.com/.

44. Robbins, "Recognition, Reciprocity, Justice," 185, quoting from Marilyn Strathern, *Kinship, Law, and the Unexpected: Relatives Are Always a Surprise* (Cambridge: Cambridge University Press, 2005), 114.

45. Robbins, "Recognition, Reciprocity, Justice," 185, quoting from Strathern, *Kinship, Law, and the Unexpected*, 15.

46. See, e.g., Cyndi Banks, "Women, Justice, and Custom: The Discourse of 'Good Custom' and 'Bad Custom' in Papua New Guinea and Canada," *International Journal of Comparative Sociology* 42, no. 1–2 (May 2001): 101–22; Melissa Demian, "On the Repugnance of Customary Law," *Comparative Studies in Society and History* 56, no. 2 (2014): 508–36; Deborah Gewertz and Frederick Errington, *Emerging Class in Papua New Guinea: The Telling of a Difference* (Cambridge: Cambridge University Press, 1999); Perveez Mody, "Forced Marriage: Rites and Rights," in *Marriage Rites and Rights*, ed. Joanna Miles, Perveez Mody, and Rebecca Probert (Oxford: Hart Publishing, 2015), 193–210; and Marilyn Strathern, "Losing (Out On) Intellectual Resources," in *Law, Anthropology, and the Constitution of the Social*, ed. Alain Pottage and Martha Mundy (Cambridge: Cambridge University Press, 2004), 201–33.

47. Robbins, "Recognition, Reciprocity, Justice," 185.

48. See the description of this three-part framework for considering human rights subjectivity in the introductory section of this chapter, taken from Celermajer and Lefebvre, *Subject of Human Rights*.

49. Niezen, *Rediscovered Self*.

50. Pheng Cheah and Bruce Robbins, eds., *Cosmopolitics: Thinking and Feeling beyond the Nation* (Minneapolis: University of Minnesota Press, 1998).

51. Although much of the empirical support for relationality as an alternative basis for human rights subjectivity comes from the anthropology of human rights and justice, some legal scholars have considered the ways in which relationality offers a more sustainable framework for law itself. The work of Jennifer Nedelsky is particularly critical in this respect. See, e.g., Jennifer Nedelsky, *Law's Relations: A Relational Theory of Self, Autonomy, and Law* (Oxford: Oxford University Press, 2011); and Jennifer Nedelsky, "Reconceiving Rights and Constitutionalism," *Journal of Human Rights* 7, no. 2 (2008): 139–73.

52. Holcombe, *Remote Freedoms*, 48.

Chapter 8

1. This discordant, if fascinating, structure fell into disuse throughout the twentieth century and was slated to be demolished before being resurrected through national legislation, which created the National Building Museum, a private institution dedicated to the history of architecture, engineering, and design. See www.nbm.org/about/.

2. Victor Mallet, "Outside Edge: The Party Spain Is Desperate to Crash," *Financial Times*, October 31, 2008, www.ft.com/content/450ddf26-a76c-11dd-865e-000077b07658.

3. See Anthony Giddens, *Beyond Left and Right: The Future of Radical Politics* (Stanford, CA: Stanford University Press, 1994); and Anthony Giddens, *The Third Way: The Renewal of Social Democracy* (Cambridge: Polity, 1998).

4. Francis Fukuyama, *The End of History and the Last Man* (New York: Free Press, 1992).

5. Evan Osnos, *Age of Ambition: Chasing Fortune, Faith, and Truth in the New China* (New York: Farrar, Straus and Giroux, 2014).

6. Saskia Sassen, *Expulsions: Brutality and Complexity in the Global Economy* (Cambridge, MA: Harvard University Press, 2014).

7. Fredric Jameson, "Future City," *New Left Review* 21 (May/June 2003): 76.

8. Erik Olin Wright, *Envisioning Real Utopias* (London: Verso, 2010). See the discussion in chapter 1 in this volume of how Wright's sociology of the future informs my approach to the future of human rights.

9. As he described it, in his inimitable way, projects for change must nevertheless maintain "some methods for distinguishing the real from the illusory, real mountain peaks from cloud formations, real palms and springs from mirages in the desert, real characteristics of an age or a culture from fanciful reconstructions, real alternatives which can be realized at a given time from alternatives realizable, it may be, in other places and at other times, but not in the society or period in question." Isaiah Berlin, *The Sense of Reality: Studies in Ideas and their History* (New York: Farrar, Straus and Giroux, 1996), 5.

10. David Harvey, *The New Imperialism* (Oxford: Oxford University Press, 2003), 87.

11. See Sonya Sceats and Shaun Breslin, *China and the International Human Rights System* (London: Royal Institute of International Affairs, 2012).

12. See Mark Goodale, "UNESCO and the UN Rights of Man Declaration: History, Historiography, Ideology," *Humanity* 8, no. 1 (2017): 29–47.

13. For a longer description of this December 1947 closed session of the UN CHR, which took place in Geneva, see Mark Goodale, ed., *Letters to the Contrary: A Curated History of the UNESCO Human Rights Survey* (Stanford, CA: Stanford University Press, 2018), 23.

14. Even the idea of human rights exceptionalism has proven to be a way for the United States to try and shape human rights diplomacy, for example, in relation to the ICC. See Brianne McGonigle Leyh, "'We Will Let It Die on Its Own': Culture, Ideology, and Power at Play between the United States and the International Criminal Court," in *Intersections of Law and Culture at the International Criminal Court*, ed. Julie Fraser and Brianne McGonigle Leyh (Cheltenham, UK: Edward Elgar, 2020), 337–57.

15. Rana Siu Inboden, *China and the International Human Rights Regime: 1982–2017* (Cambridge: Cambridge University Press, 2021).

16. Rosa Freedman and Ruth Houghton, "Two Steps Forward, One Step Back: Politicisation of the Human Rights Council," *Human Rights Law Review* 17, no. 4 (2017): 753–69, 754.

17. For a diverse, if critical, survey of the ways in which international institutions can catalyze positive change under certain circumstances, see Ronald Niezen and Maria Sapignoli, eds., *Palaces of Hope: The Anthropology of Global Organizations* (Cambridge: Cambridge University Press, 2017).

18. Inboden, *China and the International Human Rights Regime*.

19. The status of Saudi corporations is complicated by the fact that the country is an absolute monarchy controlled by the royal family. For example, one of the largest chemical manufacturers in the world, Saudi Basic Industries Corporation (SABIC), is almost entirely owned by Saudi Aramco, which holds a 70 percent stake in the company. Saudi

Aramco, with assets of almost $400 billion, is itself owned by the government of Saudi Arabia. Beyond China and Saudi Arabia, other notable examples of state ownership of major multinational corporations would include Norway's Statoil (assets of $115 billion, now called Equinor) and Russia's Rosatom (assets of over $45 billion).

20. For a case study of the use of the Alien Tort Statute, see John Dale, "Transnational Legal Conflict between Peasants and Corporations in Burma: Human Rights and Discursive Ambivalence under the US Alien Tort Claims Act," in *The Practice of Human Rights: Tracking Law between the Global and the Local.*, ed. Mark Goodale and Sally Engle Merry (Cambridge: Cambridge University Press, 2007), 285–319.

21. Stéfanie Khoury, "Transnational Corporations and the European Court of Human Rights: Reflections on the Indirect and Direct Approaches to Accountability," *Oñati Journal of Emergent Socio-Legal Studies* 4, no. 1 (2010): 68–110.

22. Bittle and Snider argue that the failure to acknowledge that "profit maximization" is the "raison d'être" of multinational corporations has been a critical obstacle in efforts to hold corporations accountable for human rights violations. Steven Bittle and Laureen Snider, "Examining the Ruggie Report: Can Voluntary Guidelines Tame Global Capitalism?," *Critical Criminology* 21, no. 2 (2013): 177–92.

23. The threat by the socialist Allende government to nationalize mines owned by the two big American companies, Anaconda and Kennicott, is usually cited as one of the main factors behind the CIA-orchestrated coup. However, documents leaked before the coup reveal that another US-based corporation, International Telephone & Telegraph (ITT), was even more aggressive in imploring the Nixon administration to act on its behalf. Memos from 1972 showed that ITT was working closely with the US State Department, the CIA, and even Nixon himself, to bring the Allende government down (the company was the majority shareholder in the Chilean Telephone Company). As the editorial board of the *New York Times* put it, this was a "classic example of how a giant international corporation should never behave, particularly in a democratic country with every right to work out its political destiny without outside interference." New York Times Editorial Board, "The I.T.T. and Chile," *New York Times*, March 26, 1972, section E, 12.

24. Quoted in Karl Sauvant, "The Negotiations of the United Nations Code of Conduct on Transnational Corporations," *Journal of World Investment and Trade* 16, no. 1 (2015): 11–87, 21.

25. Sauvant, "Negotiations of the United Nations Code of Conduct on Transnational Corporations," 54.

26. Christian Scheper, "From Naming and Shaming to Knowing and Showing: Human Rights and the Power of Corporate Practice," *International Journal of Human Rights* 19, no. 6 (2015): 737–56.

27. Elsewhere, Scheper has described CSR as a process of "corporatizing rights." Christian Scheper, "Corporatizing Rights: The Politics of Corporate Responsibility for Human Rights under Regimes of Global Production" (PhD diss., Department of Political Science, University of Kassel, 2016).

28. Christelle Genoud, "Vernacularisation from Above: Finance's Appropriation of Human Rights in Land Governance," *International Journal of Human Rights* 24, no. 11

(2020); see also Christelle Genoud, "Transnational Private Regulation of Financialized Land Grabbing: Can Human Rights Regulate Finance?" (PhD diss., Institute of Political Studies, University of Lausanne, 2020).

29. Genoud, "Vernacularisation from Above."

30. Marina Welker, *Enacting the Corporation: An American Mining Firm in Post-Authoritarian Indonesia* (Berkeley: University of California Press, 2014), 31.

31. Harvey, *New Imperialism*, 110.

32. Samuel Moyn, *Not Enough: Human Rights in an Unequal World* (Cambridge, MA: Belknap Press of Harvard University Press, 2018), xii.

33. Shoshana Zuboff, "Surveillance Capitalism and the Challenge of Collective Action," *New Labor Forum* 28, no. 1 (2019): 10–29, 14.

34. See Shoshana Zuboff, *The Age of Surveillance Capitalism: The Fight for a Human Future at the New Frontier of Power* (London: Profile Books, 2019); Zuboff, "Surveillance Capitalism and the Challenge of Collective Action."

35. Zuboff, "Surveillance Capitalism and the Challenge of Collective Action," 11.

36. Zuboff, "Surveillance Capitalism and the Challenge of Collective Action," 22.

37. Zuboff, "Surveillance Capitalism and the Challenge of Collective Action," 22.

38. Zuboff, "Surveillance Capitalism and the Challenge of Collective Action," 25.

39. Zuboff, "Surveillance Capitalism and the Challenge of Collective Action," 25.

40. For an important study of how contemporary surveillance technologies are also being used to mediate and perpetuate racial hierarchies, see Simone Browne, *Dark Matters: On the Surveillance of Blackness* (Durham, NC: Duke University Press, 2015).

41. Paul De Hert, "Biometrics and the Challenge to Human Rights in Europe," in *Security and Privacy in Biometrics*, ed. Patrizio Campisi (London: Springer-Verlag, 2013), 367–411, 368.

42. De Hert, "Biometrics and the Challenge to Human Rights in Europe," 367–411, 368.

43. De Hert, "Biometrics and the Challenge to Human Rights in Europe," 369.

44. Étienne Balibar, "L'introuvable humanité du sujet moderne: L'universalité 'civique-bourgeoise' et la question des differences anthropologiques," *L'Homme* 3–4, no. 203–4 (2012).

45. Irma van der Ploeg, "The Illegal Body: 'Eurodac' and the Politics of Biometric Identification," *Ethics and Information Technology* 1, no. 4 (1999): 295–302.

46. Ploeg, "Illegal Body," 295.

47. Ploeg, "Illegal Body," 301.

48. See Irma van der Ploeg, *The Machine-Readable Body: Essays on Biometrics and the Informatization of the Body* (Maastricht, Netherlands: Shaker Publishing, 2005).

49. Harvey, *New Imperialism*.

50. Harvey, *New Imperialism*, 148.

51. Harvey, *New Imperialism*, 179.

Index

value pluralism, 100–102, 118
vernacularization, 102; into Aboriginal
    Australian languages, UDHR transla-
    tion, 11, 111–12, 129, 140; in Bolivia,
    114–16, 128; in Iran, 112–14
Vienna Declaration (1993), 55–56
Virginia Declaration of Rights, 173n10
voluntary regimes, 154–55

waltja, 129, 140
Welker, Marina, 155
Westphalia, Peace of (1648), 49, 187n27
Westphalian system, 49, 51, 59–60, 151,
    187n27
White, James Boyd, 72

Whyte, Jessica, 32, 172n26
Wilson, Richard A., 116–17
Wood, Gordon S., 184n2
World War II, 73, 87, 182n34
The Wretched of the Earth (Fanon), 79
Wright, Erik Olin, 4, 145

Yugoslavia, former, 69

Zapatista communities, 172n23,
    196n31
*Zen and the Art of Motorcycle
    Maintenance* (Pirsig), 24
Zinn, Howard, 8
Zuboff, Shoshana, 157–58, 162

*The Politics of Love in Myanmar: LGBT Mobilization
and Human Rights as a Way of Life*
Lynette J. Chua
2018

*Branding Humanity: Competing Narratives of Rights,
Violence, and Global Citizenship*
Amal Hassan Fadlalla
2018

*Remote Freedoms: Politics, Personhood and Human Rights
in Aboriginal Central Australia*
Sarah E. Holcombe
2018

*Letters to the Contrary: A Curated History of the
UNESCO Human Rights Survey*
Mark Goodale
2018

Just Violence: Torture and Human Rights in the Eyes of the Police
Rachel Wahl
2017

*Bodies of Truth: Law, Memory, and Emancipation
in Post-Apartheid South Africa*
Rita Kesselring
2016

*Rights After Wrongs: Local Knowledge
and Human Rights in Zimbabwe*
Shannon Morreira
2016

If God Were a Human Rights Activist
Boaventura de Sousa Santos
2015

Digging for the Disappeared: Forensic Science after Atrocity
Adam Rosenblatt
2015

The authorized representative in the EU for product safety and compliance is:
Mare Nostrum Group
B.V Doelen 72
4831 GR Breda
The Netherlands

www.ingramcontent.com/pod-product-compliance
Lightning Source LLC
Chambersburg PA
CBHW030817270326
41928CB00007B/777